Exploring the Language of Drama

This edited collection introduces students to the stylistic analysis of drama. Written in an engaging and accessible style, the contributors use techniques of language analysis, particularly from discourse analysis, pragmatics and cognitive linguistics, to explore the language of plays.

Exploring the Language of Drama:

- has chapter summaries and follow-up exercises;
- offers practical advice on how to analyse a play extract and write up an assignment;
- includes contributions from some of the world's leading scholars in the field, and the plays analysed range from the works of Shakespeare to those of Arthur Miller and Tom Stoppard.

The contributors demonstrate the validity of analysing the text of a play, as opposed to focusing on performance. Divided into four broad yet inter-connecting groups, the chapters:

- open up some of the basic mechanisms of conversation and show how they are used in dramatic dialogue;
- look at how discourse analysis and pragmatic theories can be used to help us understand characterization in dialogue;
- consider some of the cognitive patterns underlying dramatic discourse;
- focus on the notion of speech as action.

Contributions from Mick Short, Vimala Herman, Paul Simpson, Marilyn M. Cooper, Neil Bennison, Jonathan Culpeper, Donald C. Freeman, Jean Jacques Weber, Valerie Lowe, Michael Toolan and Peter K. W. Tan.

Based at the Department of Linguistics and Modern English Language, Lancaster University, **Jonathan Culpeper** is Lecturer and **Mick Short** is Professor of English Language and Literature. **Peter Verdonk** is Professor in the Department of English Language and Literature at the University of Amsterdam.

The INTERFACE Series

> A linguistic deaf to the poetic function of language and a literary scholar indifferent to linguistic problems and unconversant with linguistic methods, are equally flagrant anachronisms – Roman Jakobson.

This statement, made over twenty-five years ago, is no less relevant today, and 'flagrant anachronisms' still abound. The aim of the INTERFACE series is to examine topics at the 'interface' of language studies and literary criticism and in doing so to build bridges between these traditionally 'divided' disciplines.

Already published in the series:

Narrative
A critical linguistic introduction
Michael J. Toolan

The Discourse of Advertising
Guy Cook

Language, Literature and Critical Practice
Ways of analysing text
David Birch

Literature, Language and Change
Ruth Waterhouse and John Stephens

Literary Studies in Action
Alan Durant and Nigel Fabb

Language in Popular Fiction
Walter Nash

Language, Text and Context
Essays in stylistics
Edited by Michael J. Toolan

The Language of Jokes
Analysing verbal play
Delia Chiaro

Language, Ideology and Point of View
Paul Simpson

A Linguistic History of English Poetry
Richard Bradford

Literature about Language
Valerie Shepherd

Twentieth-century Poetry
From text to context
Edited by Peter Verdonk

Textual Intervention
Critical and creative strategies for literary studies
Rob Pope

Feminist Stylistics
Sara Mills

Twentieth-century Fiction
From text to context
Peter Verdonk and Jean Jacques Weber

Variety in Written English
Texts in society: societies in text
Tony Bex

English in Speech and Writing
Investigating language and literature
Rebecca Hughes

Language through Literature
An introduction
Paul Simpson

Patterns in Language
An introduction to language and literary style
Joanna Thornborrow and Shân Wareing

The Series Editor
Ronald Carter is Professor of Modern English Language at the University of Nottingham and was National Coordinator of the 'Language in the National Curriculum' Project (LINC) from 1989 to 1992.

Exploring the Language of Drama

From Text to Context

Edited by Jonathan Culpeper,
Mick Short and Peter Verdonk

London and New York

First published 1998
by Routledge
11 New Fetter Lane, London EC4P 4EE

Simultaneously published in the USA and Canada
by Routledge
29 West 35th Street, New York, NY 10001

Typeset in Baskerville by BC Typesetting, Bristol
Printed and bound in Great Britain by
Creative Print and Design (Wales), Ebbw Vale

British Library Cataloguing in Publication Data
A catalogue record for this book is available from the British Library

Library of Congress Cataloging in Publication Data
Exploring the language of drama: from text to context/[edited by]
 Jonathan Culpeper, Mick Short, and Peter Verdonk.
    p.   cm.
  Includes bibliographical references and index.
   1. English drama–History and criticism.   2. English language–
Style.   3. Drama–Technique.   I. Culpeper, Jonathan, 1966–.
II. Short, Mick, 1947–   III. Verdonk, Peter, 1935–.
PR627.E9   1998
822.009–dc21   97-42989

ISBN 0–415–13794–2
ISBN 0–415–13795–0

Contents

Notes on contributors

Neil Bennison taught in Lancaster University's English Department between 1991 and 1996, and is currently completing a doctorate on the relationship between character and narrative in George Eliot's novels. His chapter in this book is based on an article which he published in the journal *Language and Literature* in 1993. Pursuing his interest in orchestral music, he now works for the National Youth Orchestra of Great Britain.

Marilyn M. Cooper is Associate Professor of Humanities at Michigan Technological University. She is the author (with Michael Holzman) of *Writing as Social Action* (Heinemann–Boynton/Cook: 1989) and is working on a book on postmodern subjects in writing classrooms. Her work focuses on writing pedagogy as informed by, and related to, issues in sociolinguistics, critical theory, and cultural studies.

Jonathan Culpeper is a lecturer in the Department of Linguistics and Modern English Language at Lancaster University. He teaches in the areas of English language, stylistics and pragmatics. He has published in a number of international journals, and has written *History of English* (1997) for the Routledge workbook series. Currently, he is preparing a book on language and characterization in plays and other texts.

Donald C. Freeman is Professor of English at the University of Southern California in Los Angeles. He edited *Linguistics and Literary Style* (Holt, Rinehart and Winston: 1970) and *Essays in Modern Stylistics* (Methuen: 1981), and has published many scholarly articles in journals throughout the English-speaking world. Freeman is a member of the editorial boards of *Language and Style* and *Language and Literature*. He was the founding head of the Department of Linguistics at the University of Massachusetts, Amherst, and has held visiting professorships at McGill University, the Technische Universität Berlin, and the universities of Lancaster, Salzburg, and Regensburg.

Vimala Herman is Senior Lecturer at the Department of English Studies at the University of Nottingham. Her book *Dramatic Discourse: Dialogue as Interaction in Plays* (Routledge: 1995) is a major research monograph which covers the area of discourse and drama comprehensively. She has published extensively in the area of language and literature and drama. She is currently completing a book, 'Poetic Language', for Oxford University Press. Her research interests include literary-linguistics, drama and discourse, pragmatics, and cognition.

Valerie Lowe is currently completing her Ph.D. in stylistics at Lancaster University. Her primary interests are in the area of women's writing and issues connected with language and gender. Her doctoral thesis investigates the relationship between the gender of the reader and point of view in short stories written by Virginia Woolf and Margaret Atwood. Her chapter in this book is based on an article which she published in the journal *Language and Literature* in 1994. She has also written papers on *Jane Eyre* and mountaineering literature.

Mick Short is Professor of English Language and Literature at Lancaster University. He has written *Exploring the Language of Poems, Plays and Prose* (Longman: 1996) and, with Professor Geoffrey Leech, *Style in Fiction* (Longman: 1981). He has edited *Reading, Analysing and Teaching Literature* (Longman: 1988), and, with Professor Jenny Thomas, *Using Corpora for Language Research* (Longman: 1996). He founded the Poetics and Linguistics Association, and was also the founding editor of its international journal, *Language and Literature*.

Paul Simpson is a reader in the School of English at Queen's University Belfast, where he teaches undergraduate and postgraduate courses on English language, linguistics and stylistics. He has published books and articles on stylistics, critical linguistics and related fields of language study. His books for Routledge include *Language, Ideology and Point of View* (1993) and *Language Through Literature* (1997).

Peter K. W. Tan is a senior lecturer in the Department of English Language and Literature, National University of Singapore, where he teaches literary stylistics, discourse analysis and sociolinguistics. He obtained his degrees from the universities of Malaya and of Edinburgh, and is author of *A Stylistics of Drama* (Singapore University Press: 1993). He also has an interest in the history of English and the development of New Englishes in South-East Asia, and was a member of the editorial team for the second edition of the Times–Chambers *Essential English Dictionary* which incorporated lexical items from Singaporean and Malaysian English.

Michael Toolan is Professor of Applied English Linguistics at the University of Birmingham. He has published extensively in stylistics, narrative, and language theory. Recent publications include *Total Speech: An Integrational Linguistic Approach to Language* (Duke University Press: 1996) and *Language in Literature: An Introduction to Stylistics* (Arnold: 1997).

Peter Verdonk is Professor of Stylistics in the English Department of the University of Amsterdam. He edited *Twentieth-Century Poetry: From Text to*

Context (Routledge: 1993), and co-edited (with Roger D. Sell) *Literature and the New Interdisciplinarity: Poetics, Linguistics, History* (Rodopi: 1994) and (with Jean Jacques Weber) *Twentieth-Century Fiction: From Text to Context* (Routledge: 1995). His research interests include rhetoric and cognitive stylistics, and he is currently writing a book on stylistics.

Jean Jacques Weber is Professor of English at University Centre, Luxembourg, and has published widely on English language and literature. He is the author of *Critical Analysis of Fiction* (Rodopi: 1992), as well as the editor of *The Stylistics Reader* (Arnold: 1996) and, with Peter Verdonk, of *Twentieth Century Fiction: From Text to Context* (Routledge: 1995).

Acknowledgements

Thanks are due to the contributors of this volume for providing us with their illuminating papers and for good-heartedly forbearing the nit-picky demands of the editors. In addition, we would like to thank Kevin Marshall for his assiduous work in helping us lick the papers into the required format and Dawn Archer for help with the index.

Acknowledgement is due to the copyright holders of the following works for their kind permission to reprint extracts in this book:

Alan Ayckbourn: *The Revengers' Comedies*. Extract reproduced by permission of Faber and Faber Ltd, London. Caryl Churchill: *Cloud Nine*, published by Methuen. John Cleese and Connie Booth: 'Communication Problems' in *The Complete Fawlty Towers*. Extract reproduced by permission of David Wilkinson Associates. David Hare: *The Secret Rapture*. Extract reproduced by permission of Faber and Faber Ltd, London. Eugene Ionesco: 'Victims of Duty' in *Plays: Volume 2*. Copyright © 1954 by Gallimard, Paris. Extract reproduced by permission of Éditions Gallimard. David Mamet: *Oleanna*. Copyright © 1992 by David Mamet. Reprinted by permission of Vintage Books, a Division of Random House Inc. Arthur Miller: *The Crucible*. Copyright 1952, 1953 by Arthur Miller. Extract reproduced by permission of Greene and Heaton Ltd. Copyright 1952, 1953, 1954, renewed © 1980 by Arthur Miller. Used by permission of Viking Penguin, a division of Penguin Books USA Inc. John Osborne: *Look Back in Anger*. Extracts reproduced by permission of Faber and Faber Ltd, London. Tom Stoppard: *Professional Foul*. Extract reprinted by permission of Faber and Faber Ltd, London, and copyright © 1988 Grove/Atlantic, Inc., US rights only.

The *Monty Python* extract is reprinted by permission of INK GROUP. The extracts from *Scent of a Woman* are reproduced by permission of Universal City Studios. Copyright © 1998 by Universal City Studios, Inc. Courtesy of Universal Studios Publishing Rights. All Rights Reserved.

Neil Bennison's chapter is a revised version of an article that first appeared in *Language and Literature*, Vol. 2, No. 2, N. Bennison 'Discourse Analysis, Pragmatics and the Dramatic "Character": Tom Stoppard's *Professional Foul*', pp. 79–99, 1993, printed with kind permission of Sage Publications Ltd. Donald C. Freeman's chapter is a revised version of an article that first appeared in *Journal of Pragmatics*, Vol. 24, No. 6, Donald C. Freeman, ' "Catch[ing] the Nearest Way": Macbeth and Cognitive Metaphor', pp. 689–708, 1995, printed with kind permission from Elsevier Science – NL, Sara Burgerhartstraat 25, 1055 KV Amsterdam, The Netherlands. Valerie Lowe's chapter is a revised version of an article that first appeared in *Language and Literature*, Vol. 3, No. 3, V. Lowe ' "Unsafe Convictions": "Unhappy" Confessions in *The Crucible*', pp. 175–195, 1993, printed with kind permission of Sage Publications Ltd.

1 Introduction

Jonathan Culpeper, Mick Short and Peter Verdonk

EXPLORING DRAMATIC TEXTS

This book is designed to help students to explore the language of dramatic texts through the approach usually known as 'stylistic analysis', an approach which is already well-established for the analysis of poetry and prose fiction (see, for example, this book's companion volumes: *Twentieth-century Poetry: From text to context*, edited by Peter Verdonk, and *Twentieth-century Fiction: From text to context*, edited by Peter Verdonk and Jean Jacques Weber).

How does the stylistic analysis of drama differ from the stylistic analysis of poetry or prose? Let's explore this issue through an example. In Shakespeare's *Henry IV (Part 1 and Part 2)* Falstaff – a disreputable knight who spends his time drinking in taverns and mixing with highwaymen and prostitutes (and creating much comedy for the audience in the process) – befriends Hal, the future King. At the end of *Henry IV (Part 2)* Hal has succeeded to the throne to become Henry V. Falstaff, of course, is overjoyed, imagining all sorts of imminent privileges. Outside Westminster Abbey, Falstaff meets the King:

FALSTAFF: My King! My Jove! I speak to thee, my heart!
KING: I know thee not, old man. Fall to thy prayers.

This must be one of the greatest snubs in the world of fiction. How does Shakespeare make it so effective? Shakespeare's play is largely written in verse, of course, and so one approach will be to examine the poetry. If we take our stylistics 'tool kit' for the analysis of poetry, how far would it take us in providing an explanation? Typically, poetry has been analysed by examining foregrounded features, usually achieved through the manipulation of phonology, grammar and lexis – areas of linguistic organization which are often considered as the 'core' of linguistics. In Falstaff's line, we might note the syntactic parallelism built out of terms of address – 'My King! my Jove! . . . my heart!' All consist of the same possessive pronoun followed by a noun and end with an exclamation mark. We might note the phonological parallelism: the line is metrically regular (five stressed syllables alternating with five unstressed syllables), a perfect iambic pentameter. This regularity is re-inforced by the fact that the grammatical boundaries and the punctuation boundaries coincide with the metrical units. We might also note the semantic deviation created through the hyperbolic metaphor 'my Jove! . . . my heart!' All this can be seen as reflective of Falstaff's joyful enthusiasm. The King's line deviates from the patterns set up in Falstaff's. There is no syntactic regularity here. There is no phonological regularity. Note the mid-line sentence boundary disrupting the rhythm, and the two adjacent stressed syllables falling across the grammatical juncture, followed by two unstressed syllables:

$$x \quad / \quad x \quad / \quad x \quad / \quad x \quad / \quad x \quad /$$
FALSTAFF: My King! My Jove! I speak to thee, my heart!

$$x \quad / \quad x \quad / \quad x \quad / \quad / \quad x \quad x \quad / \quad x$$
KING: I know thee not, old man. Fall to thy prayers.

In addition, the hyperbole has disappeared, along with the metaphors and the exclamatory quality. This change reinforces a difference in mood, a difference in attitude. The King is not overjoyed to see Falstaff and in fact claims that he doesn't even know Falstaff. More than this, the King, perhaps punning on Fall and Falstaff, commands Falstaff to start praying for his sins.

Whilst our poetry analysis 'tool kit' has helped us quite a lot in understanding the force of the opposition between the two lines, it has left whole areas unexplained. Nothing has been said about the fact that this is a conversational *exchange*. How is meaning constructed in this interaction? Falstaff says 'I speak to thee'. What does he mean by that? It's obvious to one and all that Falstaff is speaking to the King. He provides unnecessary information; in other words, he flouts the Maxim of Quantity (Grice 1975). What are we to infer? Given Falstaff's expectations about wealth and privileges, what he means is 'acknowledge me, acknowledge your old friend Falstaff'. What about the King's response, 'I know thee not'? This is obviously untrue, Hal had formerly spent many a night carousing with Falstaff. He flouts the Maxim of Quality (Grice 1975). What are we to infer? Hal had said in a soliloquy at the beginning of *Henry IV (Part I)* that when he was King he would turn away from all his former roguish friends. Thus, the King means he wishes to have absolutely nothing to do with Falstaff, he intends to behave as if he doesn't know him at all. Another important dramatic point here is that, although the audience works out this inference, Falstaff fails to pick it up. After these lines we find out that he assumes that the King feels that he has to put on a public face but will speak to him in private.

Our poetry analysis 'tool kit' also says nothing about the social dynamics of interaction. The essence of the snub is that they have decidedly different conceptions of their relationship. In terms of power and social distance, for Falstaff they are familiar and equal, while for the King they are distant and Falstaff is subordinate. Falstaff is not invited to speak: he initiates the conversation and thus from the King's perspective, but not his own, he speaks out of turn. He fails to pay the respect that Hal's new position of power demands. Moreover, having referred to the King in extremely deferential terms ('My

King! My Jove!'), he now refers to Henry in terms that suggest an intimate social relationship: 'my heart' seems to say that the King is so dear to him that it is as if the King is his very heart. However, the King makes it abundantly clear to Falstaff that there has been a change in the relationship. Not only does he deny that he knows Falstaff, but he deliberately offends him by addressing him as 'old man' (not the 'Jack' of former times). Note also that Hal's change in power, now that he has ascended to the throne, is signalled by his use of a direct command, 'Fall to thy prayers'. It is because he is now in a position of power that he can afford to be rude and direct. Interestingly, the pragmatic interpretation of the two men's use of the second person pronoun 'thee' as opposed to 'you' (the more common form in this period) differs: Falstaff uses the 'thee' of familiarity, the King uses the 'thee' of condescension.

Needless to say, discussion of this brief example cannot do justice to either the stylistics of poetry or the stylistics of drama, and we have said nothing about the stylistics of prose. However, it does illustrate the fact that to explain the dynamics of plays properly, we need much help from areas of linguistics – notably pragmatics and discourse analysis – which do not play a leading role in the analysis of poetry or prose. This is not to say that poetry analysis does not have a role in the study of drama. Our analysis above indicates its value. Indeed, there are points where there is a strong link between poetry analysis and interactional analysis. Note, for example, that an interpretation of Falstaff's 'my heart' involves both an appreciation of the fact that it is a metaphor and the fact that it signals Falstaff's perception of his intimate social relationship with the King. And it should also be noted that the interactional modes of analysis used to explore drama in this volume also have applications in the study of poetry, particularly those with a conversational structure, like Browning's 'dramatic monologues' or Coleridge's *The Ancient Mariner*.

DRAMA: THE NEGLECTED CHILD

If we compare them with poems and fictional prose, play-texts have in general received relatively little attention from both twentieth-century literary critics and stylisticians. Part of the problem may lie in the fact that spoken conversation has for many centuries been commonly seen as a debased and unstable form of language, and thus plays, with all their affinities with speech, were liable to be undervalued. For some literary critics, Shakespeare and some other Elizabethan playwrights were reprieved by the fact that their plays were often written in verse. In fact, within the literary-critical movements of New Criticism in the USA and Practical Criticism in Britain, which dominated the criticism of the mid-twentieth century, such plays were treated as 'dramatic poems'. By denying these plays their status as 'spoken conversation to be performed', they were considered stable texts worthy of close analysis. Similarly, the early stylistics of the 1960s tended to concentrate on the analysis of poetry (e.g. Jakobson 1960; Jakobson and Jones 1970; Leech 1969). This was partly because of the influence of New Criticism and Practical Criticism, but also because of the heritage of Russian Formalism. The formalist notions of foregrounding, deviation and parallelism could be most easily seen in the phonetic, grammatical and lexical patterning of poetry.

The development of stylistics since the 1960s has been spurred on by new developments in linguistics, and it is these developments which have enabled stylisticians to get to grips with other genres. For example, Michael Halliday's (1971) application of systemic functional grammar to William Golding's novel *The Inheritors* inspired the investigation of how ideational patterns (language used to convey experience and information about the context) can be used to convey a particular point of view in prose fiction (Fowler 1977, 1986; Leech and Short 1981; Simpson 1993). More recently, in the late 1970s and in the 1980s, developments in discourse analysis, conversation analysis and pragmatics (methods of analysis developed by linguists to deal with face-to-face interaction) have equipped stylisticians with tools to analyse the meanings of utterances in fictional dialogue. Some studies have focused on the linguistic structure of dramatic dialogue (e.g. Burton 1980; Herman 1991); some have used politeness theory to illuminate the social dynamics of character interaction (e.g. Simpson 1989; Leech 1992); and others (e.g. Short 1989) have drawn eclectically from pragmatics and discourse analysis, in order to shed light on aspects such as characterization and absurdity.

However, in spite of the availability of suitable linguistic frameworks, stylisticians have been somewhat tardy in investigating play-texts. Apart from a few articles and the odd book (e.g. Herman 1995), the stylistics of drama remains relatively unexplored. Calvo (1997) points out that out of thirty-nine articles published so far in the journal *Language and Literature* only five examine texts taken from plays. We hope that this book will go some small way towards filling the gap.

USING THIS BOOK

The second and the last chapters act to sandwich the others. The second chapter, by Mick Short, justifies the whole enterprise behind a stylistics of drama. It explains why it is valid to analyse the text of a play, as opposed to focusing on performances. Peter Tan's concluding chapter pulls together some of the threads of the book and offers some practical advice on how you might analyse a play extract and write it up as an assignment. The remaining chapters (the 'filling' of the sandwich) are organized into four broad groups which interconnect with one another. The first group (Vimala Herman, Paul Simpson and Marilyn Cooper) opens up some of the basic mechanisms of conversation and shows how they are used in dramatic dialogue. The second group (Neil Bennison and Jonathan Culpeper) looks at how discourse analysis and pragmatic theories (particularly politeness theory) can be used to help us understand characterization in dramatic dialogue. The third group (Donald C. Freeman and Jean Jacques Weber) considers some of the cognitive patterns underlying dramatic discourse. The fourth group (Valerie Lowe and Michael

Toolan) focuses on the notion of speech as action. References are made backward and forward among the chapters to help you see inter-connections among them.

Each chapter has a preface which is intended to give you a general idea of what the chapter is about. At the end of each chapter you will find a set of suggestions for further work. Typically, these will suggest other passages you can analyse or ask you to think harder about a particular aspect raised in the body of the chapter. It is worth bearing in mind that, as we said earlier, the theories and analytical frameworks described in this book need not be confined to the study of drama, but could be used to shed light on the dialogue in other text types, such as prose fiction or advertisements.

2 From dramatic text to dramatic performance

Mick Short

EDITORS' PREFACE

If we want to understand plays, can we sit in a classroom – or even in an arm-chair – and read them or should we be sitting in a theatre? Mick Short addresses this fundamental question. It is fundamental, because a stylistics of drama is based upon the premise that one can gain a rich and sensitive under-standing of a play by analysing the text. Firstly, Short presents a brief list of arguments for the adequacy of reading a play-text. In sum, he argues that, whilst the three aspects of a play – text, production and performance – are distinct in a number of ways, the production and performance are based on, and constrained by, inferences drawn from a reading of the text. To support this view, Short analyses extracts from the script of an episode of the TV series *Fawlty Towers*. He shows how a considerable number of unwritten performance features can be inferred from the dialogue, and introduces analytical frameworks by which we can recover these inferences. Most of these analytical approaches are then dealt with in more detail in later chapters of the book.

INTRODUCTION

The vast majority of plays are written to be performed.[1] As a consequence, many modern drama critics tell us that plays can only be properly understood and reacted to in the theatre. For example, J. L. Styan (1971 [1965]: 1) says that 'the fullness of music is only heard in performance, so it is with drama' and the Shakespearean critic Stanley Wells (1970: ix) that 'the reading of a play is a necessarily incomplete experience'. Writers and directors have also taken this position. Brecht tells us that 'Proper plays can only be understood when performed' (1964: 15), and Stanislavski says that 'it is only on the stage that drama can be revealed in all its fullness and significance' (1968: 115). But if merely reading a play is truly inadequate, much traditional drama criticism would need an interpretative 'health warning' appended to it, and our common educational practice of reading play-texts and discussing them in seminars and tutorials would need to be replaced by performance-based theatre studies. However, I want to suggest that the situation is nothing like as dire as this.

In this chapter I want to argue that sensitive understandings of plays can be arrived at through 'mere reading'[2] and will try to demonstrate, through detailed linguistic analysis of a dramatic extract, that dramatic texts contain very rich indications as to how they should be performed. In other words a play is a detailed 'recipe for pretence', as Searle (1975a: 328) puts it: the author of a play gives 'directions as to how to enact a pretence which the actors then follow'. This position overlaps with that outlined by semioticians of theatre like Elam (1980) and Aston and Savona (1991), which I would recommend as further reading (Aston and Savona is more accessible than Elam). As Aston and Savona (1991: 3) remark, studies like Styan (1971 [1965]) and Hayman (1977) 'which still have currency as introductions to theatre, are written in seeming ignorance of the relevance of semiotics to theatre studies, despite the development of this approach since the turn of the century'.

I should make it clear that I have nothing against performances, and am not trying to suggest that you shouldn't go to the theatre or study performances. Plays are written to be performed, and going to the theatre is usually an exhilarating and instructive experience. Moreover, theatrical performance is just as deserving of study as dramatic text (indeed, I am wanting to argue a relationship between them which is closer than most theatre critics would have us believe). In any case, I would argue that if you have never been to the theatre and don't know anything at all about the nature of theatrical conventions you probably can't read a play-text accurately enough to guarantee a sensitive understanding of it. But I do want to claim that if you have reasonable experience of going to the theatre then you can read play-texts sensitively, and with understanding.

TEXT, READING AND PERFORMANCE

As I have only limited space and want to concentrate mainly on analysing a text and predicting how it would be performed, my arguments in favour of the adequacy (even necessity) of reading play-texts will be a rather schematic list of points. However, these points will make clear my analytical assumptions and, at the very least, afford some areas for you to think harder about and discuss with others.

1 In order to put on a play, the director and actors must first read it, and presumably understand it. How else could they decide it was worth putting on and how to do it. Of course, they read the script many times, and some aspects of their understanding and how to perform the play may become clearer as they read and rehearse. But restricting full understanding to theatrical experience alone would appear to have the logical consequence that plays could never be sensibly performed.

2 In ontological terms, each production of a play would appear to be a play
PLUS an interpretation of it, in that the director and actors have to
decide which elements to focus on, emphasize in performance, etc. Note
also that some ambiguities which you can see when you read a text may,
of necessity, be forced one way or the other by the production. Films,
incidentally, don't appear to have the same ontological status as plays.
The scriptwriter is much less important and the director much more. Moreover, in most cases (apart from 'remakes'), with films there is only one
performance of one production, which is copied many times (just as books
are).

3 If what I have said in 2 above is right, *and* you also assume that plays can
only be properly understood in the theatre, there is a logical problem if we
want to discuss, say, *Hamlet,* unless we have both seen the same production.
We couldn't be sure that we were discussing the same thing, and so might
be talking at cross purposes.

4 Clearly, each production of a play will differ from all of the other productions. Whether they all differ enough for each to constitute a different
interpretation of the play is another matter. In part, working out the answer
to this question depends on your definition of 'interpretation'. I would
want to argue that many productions of plays are merely *variations on the
same interpretation.* Does putting on *Julius Caesar* in modern dress produce a
different interpretation of the play, as many newspaper drama critics
would have us believe? I would suggest not. It might help the audience to
feel more clearly the relevance of the play for modern times, but that is not
the same thing.

5 It is worth remembering that modern directors and actors have a pressure
on them to 'do something different' with plays that have been put on
many times before. They have to create theatrical 'news' in order to be
noticed, and, in an era when films and videotapes of previous productions
of plays are easily available, it is likely that productions and performances
will become more outrageous to gain critical attention and this can often
mean treating the text in a fairly cavalier fashion.

6 The problem, outlined in 3 above, of holding constant the object under
critical discussion becomes even more difficult when we remember that
each nightly performance of a particular production of a play will vary to
some extent from each of the other performances. How do we resolve this
conundrum? I would argue that each performance of a production of a
play is in essence a different *instantiation* of the same production. This
allows us to capture the fact that the performances will all be different,
and yet will also all be the same in other (usually more important) respects.
To use an analogy, think of two oak trees that you are familiar with. In
detail they will be different from one another, and indeed all other oak
trees. Yet they are both oak trees and not, say, sycamore trees. In other
words, some differences are more salient than others. This same point is
true of interpretations (see 4 above).

7 I think you can even watch a production of a play you have never seen or read before and distinguish between the contributions of the playwright and those involved in the production of the play in the theatre. I don't think you can do it in every single respect, but I would suggest that even if you have not read or seen the play before you can decide (a) whether the production you have seen was a reasonable rendering of the play, (b) whether the play is a good play or not and (c) whether the theatrical experience was good or not. For example, some years ago I saw a production of Shakespeare's history play, *King John*, directed by Buzz Goodbody at Stratford-upon-Avon, where the actors pretended to be puppets throughout. This production was an interesting and enjoyable theatrical experience, but was unfaithful to the original script. Although it used the words of the original, it did so in a way which was entirely different from the original intention, turning a history play into a puppet show farce. *King John* is arguably Shakespeare's most boring play, and the director probably had little choice if she was going to keep the audience in their seats. I have also seen a repertory production of *Macbeth*, a play I admire, which was at the same time both unreasonable (unfaithful) and a poor theatrical experience (more than half the audience had walked out before the end of the performance I saw). This production treated *Macbeth* as a comedy, with the action taking place in a lunatic asylum and with the three witches acting as nurses to the other characters, all of whom were inmates of the asylum. In this case, it was also possible on occasion to distinguish clearly the poor qualities of the acting from those of the production. The actress playing Lady Macbeth even managed to ruin her rendering of the famous lines 'The multitudinous seas incarnadine/Making the green one red' (II. ii. 63–4), interpreting the second of them as 'Turning the green one (i.e. the green sea, as compared with seas of other colours) red' instead of 'Turning the green (i.e. all the seas) red'.

8 Reading and watching plays both appear to have advantages and disadvantages. When you read, you can try things more than one way in your head, and you can go back to something you didn't understand. You can't do this in performance, but the acting, lighting, etc. (a) help you feel more vividly what is in the play and (b) help you to understand what is happening more easily, as you have both visual *and* aural information to help you. When you 'see' a play while reading it, the 'performance' is always perfect: the actors never fluff their lines, for example. On the other hand you can never be pleasantly surprised.

In general terms, then, I would argue that when sensitive and experienced readers interact with a play-text they in effect infer how the play would be performed on the stage. But if I am to persuade you of this view, I will need to provide an account of the reading experience which is rich enough to show how we can infer (a) what is often referred to as 'the meaning between the lines' and (b) how the play should be staged and performed.

INFERRING PERFORMANCE FROM TEXT: A SMALL EXAMPLE

Let us begin this section by examining a small extract from the very beginning of the 'Communication Problems' episode of the John Cleese/Connie Booth *Fawlty Towers* TV series. I choose the very beginning as there are no complications concerning assumptions of knowledge from previous parts of the text:

> [*The hotel lobby. Things are busy; Sybil and Polly are dealing with guests; Basil is finishing a phone call. He goes into the office. Mr Mackintosh comes to the reception desk.*]
> MACKINTOSH: [*to Polly*] Number seventeen please.
> SYBIL: [*to her guest*] Goodbye. Thank you so much. [*He moves off . . .*]
>
> (John Cleese and Connie Booth, *The Complete Fawlty Towers*,
> 'Communication Problems': 161)

It is well-known that stage directions constitute instructions to the director and actors. There is, however, considerably more direction over and above what the four initial sentences state. Once we know that the scene is a hotel lobby, even if we do not know the *Fawlty Towers* series, our schematic assumptions about hotels will lead us to expect to find all those things which hotel lobbies typically exhibit – for example a reception desk, and somewhere to store the room keys. The telephone is likely to be at the desk, and so Basil, Sybil and Polly will probably be behind it. The office which Basil enters will be behind the desk, and the customers will be on the other side. If things are busy, there must be quite a lot of people at the reception desk, coming and going. Sybil and Polly must also be performing appropriate actions (giving directions, settling bills, etc.). Basil must be talking on the telephone, even though his words are not specified, and must perform an appropriate telephone conversation ending routine and put the phone down before moving away.

Already we can see that the initial stage direction is very rich in terms of the performance detail which it specifies. It does not tell the performers *exactly* what to do or how, but it demarcates a clearly specified range of appropriate behaviour. The actress playing Polly can choose what behaviour to be performing behind the desk, but it must be appropriate for the hotel schema. She can't kiss the guests goodbye, munch a carrot or take her clothes off. She, like the other actors, is free to choose, but only from a limited set. Our schemata for telephone conversations will also help us to imagine Basil going through a 'thank you, goodbye' routine, with all the appropriate head nods, facial expressions and actions. Even the sequencing of the last two sentences of the stage direction tells us something: Basil must have gone into the office, or already be on his way there before Mr Mackintosh comes to the desk.

It is clear from his utterance that Mr Mackintosh must not come down the stairs to the desk. He is more likely to come from outside. He is obviously already resident, as he knows his room number, and if he is asking for his key he must have left it behind the desk, which typically happens when guests go out from a hotel. In this case, then, schematic assumptions concerning Mackintosh's utterance have a 'backwash logic' effect of delimiting earlier behaviour. He uses the politeness marker 'please', and, given this and our schematic assumption concerning the behaviour of hotel guests, it is likely that his facial expression and gestures will be polite and socially cohesive too. And Polly will have to find the key, probably from a rack behind the desk, and give it to him.

When Mackintosh says his line he will have to perform it with one over-arching intonation (tone) group, with the tonic syllable on the '-teen' of 'seventeen'. The politeness marker and the word 'number' can be assumed as given information in this context. If he is asking for his key it will have to have some number, and we would expect polite behaviour in this context too. The significant piece of information is the number itself, and except in lists of numbers, the normal place for the tonic to occur in this word is on the final syllable. Other 'performances' of the line are conceivable but extremely unlikely. It is hard to provide a sensible contextualization for placing the tonic on either of the syllables of 'number', for example, and placing it on the first syllable of 'seventeen' would presuppose a situation where there was some other issue about the number – for example that Polly had earlier mis-heard Mackintosh, and had tried to give him another key. Similarly, giving 'please' the tonic or dividing the utterance into two tone groups, by assigning 'please' to a tone group of its own would lead to a highlighting of that word, and hence to a social relationship between the two characters, which would be out of line with a normal hotel lobby transaction.

When Sybil says goodbye to her guest, it is clear that he must be leaving the hotel at the end of his stay (otherwise she would not need to thank him). This leads us to assume that Sybil and the guest must have been going through a payment routine, where she gives him the bill, he pays for it, she gives him a receipt, and so on. Although we are not explicitly told, when he moves off he will presumably have to exit by the front door, the one Mr Mackintosh entered through. Things have apparently gone well, and so Sybil and the leaving guest will have to exhibit appropriate facial expression and beha-viour. The fact that Sybil's utterance assigns the word 'goodbye' to a sentence of its own suggests that it will have to have its own intonation group; and to receive that kind of weighting it will need to be said fairly loudly and with quite a wide range of pitch movement (contrast this with Mr Mackintosh's 'please').

LESSONS TO BE LEARNED FROM THE ABOVE ANALYSIS

I have not specified all of the directing and acting consequences of this tiny and unimportant sequence, but it should now be clear that the amount of direction we can intuitively infer from the text is extremely high. I am not, of course, wanting to suggest that what I have outlined is the only possible way of acting this part of the script; and great directors and great actors will often be able to make something more of the text than mere analysts. But I would want to claim (a) that what I have outlined in terms of performance is extremely likely, given the evidence, (b) that an alternative way of acting the extract should be in principle supportable in a similar way and (c) that much more about performance is specified by the text than many drama critics would have us believe. For most non-linguists, because they operate so habitually and so fast with language, they do not realize the power that it has to lead us to infer aspects of meaning and significance.

The situation is somewhat different in the theatre, where we receive linguistic and non-linguistic information in concert, but in terms of reading dramatic texts and imagining aspects of performance, the following chain of reasoning applies:

Inferring performance from text:

What is said (in the dialogue and stage directions)
leads, via processes of inference, to
What is meant
which in turn leads, via inference, to

Performance features:

Action
What is done on stage (movement, placing of objects and other 'business'),
Gestures,
Body position and posture changes,
Facial expression,
Direction of gaze.

Speech
Assignment of general pronunciation features (e.g. non-standard accents, and
    unusual speech features, like stutters).
Assignment of intonation contours and tonic placement for each line.
Paralinguistic phenomena (e.g. tone of voice, loudness, speed of delivery,
    pauses, etc.).

Appearance
Gender, age and physical size of actors.
Skin colour, hair colour and other physical features.
What the characters wear.

The above list is almost certainly not complete. There also appears to be some ordering with respect to particular utterances in terms of chains of inference leading to performance phenomena. In the case of Sybil's utterance above, for example, we move from the syntactic and intersentential arrangement of the sentences to inferences about intonation, which in turn lead to paralinguistic specification (she can't shout what she says angrily, but has to be polite) and hence to inferences concerning facial expression and body posture.

Most of the above list of factors have been referred to in my discussion of the *Fawlty Towers* extract above. But we have not discussed what the characters look like and how they are dressed. There are no specific stage directions to this effect, and so there is some variation possible. It is unlikely, though, that the women behind the counter will be old, and, given their jobs, the people behind the counter will need to be tidily and relatively formally dressed. The customers could be more varied, of course, although if you know from previous episodes what sort of hotel *Fawlty Towers* is, you will probably have assumed middle-aged customers who will also be relatively formally dressed (suits, ties, etc.). So even dress and who is chosen to play a part are restricted. There are famous counter-examples (Sarah Bernhardt playing Juliet when an old woman, for example), but the script still has a massive effect in predisposing production and performance decisions.

Now let us outline some of the informational sets and 'systems' that are available to us to infer performance features from dramatic text. For reasons of space I won't discuss these systems in any detail here, but, where appropriate, refer you to relevant sections in later chapters of this volume where they are outlined:

- Background information about the world and how it works, often arranged into pre-packaged schemata (e.g. the hotel lobby schema, the telephone conversation schema – see Weber's contribution);
- Implicature/inference theory (see Cooper's contribution);
- Politeness theory (see Culpeper's contribution);
- Turn-taking conventions (see Herman's contribution);
- Speech acts (see Lowe's and Toolan's contributions);
- Sociolinguistic conventions;
- Graphological information;
- Sound structure;
- Grammatical structure;
- Lexical patterning.

A MORE EXTENDED EXAMPLE

Now let us have a look at a more interesting stretch of the *Fawlty Towers* sketch. A little after the opening I discussed above, Polly is dealing with a guest, Mr Thurston, when a new guest, Mrs Richards, arrives. She brusquely interrupts Polly (addressing her rudely as 'girl') and Mr Thurston in order to get some change to pay the taxi driver. Mrs Richards goes to pay the taxi driver. When she returns, Polly and Mr Thurston have not yet completed their transaction:

(1) THURSTON: Can you tell me how to get to Glendower Street . . .
     [*Mrs Richards has paid the driver, who exits. She turns back to Polly.*]
(2) MRS RICHARDS: Now, I've booked a room and bath with a sea view
     for three nights . . .
(3) POLLY: [*to Thurston*] Glendower Street? [*gets a map*].
(4) THURSTON: Yes.
(5) MRS RICHARDS: You haven't finished with me.
(6) POLLY: Mrs?. . .
(7) MRS RICHARDS: Mrs Richards. Mrs Alice Richards.
(8) POLLY: Mrs Richards, Mr Thurston. Mr Thurston, Mrs Richards.
     [*Mrs Richards, slightly thrown, looks at Mr Thurston.*] Mr Thurston is the
     gentleman I'm attending to at the moment.
                              [. . .]
(9) MRS RICHARDS: Isn't there anyone else in attendance here? Really,
     this is the most appalling service I've ever . . .
(10) POLLY: [*spotting Manuel*]. Good idea! Manuel! Could you lend
     Mrs Richards your assistance in connection with her reservation.
                    (John Cleese and Connie Booth, The Complete *Fawlty Towers*,
                                            'Communication Problems': 162)

In terms of conversational turn-taking rules Thurston's request for directions
clearly requires an answer from Polly, but before she can provide it
Mrs Richards interrupts again, with a rather peremptory statement, containing no politeness markers (note how the initial 'now' assumes that she has
the right to control the conversation, thus making it likely that it will be said
loudly and with a high falling intonation). She has now interrupted Polly
twice, as well as using the demeaning address term 'girl' earlier to get her
attention. All this clearly constitutes rude behaviour towards Polly in particular, but also to some extent towards Mr Thurston. Polly chooses to continue
to respond to Mr Thurston, not Mrs Richards, thus being polite to him but
not to her, by ignoring her. All this will have consequences for the facial
expressions of both Polly and Mrs Richards, and given that it is now clear
that an issue is developing between them, it is likely that when Mrs Richards
originally called Polly 'girl', Polly will have indicated her displeasure via
facial expression. Note how what occurs in later stretches of text may have
performance consequences for earlier parts.
    Polly and Mr Thurston return to the business of directions in turns 3 and 4,
and clearly they will have to be looking closely at the map. But before they
have finished the direction-giving sequence, Mrs Thurston interrupts again
in turn 5 with a statement of complaint which assumes that she had priority
and that Polly has not properly attended to her. Mrs Richards is thus likely
to be looking and acting annoyed. But from the viewpoint of Polly and
Mr Thurston, turn 5 itself constitutes another interruption by Mrs Richards.
Mr Thurston never responds to Mrs Richards, suggesting that he should
either seethe quietly with anger or be such a nice man that he doesn't mind.

The latter interpretation and consequential actions and facial expressions seem most likely. If he was getting annoyed, he would be unlikely to stay quiet, and in any case he has earlier indicated that he was happy to be interrupted in order for Mrs Richards to get her change for the taxi driver.

Mrs Richards has now been impolite to Polly at least four times, and so we can infer that by now Polly must be getting cross. It is this context which allows us to interpret turns 6–8 as heavily ironic on Polly's part. 'Mrs? . . .' is clearly an incomplete utterance, and the question mark predicts a rising and incomplete intonation contour. As it is the first word in a 'title + last name' sequence, it thus functions as a request for Mrs Richards's family name, which she supplies. Polly then goes through an introduction sequence for Mrs Richards and Mr Thurston. Given that they have no need to be introduced, we can infer that Polly's unnecessary behaviour constitutes a rebuke to Mrs Richards for interrupting Mr Thurston. She is thus likely to perform the introduction in a very exaggerated way, with exaggeratedly appropriate hand gestures, expressions, etc. A member of the hotel staff is thus being rude to a new guest, but in a rather indirect and apparently polite way. In other words, Polly has decided to do battle with Mrs Richards, but in a way which will not produce open warfare. The stage direction tells us that Mrs Richards is '*slightly thrown*', and so she will have to look puzzled.

Polly has now got the upper hand. She goes on to state to Mrs Richards that she is currently attending to Mr Thurston. This also counts as an indirect criticism of Mrs Richards, for if Mrs Richards was herself sensitive to the code of polite behaviour she would not have interrupted Polly's conversation with Mr Thurston. Polly also suggests that Mrs Richards will now have to wait until Mr Thurston's needs have been met, another act of indirect impoliteness towards Mrs Richards while at the same time being polite to Mr Thurston. By now, even if we have not seen these characters in *Fawlty Towers* before, we can infer quite a lot, not just about the facial expressions and gestures of the characters, but also about what they are like as people. Mrs Richards is clearly overbearing and self-centred. Polly, although she is just a hotel receptionist, is clearly a formidable woman: she possesses considerable verbal skills, enabling her to defeat Mrs Richards comprehensively, but subtly. These inferences concerning the characterizations of the two women will help us to work out how to predict their behaviour appropriately in later scenes.

There are another five turns in between what we have examined so far and the final two turns I have quoted above. In these intervening five turns the battle continues, with Mrs Richards losing her temper and shouting. We also discover that Mrs Richards is a bit deaf, which helps, to some extent, to explain her overbearing behaviour.

In turn 9, Mrs Richards produces a question and statement which clearly constitute the speech act of complaining. It is a very strong complaint (cf. 'most appalling service') and so we are likely to see her becoming very angry now, with appropriate gestures and expression. Polly then spots Manuel, the

Spanish waiter/porter who, as regular viewers of the *Fawlty Towers* series will know, has considerable difficulty in understanding English. Manuel has not been mentioned in this script until now, so it is likely that he is passing through the entrance hall on his way from one part of the hotel to another. As it is clear that he is later going to have to help Mrs Richards with her bags, he is unlikely to be carrying anything when he enters, or, if he is, he will have to put whatever it is down.

Polly now sees an opportunity to deflect Mrs Richards, allowing her to get back to Mr Thurston. The exclamatory 'Good idea!', with its accompanying exclamation mark, suggests a high falling intonation and a joyful expression on Polly's face. The exclamation mark for 'Manuel!' indicates another high fall intonation contour, said in a loud voice to attract Manuel's attention, and he must now look towards her. But perhaps the most interesting thing is what Polly then says to Manuel. She could have said something straight-forward and direct like 'Please help Mrs Richards with her bags.' But what she actually says is full of complex lexical items ('assistance . . . connection . . . reservation'), is grammatically complex and is also indirect in speech act terms. Instead of telling Manuel what to do, she produces an extremely indirect and polite request by asking Manuel a question about his ability to give Mrs Richards some help. Given Manuel's lack of skill in English, it is clear that Polly has asked Manuel to help in a manner that she knows is bound to confuse him. She is thus being apparently helpful to Mrs Richards while actually plotting to make her life difficult. Polly is thus likely to look self-satisfied, if not triumphant, and Manuel will look very puzzled. Mrs Richards will look expectant, as she thinks she is being helped, but we can predict that she is about to become very confused indeed by whatever Manuel says and does. This in turn begins to predict the range of future beha-viour in the scene for Manuel and Mrs Richards. Now read on . . .

CONCLUSION

I hope to have demonstrated that if you pay close attention to the linguistic form of (parts of) dramatic texts you can infer a huge amount of information about an appropriate way to perform them. This comes about because we carry with us a large amount of information about how to interpret utter-ances, and hence how they will be said, what gestures and actions will be appropriate, and so on. Not everything is predictable, and there is plenty of room for the director and actor to make their contributions to performance. But the range of appropriate behaviour is considerably more restricted than many critics would have us believe. Interestingly, it is the same process of inference concerning characterization, theme and so on which allows us to predict appropriate behaviour, and hence performance.

In discussing the short extract from the *Fawlty Towers* sketch, I have also referred very informally to a number of methods of analysis which will be described and used later in this collection, for example schema theory (see Weber), turn-taking (see Herman), speech acts (see Lowe and Toolan), politeness theory (see Culpeper) and the inferring of meaning through what is usually called the 'Co-operative Principle' of conversation (see Cooper). So, by the time you have finished reading the other chapters in this book you should be able to examine the performance characteristics of texts with considerably more precision than I have managed in this introductory chapter.

SUGGESTIONS FOR FURTHER WORK

You will get most out of the exercises below if you work at them in discussion with other students.

1 Consider each of the points made above in the section called 'Text, reading and performance'. Make up your own mind on each of the issues. Then write down any other considerations you can think of, and finally come to your own conclusion about whether you can understand a play without seeing it performed.
2 Note that poetry is also often performed in poetry readings. In that sense, drama is not the only performance genre. Is each performance of a poem a different interpretation of it? What consequences do your conclusions have for what differences constitute different interpretations? How does this relate to your consideration of interpretation in drama?
3 Take a 10-line sequence from any of the play extracts used in other chapters of this book which can be seen in videotaped form. Part of the text from *Cloud Nine* in Michael Toolan's chapter would be an interesting choice, as Toolan suggests a few performance characteristics in his commentary on it. Make detailed proposals for how each line should be performed. Note down, as carefully as you can, the evidence for your performance predictions. Then watch the videotape of the lines you have examined and compare your predictions with what happens on the tape. Estimate how close you were (give a rough percentage estimate?). Now look more carefully at the videotape, line by line. For each line, were the differences between your version and what is on the videotape reasonable alternative realizations of what you were predicting or more substantially different? Do you want to change your percentage estimate? If you prefer, you could watch the *Fawlty Towers* videotape and mark the performance predictions I make in this chapter!

NOTES

1 There are a few plays, *Otho the Great* by John Keats, for example, which were never intended to be performed. These are at one end of the dramatic spectrum. At the other end are avant-garde 'happenings' and 'recipe plays', where the actors are given only very general direction and are otherwise free to make things up as they go along, including the words they say. But most plays specify the words to be spoken and also give some stage directions. It is this prototypical kind of play that my comments relate to.
2 Some discussion of this matter can also be found in Short (1989).

3 Turn management in drama

Vimala Herman

EDITORS' PREFACE

Vimala Herman explores the insights that Conversation Analysis, developed by the ethnomethodologists, might afford the study of drama. In particular, she examines the concept of 'the turn': when someone speaks, they take a turn at speech, and when speech alternates, turns alternate as well. Drama as dialogue is a multi-input form, and this raises the issue of the distribution of turns and their management. After briefly reviewing the work of the Conversation Analysts, Herman considers the contribution that turn-taking patterns make to the understanding of situation and character in plays. She conducts an analysis of an extract from John Osborne's *Look Back in Anger*, and shows how turn-taking choices (e.g. who speaks to whom, length of turns, pauses, interruptions) affect the reader's interpretation of the characters' speech.

INTRODUCTION

The study of dramatic dialogue as interaction is a complex matter (Herman 1995), involving various frameworks of analysis, but central to the dynamics of interaction is the concept of *the turn*, which can be glossed, informally, as the enactment of a speaker's right to speak by taking an opportunity to speak in a speech event or situation. Although the scope of the concept of 'the turn' is debated in studies of conversation (see Edelsky 1993, for a review), the above suffices for our present purposes. When a speaker speaks, he or she takes a turn at speech and as speech alternates, turns alternate as well. The distribution of turns has, however, to be managed to mitigate the threat of speech chaos when numerous interacting participants have rights to speak and wish to take turns. The 'systematics' involved in turn-taking and turn management have been explored by the Conversational Analysts of the ethnomethodological school. The work of these analysts will be detailed briefly below.

TURN AND FLOOR MANAGEMENT

In a seminal article entitled 'A simplest systematics . . .' the Conversational Analysts of the ethnomethodological school, Sacks *et al*. (1978), attempted to describe the systematic properties involved in turn-taking and turn management in ordinary conversation. Out of the analysis of a large body of data, collected from contexts of naturally occurring speech, the authors revealed that spontaneous conversation, contrary to our habitual expectations, was both ordered and orderly and responsive to unconscious 'rules' that were being observed by participants in daily talk. Generalizing over the regularities identified, a 'system' or 'systematics' for talk regulation was proposed, which is composed of two components: (a) a turn-allocational component and (b) a turn-constructional component (Sacks *et al*. 1978; Levinson 1983: 296–303).

The *turn-allocational component* regulates the changeover of turns. In general, turn change proceeds smoothly: one participant talks, stops, the next participant talks, stops, and so on, but there can also be conflict at the changeover point, termed the Transition Relevance Place (abridged to TRP). A 'one-party-speaks-at-a-time' rule ensures that where there is interruption of the current speaker's turn, or the overlapping of speech either at the end or the beginning of turns, one speaker will drop out so that the turn-holder can proceed with his or her speech. Where this is not the case, and overlaps hold across most or all of the duration of the current speaker's turn, according to the 'one-party-speaks-at-a-time' rule, it could be assessed as conflict, but this is not the only option (see below), since other conventions might well be in force, which could complicate and problematize assessments of what is or is not an interruption or overlap. At any rate, turns have to be relinquished, so that the alternating course of the dialogic structure of turns comes into existence for the interactive possibilities of dialogue to be realized.

And the changeover can be accomplished in different ways. Firstly, *the current speaker can select next speaker* by indicating preference by naming, by the use of pronouns or address forms, by pointing, or by eye contact and gazing at the selected speaker, etc. Secondly, *the next speaker can self-select*, especially if the first option was not used. The selected speaker may not respond so that there is a *turn-lapse*, and the current speaker can incorporate the ensuing silence as 'lapse' into current turn and transform it into a 'pause', and continue with the turn and attempt to relinquish the turn at the next TRP by the use of either of the two methods described above. In the case of a lapsed turn, the silence that follows is regarded as an *attributable* silence, and attributed to the lapser as his or her silence. The lapser 'owns' the silence, as it were, although both parties could well be covertly active in different ways for its duration so that the silence is shared, but disparately. And there are other kinds of silence (Tannen and Saville-Troike 1985; Herman 1995: 96–9). Intra-turn speaker silences could be assessed as *pause*, and these can signify hesitation, or be used as a ploy for emphasis. Pause-ridden speech can also be used to dramatize the trials of bringing thought and language into alignment (Chafe 1985). *Gaps* can stretch from initial non-responsiveness followed by a response to full-scale silence. In the former case, when initial silence occurs between turns, gaps may constitute *switching pauses* when it is unclear as to whether the silence should be attributed to the first or second speaker or to both. An initial stretch of silence in response to another's speech can also be interpreted as caution, the speaker following the 'think before you speak' maxim. If nobody were selected or a potential next speaker does not self-select, the gap that follows can bring about closure. Silences are generally interpreted in relative terms; relative, that is, to the various cultural or inter-personal values associated with the performance of speech in context. For instance, interactants who privilege a fast tempo and verbosity in speech could find slower, deliberate, disfluent or laconic speakers a trial – and vice versa.

Turn allocational strategies can construct the *order* of turns via the various next speaker selection strategies mentioned above. In two-party speech, turns may alternate in A–B–A–B . . . fashion. In multi-party instances, the order may sanction speech rights for only some selected or self-selected other or others within the pool of possible participants, and flout the democracy of turn rights which is the unstated norm believed to be operative in Western, English-speaking contexts, which is where most turn-taking research has been conducted. Turn-allocational strategies, however, can control the turn order adopted. And the order is significant, since who speaks to whom and who is not spoken to within the contingencies of a situation can colour the way in which the situation itself develops. For instance, if in three-party speech the order were to be A–C–A–B–A–B–A–B . . . C's exclusion from speech by the selection strategies used by the other two could create a notice-ably asymmetrical situation.

The *turn-constructional component* regulates variables like the size or length and linguistic texture of a turn. Again, where democracy of turn rights is a strong expectation, long speeches require negotiation, and in conversation speakers who require extra turn time usually signal the need, and attempt to get ratification prior to taking a long turn, as is evident in instances when speakers wish to narrate some personal experience. Bids for 'the floor' are made and, if accepted, the narrative proceeds, as in *A: You know what happened on my street the other day?/B: What?/A: Well, there was this . . .*, where B, via the responsive question, hands the turn back to A for further elaboration as answer. Long turns place a burden of listening on recipients and, hence, should be used judiciously if the threats of boredom, hostility, etc. on the part of listeners are to be countered. Long turns also block access to the floor for other potential speakers and can function as a ploy for dominance, exclu-sion or coercion, depending on whether resistance or challenge or counter-measures are undertaken in response.

Short turns, too, are dependent on the responsive dimension for their value interactively – and could be used to signify indifference, urgency, the need for extra detail if questions are relayed in succession on the same topic, and so on. Various speech repertoires and styles could be used to vary the linguistic structure and texture of the turn – different registers, markers of formality or informality, fluency or disfluency, dialects, code-switching, bilingualism, one-word versus multi-clause turns, poetic or rhetorical styles, etc. could be mobilized as the occasion demands.

Turns also have a joint orientation to the *topic* of talk, i.e. what is talked about, which can form a point of focus as participants initiate, develop, close or change topics via the course of talk. The cohesiveness of a stretch of talk is achieved by various means, but the glue of topic is one important factor. Successive turns and speakers can orientate collaboratively to develop a topic, or negotiate change or closure. Turns in sequence have a projective and a retroactive dimension to them; they can point back to a previous turn, as when an answer is given to a question issued in a previous turn, or constrain the nature of the next turn, as when one issues a greeting to another. But *turn skips* are also possible when one speaker does not orientate to a previous speaker's turn or concerns, but orientates to topics raised in one's own which involves skipping the other's turn. Thus, although each participant takes a turn in alternating fashion, a double strand of talk running more or less independently can also occur. Thus different degrees of co-operativeness and intermeshing of concerns are possible.

The system, as described by Sacks *et al.* (1978) is a general system as well as one that is *locally* managed by participants themselves within the contingencies of a situation. The local management aspects of the system can exploit the different features and variables for specific functional uses.

FLOORS AND TURNS

The above description of the turn-taking system provides one set of conventions for the conversational 'floor' and the 'rules' by which turns are managed within it. '*The floor*' in Conversational Analysis is actually a complex concept and is understood differently by different analysts (Edelsky 1993). The most usual usage is to conflate 'turn' and 'floor', so that taking a turn involves taking the 'floor', or 'having' the floor. Where 'schisms' occur, and different groupings and participant structures develop more or less simultaneously, as in large dinner parties, and there are different foci for talk among different participants, multiple floors can occur (Shultz, Florio, and Erickson 1982), while the overall situation remains the same. In 'free-for-all' floors (Edelsky 1993) much talk is conducted in overlap, with interactive business being jointly constructed via simultaneous speech which is not assessed as either conflictual or competitive.

Other turn-taking conventions can create different types of 'floor' and thus organize the flow of talk differently. In institutional settings, the order of turns is controlled not spontaneously but by appropriate institutional conventions. For instance, in a formal board meeting, the Chair would authorize who speaks when, as the Speaker would in the House of Commons. Legal contexts have elaborate arrangements regarding who speaks when and to whom. Different cultures, too, could adopt turn orders which award precedence to seniority by age or social rank even in non-institutional settings, as for instance, the Japanese 'round robin' type of floor arrangements in mixed-sex interactions (Watanabe 1993).

The 'one-speaker-speaks-at-a-time' requirement in the turn-taking model described above privileges the lone speaker and its turn, which assumes centrality and becomes the focus of others' attention. The consequence is that a focused and homogeneous 'floor' results via turn-taking rules which preserve the requirement. Where there are dual starts, for instance, one speaker must drop out so that the integrity of the speaking turn can be maintained and the turn can proceed unsullied by other voices. Interruption and overlap are thus assessed as 'competition' for the floor in this model. And in most cases, these conventions appear to operate as predicted, not least because participants wish to hear what the speaker has to say.

'Free-for-all' floors, on the other hand, as Edelsky (1993) notes, are characterized by much simultaneous speech with partial or full *overlaps* enacting collaboration of a different kind, with multiple speakers using the same next turn in answer to a question, or building up different aspects of a joke in different ways simultaneously to tease previous speakers, or by different speakers and different utterance units and contents, contributing to the development of an idea, again simultaneously, with multiple speakers displaying thereby that they are on 'the same wavelength'. Collaboration in this kind of floor uses simultaneous speech, overlaps, etc. positively. These aspects are generally negatively assessed in the singly constructed floor. Different conventions for turn-taking result with the same structural and behavioural features being open to different interpretations. The 'free-for-all' or 'collective' floor is more multi-dimensional than linear, with different kinds of speech business proceeding simultaneously, and with overlaps and simultaneous speech not seen as conflictual. The central speaker role is more circumscribed by comparison, and self-selection in the 'free-for-all' floor can produce multiply occupied speech turns as a matter of course, the focus to previous turn being jointly and multiply performed by others as a mode of joint collaboration. Erstwhile hearers, as speakers, may develop their own line of thought, in depth, in speech tandem with others without a sense of conflict occurring. Turn-holders have to negotiate their goals in speech and may often speak in unison with others, either sharing common goals and functions with different utterances, or even with the same utterance.

Different floor conventions generate different turn-taking strategies and the interactive structures that they authorize as 'normal'. Singly developed floors with the 'one-speaker-speaks-at-a-time' rule in force, awards a pivotal role to the *sotto voce* speaker, with 'collaboration' interpreted as respect of speaker's rights; others are cast as non-speaking 'hearers' who change discourse role to speakers with the same turn rights. Turns respect previous turns, and, if projecting future turns, require reciprocal attention, usually from one next speaker, either current-speaker-selected, or self-selected. A linear path of development ensues, with interruptions, overlaps, etc. negotiated economically so that the speaker may proceed with a turn. Any disruption of speaker rights by another speaker is generally, if not always, seen as conflictual. And the different floor conventions could be gendered. Women contribute more in collective floors, whereas single floors favour male participation. The focus of this chapter is on the single floor and its rules and conventions and the exploitation of these in drama, since the single floor is more commonly capitalized on in drama.

TURN MANAGEMENT IN DRAMA

The order of speech in dramatic texts is organized to project the order of turns to be taken by the *dramatis personae* and is in the control of the dramatist. The turn-taking conventions used can design different floor types and different situations as a result, since a great many situational kinds make their appearance in drama. Given that the fictional contexts of plays, in the 'lateral' or 'horizontal' dimension of character–character interactions, simultaneously project on a 'vertical' dimension of stage to the audience, dialogue in drama is under the necessity to be heard and understood by the receivers, and thus dramatic dialogue has generally been regarded as tidied up speech, eschewing the use of 'spoken' characteristics like false starts, repetition, interruption, overlaps, simultaneous speech, etc. In fact, a comparison between transcriptions of naturally occurring speech and even the most 'naturalistic' of dramatic speech reveals that the latter is a representation of ordinary speech, and not a mirror image of it. Yet this is to compare 'texts', graphic representations of the two, and not actual performance. In performance, where the medium or channel is the voice, the resource can be manipulated to include multiple voices in overlap, or simultaneous speech, pauses, gaps, etc., but these options, in drama, would be subordinated to some dramatic function.

The one-speaker-speaks-at-a-time kind of floor and the turn-management strategies that construct it are the dominant mode of organizing speech in drama. But within this overall mode, the use of turn-lapses, pauses, gaps, interruptions, overlaps, either partial or as full simultaneous speech, also make their appearance (see Herman 1995: Ch. 2 for fuller discussion). Such choices bring significant elements of meaning which can condition the content and function of what is 'said' or meant by a speaker's speech. For instance, where a dramatic character is consistently interrupted and the opportunity to speak is consistently denied to one or other character, and no counter-bid to speak is successful, the interrupted speaker can be interpreted as the less powerful interactant. Similarly, when dual starts are made for a turn, and become a consistent ploy which does not succeed in gaining attention and the floor, or if turn-taking choices by-pass a character's attempts to speak, the path constructed by the use of such options can dramatize or enact the fact of a character's ineffectuality. Consistent turn-lapses on the part of a targeted other who is addressed by a speaker can signal indifference, boredom, hostility, the desire to be left in peace, opting out, etc. and import negative tones into the interaction, even in silence.

In floors of this kind, the event being constructed by speech can colour the situation and interpretation of those who are jointly involved in creating it, turn by turn. The following are all variables in the system: (a) who speaks to whom, (b) who is not spoken to, (c) who listens or doesn't listen, (d) whether listeners are responsive in turn, or not, (e) whether those who respond are those targeted by the speaker or not, (f) length of speeches, (g) linguistic style and texture of a character's speech, (h) how changeovers are effected, (i) the uses of silences, either intra- or inter-turn. Situation, event and character thus emerge, develop, in the 'here and now' of speech as speech alternation is blocked or progresses in troubled or untroubled fashion.

In the analysis of the extract given below, the variables in the turn-taking system will be identified and the specific patterns and choices of uses will be interpreted for what they contribute to a reader's understanding of the dramatic situation they construct. This is inevitably a partial analysis, since other dimensions, like turn sequencing and pragmatics, and gender, are left out of account. The interest is in the use of the turn-taking system and the turn-management strategies used for what they contribute to the understanding of this extract. The extract itself is taken from John Osborne's *Look Back in Anger*. There are four dramatic characters – Jimmy and Alison are a married couple, whose marriage is in trouble. Cliff and Jimmy are enduring friends, but Cliff is also close to Alison and a confidant of hers. Helena, an actress, and a long-standing friend of Alison's, is visiting the couple. The turns are numbered for reference.

(1) JIMMY: Oh, yes, and I know what I meant to tell you – I wrote a poem while I was at the market yesterday. If you're interested, which you obviously are. [*To Helena*] It should appeal to you, in particular. It's soaked in the theology of Dante, with a good slosh of Eliot as well. It starts off "There are no dry cleaners in Cambodia!"

(2) CLIFF: What do you call it?

(3) JIMMY: "The Cess Pool!" Myself being a stone dropped in it, you see –

(4) CLIFF: You should be dropped in it, all right.

(5) HELENA: [*to Jimmy*]. Why do you try so hard to be unpleasant?
[*He turns very deliberately, delighted that she should rise to the bait so soon – he's scarcely in his stride yet.*]

(6) JIMMY: What's that?

(7) HELENA: Do you have to be so offensive?

(8) JIMMY: You mean now? You think I'm being offensive? You underestimate me. [*Turning to Alison.*] Doesn't she?

(9) HELENA: I think you're a very tiresome young man.
[*A slight pause as his delight catches up with him. He roars with laughter.*]

(10) JIMMY: Oh dear! oh dear! My wife's friends! Pass Lady Bracknell the cucumber sandwiches, will you?
[*He returns to his meal, but his curiosity about Alison's preparations at the mirror won't be denied any longer. He turns round casually, and speaks to her.*]
    Going out?
(11) ALISON: That's right.
(12) JIMMY: On a Sunday evening in this town? Where on earth are you going?
(13) ALISON: [*rising*]. I'm going out with Helena.
(14) JIMMY: That's not a direction – that's an affliction.
  [*She crosses to the table, and sits down C. He leans forward, and addresses her again.*]
    I didn't ask you what was the matter with you. I asked you where you were going.
(15) HELENA: She's going to church.
    [*He has been prepared for some plot, but he is as genuinely surprised by this as Cliff was a few minutes earlier.*]
(16) JIMMY: You're doing what?
    [*Silence.*]
    Have you gone out of your mind, or something? [*To Helena*] You're determined to win her aren't you? So it's come to this now! How feeble can you get? [*His rage mounting within.*] When I think of what I did, what I endured, to get you out –
(17) ALISON: [*recognising an onslaught on the way, starts to panic*]. Oh yes, we all know what you did for me! You rescued me from the wicked clutches of my family, and all my friends! I'd still be rotting away at home, if you hadn't ridden up on your charger and carried me off!
                    (Osborne 1965 [1957], Act 1, 50–1)

The turn-taking system proposed by Sacks *et al.* (1978) is one of the options for turn allocation and to initiate turn change. Current speaker can select next, to whom turn rights pass; or next speaker can self-select, or the turn may lapse and the original speaker may incorporate the 'lapse' into their own turn as 'pause' and continue with the turn and try to relinquish it at the next TRP by the choice of one or other of the options mentioned above. In the extract all three options are used, but with different frequencies of occurrence, and with variations on how next turns are actually taken. The two most frequent options used are current speaker selecting next and self-selection, but they often clash since the speaker selected by current speaker is not the one who speaks next, since next speaker self-selects against the rights to speak of the previously selected speaker. Jimmy is the 'dominant' character. Eight of the seventeen turns are Jimmy's and Jimmy does most of the selection. In Turn 1, Jimmy chooses Helena, but Cliff takes Turn 2. Helena self-selects in Turn 5, changing the focus and direction of the talk away from Cliff to herself. After a brief exchange with Helena, Jimmy chooses Alison in mid-turn in Turn 8. But it is Helena who takes Turn 9. After a brief interchange with Alison, whom he chooses, Jimmy's address to Alison again in Turn 14 is returned by Helena. The self-selections are therefore 'turn-grabs' by unauthorized speakers who interpose themselves between Jimmy and his targets.

Turn-grabs

Turn-grabs can have different functions, since interposing oneself into an interaction uninvited and against the rights of invited speakers can be either self-orientated, to promote one's own interests, or other-orientated. It appears to be the latter here, given that Jimmy selects his targets in order to bait them in one way or another. Thus, the sarcasm directed at Helena in Turn 1, and the potential conflict it can initiate is deflected from developing by Cliff who interjects his own contribution and makes himself Jimmy's inter-actant rather than Helena for the next two turns. Helena, however, installs herself into the interaction, and takes her delayed turn by self-selection, and, 'rising to the bait', challenges Jimmy. After a brief exchange with her, Jimmy selects Alison, but Alison's turn lapses as Helena interposes herself between Jimmy and Alison, continuing her challenge to him. In Turn 10 Jimmy chooses Alison again, but on a change of topic – as to where she is going. A brief altercation with Alison ensues, but when it gets critical, in Jimmy's insistence to be told *where* she is going, Helena interposes herself in place of Alison again in Turn 15, powerfully sidelining Alison in her use of the third person 'she' in Alison's presence, while taking her turn. Jimmy's Turn 16, addressed to Alison chiefly, gets a collective lapse, and the silence becomes a 'gap' since nobody self-selects to answer him, and Jimmy incorporates the gap into his own turn and continues, choosing first Alison, then Helena, then an aside to himself, and then Alison again in the space of one turn, leaving little room for any response. Alison cuts his turn off with an interruption and holds the floor (even though in panic, as the stage directions note) with a long turn, thus inhibiting his access to the floor.

The development of hostility reciprocally is frustrated by the others self-selecting to speak to deflect the barbs. Turn-changes in the responsive dimension are actually effected in such a way as to curtail the dominance awarded to Jimmy in the frequency of turns. Alison is the most protected in this way, usually by Helena. Cliff, too, acts on Helena's behalf, although Helena has her say, nevertheless, even in delayed mode.

Turn allocation

In defiance of canonical expectations built into turn-taking 'rules', Jimmy's turn allocation strategies via participant selection are *not* designed only to pass his turn to another. His choice of addressee is usually politic, since he targets, often midturn, the addressee most likely to be undermined by his taunts – the two women, in particular. The turn allocational strategy used first targets those he names as the butts of his speech and then the passing of turn to them is challenging, confrontational. Thus, in Turn 1, Jimmy turns to Helena and selects her by gaze, and addresses the last part of his turn to her, with the sting in the tail specifically aimed at her: 'It should appeal to you, in particular. It's soaked in the theology of Dante, with a good slosh of Eliot as well . . .'. Similarly, in Turn 8, having declared to Helena to whom his turn is addressed that she underestimates him, he selects Alison at the end with the challenge for confirmation 'Doesn't she?' In Turn 16, there are swift changes of addressee from Alison to Helena and back to Alison which brackets them, in his perception, as in collusion against him. The content of his turn becomes accusatory and negative. Although all three participants are addressees and part of the interactive 'floor', Cliff is generally omitted from the scope of the address, as the untargeted addressee, and the conflict and antagonism is directed specifically at one or both of the women.

Turn order

Turn order, too, reveals unequal distribution of turns among those present. The seventeen turns that constitute the extract can be subdivided into basically two-party interactions in succession, within the four-party floor. Jimmy is central to all the interactions and the participant structures in force. All present address Jimmy. He is thus the focal point of their speech. They do not address each other, and so no 'free-for-all' floors or 'schisms' via turn management ensue. This is the 'holding forth' 'one-speaker-speaks-at-a-time', linear development of action which single floors encourage (Edelsky 1993), which provides space for the turn-holding speaker and individuates its participatory trials and outcomes. Turn order takes up and drops participants, one at a time, in succession. Thus, Turns 1–4 have Jimmy–Cliff–Jimmy–Cliff in interaction. The pattern then changes to Helena–Jimmy until Turn 11, when it passes to Alison. Alison's selected turn at Jimmy's Turn 8 lapses as Helena proceeds. In Turn 10, Jimmy addresses Alison and the turn order takes a different course: Alison(Turn 11)–Jimmy–Alison–Jimmy. Helena takes Alison's Turn 15, and so there is yet another shift – Helena to Jimmy, but the order reverts to Jimmy–Alison. Apart from Jimmy, Helena is awarded most turns and interactive prominence in the turn distribution pattern used. Alison has to wait her turn till the last third of the extract.

Turns to speak for Alison are delayed till Turn 11. Cliff, who takes turns at the beginning of the extract, is then sidelined by the other interactions. There is a difference, however, since nobody speaks for Cliff, whereas Helena does for Alison. Nobody targets him, either, as Alison is targeted by her husband. Active measures undertaken to block the Jimmy–Alison participation marginalize Alison more, even if in her own interests, and make her the most vulnerable character in the episode. But the vulnerability can be ambiguous, and can be portrayed variously. For instance, if another option, provided by the turn-taking system but not included in the stage directions, were to be used by a director, a different interpretation of Alison's demeanour and character could be constructed. And this is dependent on the way silence is used. The above interpretation is built on the assumption that others 'turn-grab' – i.e., turns are returned with the usual split-second timing habitual in conversations. But if Alison were to play her non-responsiveness as a *turn-lapse*, so that she actively *does not answer* when addressed by Jimmy, thus intentionally and ostentatiously ignoring him and his taunts, then her performance would seem more actively resistant, even if she does not take her turn. In fact, she does perform an obvious turn-lapse to Jimmy's Turn 14 when he expresses his opinion of what he thinks of her going out with Helena: 'That's not a direction – that's an affliction.' She does not respond either in comment/comment fashion, or to the implicit demand for information as to where she is going. She indulges in stage business instead, merely crossing to the table and sitting down, which leads Jimmy to repeat his question again. The script and content of her turns does not change, but the change in the distribution of silences at TRP or turn juncture would make a significant difference to the kind of meaning that is conveyed. But whether her silences are played passively, as the consequence of others' grabs, or as turn-lapses, actively, the delay of speech turns for her does contribute to the building up of tension within her, which explodes in the final confrontation with Jimmy at the end.

The fact of ambiguities, and the multiple interpretations they generate, can be extended to cover the nature of 'the floor' and the participant structure that is configured by the turn-taking. And these are wholly dependent on which kind of turn management rules are assumed to be in force when interpreting the dialogue. They do not arise, in this instance, as a consequence of what is said in the text or script which remains constant across the different interpretations. The canonical participant structure is the 'single' floor, which is the one in use here – with one speaker speaking and the others cast as addressees, in a Speaker–Hearer(s) configuration. But the configuration in the extract could equally be characterized differently, with splits introduced between targeted and untargeted addressees at the reception end of the configuration (Levinson 1988) so that the ostensible addressees are not the real targets of speech but someone else in the participant structure, to whom the goals of a speaker's speech are actually directed, with the gazed-at or otherwise-selected addressee mediating the relay. 'Footing' changes (Goffman 1979) could thus be introduced into the participant structure, but without any change in the 'words' of the dialogue.

From this perspective, Alison is actually the targeted addressee. Most of Jimmy's speech antics to Cliff and Helena could be interpreted as having been designed for her benefit and actually directed at her, even when Cliff and Helena are Jimmy's immediate addressees. The hostility displayed to Helena is targeted at her personally as well, but relayed beyond her, the end-point including Alison. The address to Alison, while speaking to Helena, makes it evident that Jimmy's own consciousness of the participant configuration in which he is involved includes Alison. He does not attempt to get Cliff involved in this way. Again, this mode of performance of his turn could be interpreted variously. It could be either that he is being a considerate participant and wants to involve his wife within the terms of participation by selecting her for speech, or that he wishes her to know that she is also targeted, since his address to her presupposes her attention to what he is saying and doing with the others. Given the negative and interpersonally offensive nature of his speech, indirectly barbed, as it is, the 'considerate' option is less plausible than the alternative one – that the extended relay of his intentions in speech are basically directed at her, which his addressive prompt monitors and makes manifest.

Turn change, on the whole, is smoothly achieved. One speaker speaks, stops, and the next speaker speaks, stops, and so on. There is variation, however, in the two interruptions, both of Jimmy's turn, once by Cliff at the beginning in Turn 3, and again by Alison at the end in Turn 16. These are marked options given the dominant pattern of smooth turn change. But as mentioned above, turn-lapses could be introduced wherever there is a turn-grab, on Helena's part after Jimmy's first address to her, and again, to Alison after Turns 8 and 14. The two dominant participants, Jimmy and Helena, conduct their interactions via smooth turn change. They give each other a full hearing and exchange offences in equal measure, promptly and smoothly. Smooth turn change, paradoxically, does not produce comity, but facilitates an equality between them in the control of the conflict that is enacted between them. Cliff and Alison, on the other hand, interrupt Jimmy and attempt thereby to stem the flow of Jimmy's speech and block his access to the floor. Whereas Helena displays her ability to confront and engage with Jimmy on his terms, and he with hers, neither Cliff nor Alison have the stomach for it.

Turn size and texture

Turn size and texture also vary, but not drastically. Jimmy's turns are occasionally longer, multi-clause turns which he uses to develop or to intensify some personal point to be delivered to his interactant – to Helena in Turn 1 to mock her, or in Turn 16, to Alison, to magnify his feeling of outrage at the thought of her aligning herself with Helena in going to church. His turns can also include many questions, rather than one, or question and comment, and so on, although short, one-clause turns are also evident – to express surprise and disbelief, as in 'You're doing what?' to Alison about the imminent visit to church, or in the pretence of innocence to Helena in Turn 6 'What's that?' in response to her direct expression to him of his unpleasantness. Apart from Alison's Turn 17 at the end, when she matches his outburst with one of her own in equivalent fashion, all the rest are short turns. Helena's turns are all one-clause, the brevity emphasizing the directness of encounter – 'Why do you try so hard to be unpleasant?' or 'Do you have to be so offensive?' or 'I think you are a very tiresome young man', and later, 'She's going to church'.

Alison's turn-lengths vary – short, one clause, evasive answers to begin with but culminating in a long and desperate turn at the end. After her enigmatic silent presence for most of the extract she takes the floor with Jimmy, responding to his questions, but her answers are not satisfactory to Jimmy, who reinitiates his questions till Helena gives him the answer which Alison had withheld. The weapon of silence – *not saying* what he required of her – finds its mark far more effectively than either his spoken taunts or Helena's directness had done. Whereas his interactions with Helena's counter-insults to him were met, as the stage directions state, with 'delight' and roaring laughter, he responds to Alison with mounting 'rage'. In her last turn in this extract, Alison not only emerges into full speakerhood (hers is a turn as long as Jimmy's), but she interrupts Jimmy and reduces him to silence as well. Thus, the tables are turned, with the silent, often passive, long-suffering Alison taking centre stage, and using speech as weapon in active mode, back against Jimmy, whose speech profile has been high throughout the extract. But participatory, counter-speech with Jimmy, for better or for worse, is not her usual mode of interaction with him. Jimmy's excessive, aggressive speech tactics and Alison's silent, non-responsiveness and non-reactions, of the kind dramatized here, are part of their marital relationship, which construct a destructive pathology of speech and silence. Only at the end of the play does turn-taking in interpersonally collaborative fashion occur systematically between them, and speech and counter-speech approximates to the canonical requirement of interpersonality. Cliff uses one-liners, in laconic fashion, and then opts out.

The *linguistic style* is uniform for all of them – 'naturalistic', standard language prose, in informal, conversational idiom. Given that class is an issue – for Jimmy – in performance Alison's accent could well reflect her upper-class status, with the others distributed according to their class affiliations. Jimmy, however, in spite of his work at the market, and declared friendships with others of his origins and contempt for Alison's class, betrays his own 'upward mobility' class split – the literary allusions which pepper his speech to Helena (Dante, Eliot, Wilde) reflect his distance from the class origins he champions. His speech casts him as university-educated middle class, even in rebellion against it. Jimmy is thus a more ambivalent figure than his proclaimed class stances might lead one to believe, entrapped in, and resistant to, his class position. Although, in the 1950s, the play questioned hallowed myths regarding class, empire, etc., the sting in the social ambiguities of class, it would seem, is not easily overcome. Jimmy also has a more complex *speech style* – he can be indirect – targeting the women, while bantering with Cliff; sarcastic, especially to Helena, direct and challenging or expressive of personal outrage, and demanding in his interactions, especially with Alison. Helena is mostly direct in delivering questions, even 'face-threatening' ones, or answers to Jimmy. Alison's speech style is mostly composed of answers, delivered in minimalist mode, to Jimmy, except for the final long and sarcastic counter-turn.

Topic control is generally in Jimmy's hands, and others' turns orientate to his. Helena is the exception, since it is she who initiates the topic of his unpleasantness with which he engages, but the other topics, like his poem, and where Alison is going, are initiated by him. Neither Cliff nor Alison bother to challenge his topics, nor initiate their own. Cliff develops Jimmy's topic of his poem by requesting information about it but then interrupts him with a bantering, half-serious comment of his own. Alison is the minimal respondent when she is allowed to or bothers to answer at all. Thus both attempt either to opt out, or to stop development of the course they suspect is about to come into existence by aborting it with interruption.

CONCLUSION

The variables of the system have thus been used in complex fashion throughout the extract to give us cues to interpret both situation and character. The situation is a conflictual one with Jimmy central to the conflict. The situation develops in sequential fashion, with Jimmy interacting with each of the participants in turn. He is the constant participant with all of them, and all the others' turns are addressed to him, which makes him the focus of their attention. The majority of turns are also Jimmy's, and he also initiates the majority of topics. His speech style is varied and complex and adapted to his goals in speech, and he often takes marginally longer turns than the others. The others, given their limited speech presence, relative to his, are mostly short turns, except for Alison's at the end.

Jimmy's control of turn-management procedures awards him dominance, but other factors in the *responsive* dimension, in the strategies used by recipients, in the turn-by-turn unfolding of action, curtail and modulate his dominance. Next turn rarely passes to Jimmy's selected speaker, so that the turn order that actually comes into existence is outside his control, even if the turn order achieved centralizes him. He is also the only speaker to be interrupted twice, so that the intended course of his speech is blocked off by others. The breaks on Jimmy's belligerence are temporary, since he proceeds to wrangle with each of the other characters in turn. His belligerence, too, is modulated and strengthens as the episode proceeds. He interacts half-jokingly with Cliff, and then mockingly with Helena, but gets directly confrontational with Alison. The delay in bringing Jimmy into engagement with Alison only serves to intensify the incipient friction between them, since others' turn-grabs and her own silences had served to hold her at bay and deflect the tension, which then erupts into open conflict when the two are properly face to face. Alison's matching counter-speech at least temporarily silences him, since he is interrupted and given a counter-dose of sarcasm in a long turn which blocks his access to speech, and which changes the contour of the episode by giving her the upper hand.

Helena's strategies portray her as direct and confrontational and as a powerful opponent, equal to Jimmy, a fact that contributes to their sexual attraction and alliance which occurs later in the play. She is self-directed, self-selects more than once and frustrates his turn choices. She initiates her own topic, and holds her own with Jimmy, turn for turn, without either interrupting or being interrupted, but she is bypassed by Jimmy when he turns the course of his talk to Alison. Alison is the most enigmatic and ambivalent of them all – protected but sidelined by the others, but resistant and provocative in her very silences. Jimmy has to try again and again to engage her, before he finally provokes her into speech. Cliff is the foil to the more intense interpersonal dramas being enacted. A detailed examination of this extract from *Look Back in Anger* shows us that what is important in interpreting dramatic dialogue is not just the meaning of what is said, but the management of the saying itself, in the judicious use of the variables of the turn-taking system which the dialogue projects.

SUGGESTIONS FOR FURTHER WORK

Select a passage from a play and analyse it for the turn-taking mechanisms used. You might look at the passage from Arthur Miller's *Crucible* in Lowe (this volume); or the passage from Shakespeare's *Taming of the Shrew* containing the interaction between Katherina and Petruchio (discussed from a Gricean perspective by Cooper in this volume); or a passage from Shaw's *You Never Can Tell* (e.g. 1984 [1898]: 214–17). All these should prove rewarding. Questions you can ask yourself include: How many participants are there? And what strategies are used for turns to be exchanged among them and what patterns are created in the variable use of options for turn change – of current speaker selecting next/next speaker self-selecting/turn-lapse, if any? In other words you need to examine the passage for patterns of who speaks to whom, who is not spoken to, who is addressed and who speaks, etc. to get an idea of how the turn-taking rules are exploited. Also, look for smooth turn change patterns and instances of interruption, pause and overlap. Who has control of topic, and how does it develop? What does the choice of turn size and turn texture/style contribute? Who is dominant and why? And finally, why do you think the dramatist has designed speech in this way in this extract, and what does the design contribute to the portrayal of the situation and the characters who are involved in producing it via the speech strategies used?

4 Odd talk

Studying discourses of incongruity

Paul Simpson

EDITORS' PREFACE

A number of famous twentieth-century plays have been characterized as absurdist, and this has led to critical consideration of what it is that makes a play absurd. One clear aspect of absurdity is what, in this chapter, Paul Simpson calls 'odd talk'. He shows that odd talk often involves taking the assumptions and patterns from one discourse context and using them in another, where they would not normally be found. He then goes on to demonstrate the effects of this kind of discoursal 'mismatch' in absurd drama by examining in detail extracts from Ionesco's *Victims of Duty*, showing how the detective 'softens up' Monsieur Choubert through excessive politeness for what appears to be a very social minor intrusion, before suddenly launching into a savage cross-examination of him. Absurdism is often linked with humour, and Simpson goes on to explore a small extract from a sketch in the *Monty Python's Flying Circus* series where two men meet for the first time in a bar. Instead of the phatic talk which normally characterizes such first meetings, we observe one of the characters asking a series of highly personal questions of the other, generating considerable humour and the effect of absurdity at the same time.

INTRODUCTION

> The feeling of absurdity bursts from the comparison between a bare fact and a certain reality, between an action and the world that transcends it. The absurd is essentially a divorce.
>
> (Albert Camus 1984 [1955])

> A: Is this the right room for an argument?
> B: I've told you once.
> A: No you haven't!
> B: Yes I have!
>
> (*Monty Python's Flying Circus*)

This chapter looks at 'odd' talk. It examines talk which is in some way marked, aberrant or anomalous. The main focus of the analysis will be on dialogue in drama, especially dialogue in that type of drama which is conventionally labelled 'absurd'. This study of absurd dialogue will be placed in the context, on the one hand, of naturally occurring conversation and, on the other, of a certain type of dialogue used in popular comedy sketches. Building from some observations about the basic mechanisms of naturally occurring conversation, a principle of linguistic *incongruity* is identified, and it will be suggested that this principle to some extent underpins (and unites) both the absurd and the comic as genres of talk.

What can an exploration of odd talk offer the student of stylistics? The obvious answer to this is the one that is often voiced in support of any type of stylistic analysis: a language-based approach offers a valuable analytic and critical method for explaining text(s). Equally important, in view of the remit of this chapter, is the potential which a study of odd talk has for the study of *ordinary* forms of talk. It has become an axiom in discourse stylistics that the study of non-routine patterns of communication (such as those manifested by the texts examined in this chapter) can inform the routine and unexceptional in interaction. A study of 'miscommunication' thus offers a vantage point for observing what is communicatively commonplace – a point endorsed by Coupland *et al.* who stress that:

> communicative interchange becomes a foregrounded rather than a taken-for-granted process most frequently when *we recognize its inefficiencies and its unforeseen or undesirable consequences.*
>
> (Coupland *et al.* 1991: 3; emphasis added)

Explaining how a model of interaction might be developed to account for 'inefficient' interchanges will be one of the tasks of the next section.

The term 'absurd', in its current literary-critical sense, originates from Albert Camus' series of philosophical essays entitled *The Myth of Sisyphus* (1984 [1955]). In Greek mythology, Sisyphus is condemned by the Gods interminably to roll a boulder up to the top of a mountain, only to watch it fall back down again under its own momentum. Sisyphus is the archetypal absurd 'hero' and in his plight Camus saw mirrored the true absurdity of the human condition: a pointlessly preoccupied individual, perpetually alienated from his own society, whose 'whole being is exerted towards accomplishing nothing' (1984 [1955]: 108). In acknowledgement of Camus' ideas, critics have come to use the phrase 'Theatre of the Absurd' to refer to the work of a group of dramatists, writing mainly in the 1950s and early 1960s, which includes, but is not restricted to, Harold Pinter, Eugene Ionesco, Edward Albee, N. F. Simpson and Samuel Beckett.[1] Although not a literary 'movement' in the sense of any conscious initiative or allegiance from its practitioners, the tradition of absurd writing is none the less galvanized by its preoccupation with exploring the apparent futility of human existence, the alienation of the individual from an inveterately hostile society and the religious and spiritual disillusionment experienced *en masse* in the wake of the Second World War. The discourse of absurd plays is irrational, anti-realist and illogical, markedly 'devoid of the traditional attractions of the well-made drama' (Esslin 1980: 28). However, while literary critics are largely in agreement about the significance of language in these plays, their attempts to account for the nature of absurd dialogue are at best impressionistic and at worst unintelligible. In his seminal study of the genre, for instance, Esslin talks of the 'incoherent babblings' (1980: 22) which probe 'the limitations of language both as a means of communication and as a means for the expression of valid statements' (85). For Hinchliffe, the 'verbal nonsense' that is the language of the absurd is 'a dead thing, limiting communication' (1969: 54), which is at once 'very funny and very terrifying' (63) yet is 'part of the failure to know where or what we are, an impenetrable barrier' (68). Critics' insistence on the 'meaninglessness' of absurd dialogue fails to explain how absurd texts can still 'mean' on a more general communicative level. Moreover, with the notable exception of Sherzer (1978), drama critics have resolutely failed to account for this 'meaningless' dialogue within the terms of any coherent discourse or pragmatic framework. To address this issue, the next section will outline some basic principles of spoken interaction and will suggest ways in which a working model for explaining 'odd talk' might be developed.

There is also a tendency in the critical literature to assume that linguistic 'absurdity' is somehow unique or inherent to absurd drama. In my view, this assumption is simply untenable. By isolating some broad-based similarities in patterns of language use, this chapter will seek to establish connections between so-called absurd dramatic dialogue and other genres such as the verbal comedy sketch. It will concentrate particularly on a type of humour normally referred to as 'incongruity-based' (Raskin 1987: 17) which consists in the merging of incongruous concepts, discourses or frames of reference. Some of the best-known exponents of this type of humour in British radio and television are the Goons, the Monty Python team and, most recently, the pairing of Vic Reeves and Bob Mortimer. Unlike puns and other forms of verbal play, incongruity-based humour is more abstract, more surreal and ultimately more radical (Paton 1988: 217). Its relative complexity may also explain why this form is the least studied in linguistic analyses of humour. Working within this paradigm of 'incongruity', section three explores dialogue in a selection of drama extracts and then examines patterns of interaction in a short comedy sketch from the Monty Python team.

FEATURES OF SPOKEN DISCOURSE

Verbal interaction

Defining 'odd' talk is not easy, simply because such a definition needs to be based on some notion of what constitutes 'non-odd' talk. As discourse is arguably the most fluid level of language organization, a definitive account of the principles of 'normal' interaction is relatively difficult to obtain. Nevertheless, there exists among discourse analysts a broad measure of agreement about what constitutes well-formed, canonical discourse and this means that, by imputation, there exists a method for explaining relatively ill-formed, non-canonical discourse. Common to many studies in discourse analysis are a number of basic assumptions about the communicative properties of language in general and about the nature of spoken interaction in particular. Perhaps the most significant of these, following Schiffrin's observations (1987: 3), is that all interaction occurs in a *context*. The notion of context may be sub-divided into three overlapping categories:

1 *Physical context:* This is the actual setting or environment in which inter-action takes place, whether it be in the workplace, at home or in a publicly accessible area. In much spoken language, such as face-to-face conver-sation, speaker and hearer share the same physical context, although in some forms of spoken interaction, such as broadcast talk, speaker and hearer are physically displaced.
2 *Personal context:* This refers to the social and personal relationships of the interactants to one another. Personal context also encompasses social net-works and group membership, the social and institutional roles of speakers and hearers, and the relative status and social distance that pertains between participants.
3 *Cognitive context:* This refers to the shared and background knowledge held by participants in interaction. Cognitive context, which is susceptible to change as interaction progresses, also extends to a speaker's past experi-ence, cultural knowledge and world-view.

There are different methods for explaining how talk is organized, though all approaches need to be cognizant of the importance of context in the study of discourse. One approach is to focus on the way spoken discourse is *structured*; that is to say, how it is organized in a linear fashion and how its various com-ponents are bolted together. A structural analysis of discourse seeks to explain in a relatively idealized way how units such as *exchanges* are formed; how, for example, questions predict answers, statements predict acknowledgements and requests predict reactions (although whether they always do in conversa-tion is another matter). It is also possible to study discourse in terms of *strategy*. From this perspective, attention is focused on the way speakers use different interactive tactics at specific points during a sequence of talk. Take, for instance, the following three exchanges which all exhibit a superficially similar discourse *structure*:

1 A: Open the window.
   B: [*opens the window*]
2 A: Could you open the window?
   B: [*opens the window*]
3 A: Goodness me, it's hot in here!
   B: [*opens the window*]

(adapted from Simpson 1997: 136)

In structural terms, all three exchanges consist of two parts each: a request followed by a reaction. However, in terms of discourse strategy, the first elements in each exchange are markedly different from one another, with the most direct form used in 1 and the least direct in 3. Furthermore, the transition from the unmitigated command in 1, through the routinely indirect form of 2 to the oblique 'hint' in 3 marks a concomitant shift in politeness, ranging from least polite to most polite. Speakers are normally acutely aware of what sort of strategy can be used in which circumstances: there may, for instance, be little interactive risk in using strategy 1 with friends and social equals in an informal setting, but if used in a formal setting with an interlocutor who is an acknowledged social superior the interactive consequences may be grave. A speaker's communicative strategies are thus sensitive to the perceived context, so in this respect, context, in its three aspects outlined above, operates as a key strategy-framing device in discourse. A speaker's knowledge of what to say, and when and where to say it, is what ethnographers call 'communicative competence' (Hymes 1972). Communicative competence is the skill involved in matching an utterance to an appropriate context of use; in other words, knowing when to be familiar and when to be formal, knowing when to be direct and when to be indirect, or simply knowing when to talk and when to keep quiet. The notion of communicative competence will prove to be a pivotal element in the model of odd talk that follows.

Characterizing odd talk

As a first stage in the development of a model of odd talk, the importance of context as a determinant of interactive patterns needs to be re-iterated. Consider the following exchange, presented initially without any supporting explanation of the context in which it occurred:

4   A: Morning.
    B: Edinburgh?
    A: Yes.

On the face of it, this bizarre sequence may look like a prima facie candidate for inclusion in any category of odd talk, but an explanation of its context militates against this reading. This exchange occurred on the tarmac of Belfast airport where Speaker A (me) has arrived so late for a flight to Edinburgh that he is about to board an aircraft within two minutes of its official departure time. Speaker B is a flight attendant, waiting below one of the wings of the aircraft, whose routine pleasantry receives no acknowledgement from an interlocutor whose main concern is to confirm the destination of the plane he is about to board. While the exchange, amongst other things, tends to endorse Brown and Levinson's observation that politeness rituals often evaporate in situations of panic or urgency (1987: 69), a supplementary account of the discourse context of this exchange makes it look much less aberrant than it first appears. As dialogue can never be stripped from its context of use, the first principle of a model of odd talk is that it needs to be *context sensitive*.

Such a model also needs to account for the occasions when interaction breaks down; or when, in other words, there is a fracture in the *structural* development of discourse. Various reasons have been identified for breakdowns in conversational structure, but an especially common cause is interaction in cross-dialectal or cross-lingual contexts (Milroy 1984; Gass and Varonis 1991).[2] The first type occurs between speakers whose individual dialect systems, although part of the same language, are sufficiently disparate lexically and grammatically to cause a communicative breakdown. Example 5 records an encounter between two friends whom I had just introduced to one another. Speaker B uses Standard British English, speaker A the Mid-Ulster dialect system common in Northern Ireland:

5 A: Are ye just after a dander?
   B: I'm sorry?
   A: Have ye just been out for a dander?
   B: Sorry. I beg your pardon?
   A: Have you just been out for a walk?
   B: Oh . . . well no, actually.

Unlike misunderstandings, which are normally not perceived at all during conversation, communicative breakdowns require repair strategies in order for the breach in discourse structure to be mended. The tactics used in 5 include restarts (A's second and third utterances) and requests for restarts (B's first and second utterances). Other repair devices include 'metalanguage' (language about language) which is encoded in remarks such as 'What I'm trying to say is . . .', 'What I want to ask is . . .' and so on.

Breaches in discourse in terms of discourse *strategy* are qualitatively different from the communicative breakdowns just discussed. Basically, this type of violation derives from a mismatch between context and utterance. Obvious cases of this would be, for instance, baptizing a child or performing a marriage ceremony without institutionally sanctioned authority. Another would be using taboo language or introducing a taboo topic in an inappropriate context. More subtle mismatches of this sort can occur in inter-ethnic or cross-cultural encounters. In a study of job interviews in Britain, Gumperz (1992) noted that South Asian interviewees, although fluent non-native speakers of English, tended to perform less well than their native-speaker counterparts and were often found reticent and diffident by their white native-speaker interviewers. Gumperz suggests that this results from a mismatch in communicative competences, where the Asian speakers, finding themselves in the atypical situation of a formal job interview, tend to fall back on rhetorical strategies acquired in their own native-language environment. The problem is clearly not to do with the *linguistic* competence of knowing how to form the sentences of a language, but the *communicative* competence of knowing which discourse strategies are typically aligned with which discourse contexts.

A common by-product of an incongruity between strategy and context is a breakdown in discourse at the structural level. In her well-known study of courtroom discourse, Harris (1984) notes that magistrates wield institutional power to the extent that only they have the authority to ask questions. In such a situation, where social roles are so clearly defined, the following encounter therefore clearly violates expectations about the relationship of language to context:

6 MAGISTRATE: I'm putting it to you again – are you going to *make* an offer – uh – uh to discharge this debt?
DEFENDANT: Would you in my position?
MAGISTRATE: I – I'm not here to answer questions – you answer *my* question.
DEFENDANT: One rule for one and one for another – I presume.
MAGISTRATE: Can I have an answer to my question – please.

(after Harris 1984: 5)

In spite of their markedly asymmetrical power relationship, the defendant here has clearly not 'read the rule-book' so to speak, and a rather flustered magistrate is forced to invoke metalanguage, one of the repair strategies noted above, in order to re-establish the discourse framework.

It is the mismatch between communicative strategy and discourse context, rather than breakdowns in structure, which forms the central tenet of our model of 'odd talk'. Whereas structural breakdown qualifies as an oddity of sorts, the core issue, in view of the sort of texts that will be examined in the next section, concerns the type of incongruity that resides at the interface of strategy and context. Incongruity is the consequence of speakers *not* observing the familiar or expected routines that are cued by a particular context. It was established earlier in this section that discourse occurs in a context and, moreover, that it needs to be investigated with reference to this context. Awareness of context, in its physical, personal and cognitive dimensions, and the forms of communication that are appropriate to it, is what constitutes part of a speaker's communicative competence. If discoursal incongruity resides in the mismatch between context and utterance, then the concept of communicative competence will be crucial to the explanation of what Goffman (1969: 166) has called 'communicating out of character'. The next section examines discoursal incongruity in dramatic and related texts, looking particularly at situations where dramatic characters communicate 'out of character'.

ODD TALK AND DRAMA DISCOURSE

It is a truism to say that drama dialogue differs from everyday speech. Drama dialogue clearly is fabricated interaction between fictional characters, mediated and controlled by playwrights in the first instance, and, in the case of dramatic performances, by directors and actors in the second. This is not to say, however, that principles of social interaction, such as those identified in the previous section, cannot be brought to bear in the interpretation of dramatic dialogue. In fact, drama dialogue can only be accessed through its relationship to the social context outside the play-text. Dramatic action, as Herman points out, becomes meaningful in relation to the 'authenticating conventions' that are drawn from the wider world of affairs in which the dramatic activity is embedded (1995: 6). In other words, the norms, values and modes of conduct which regulate how 'real' people organize their linguistic behaviour form the basis for interpreting the speech and action of the fictional characters in the world of a play. It is the social organization of everyday language, therefore, that creates a 'commonality' of ground between playwright and audience/reader (Herman 1995: 6) and that constitutes the backdrop to the speech patterns encoded in a play-text. So while everyday speech and drama discourse are not homologous modes of communication, they are none the less parallel, and expectations about well-formedness in everyday speech form the benchmark against which aberrant and incongruous discourse can be measured.[3]

Here first of all is a brief and relatively straightforward example of how expectations about discourse act as a context-framing device for interpreting play dialogue. Recall for a moment some of the observations made about courtroom discourse at the end of the previous section. Given its context in terms of physical location, a courtroom is an institutionally designated area which is set aside exclusively for legal proceedings, and is manifestly not the sort of thing that can be set up by anybody in, for example, a domestic living room. Furthermore, in this rigidly marshalled discourse context, social roles are fixed and there are established procedures for ritualized activities such as the swearing-in of witnesses. Shared assumptions between participants about the way these routines are conducted thus form part of the cognitive context of the courtroom. Given this contextual information, look now at the following court scene from N. F. Simpson's play *One Way Pendulum* (1960: 60):

[*The Usher enters followed by Mr. Groomkirby, whom he directs into the witness box. Mr. Groomkirby takes the oath.*]

MR. GROOMKIRBY: [*holding up a copy of 'Uncle Tom's Cabin'*]
   I swear, by Harriet Beecher Stowe, that the evidence I shall give shall be the truth, the whole truth, and nothing but the truth.
JUDGE: You understand, do you, that you are now on oath?
MR. GROOMKIRBY: I do, m'lord.

Although Mr Groomkirby's 'swearing-in' contains many instantly recogniz-
able formulaic structures such as 'the truth, the whole truth and nothing but
the truth', his use of *Uncle Tom's Cabin* clearly violates the conditions which
govern this ritual (at least within the parameters of the British cultural
context informing this play). These conditions, often referred to as 'felicity
conditions', proscribe the swearing in of a witness by any text other than the
Bible – irrespective of its literary merit. However, in my view this violation
of felicity conditions is not in itself the key trigger of discoursal incongruity
here; it is, rather, the judge's lack of surprise at and subsequent endorsement
of the swearing-in ceremony. Were the Judge to have outlawed *Uncle Tom's
Cabin* and declared the swearing-in inadmissible, as presumably any judge
would do, then this appeal to everyday modes of conduct would have lessened
greatly the incongruity of the sequence. The responses of interlocutors in a
play to something that is unanticipated in context – such as the Judge's to
Mr Groomkirby's use of *Uncle Tom's Cabin* – often has a crucial bearing on
the way a discourse of oddity is established and developed. More will be said
later on the importance of monitoring interlocutors' responses in this way.
As a final comment on the discoursal incongruity here, it is worth noting that
in spite of my earlier remarks about the physical context of courts, the courtroom which is inhabited by Mr Groomkirby, the Judge and others in the
play has been assembled previously from a do-it-yourself kit and has been
situated (perhaps you have guessed!) inside a domestic living room.

Eugene Ionesco is arguably the most 'core' of the acknowledged absurdists,
and his plays the most prototypically absurd in terms of their patterns of
dialogue. A feature which unites much of Ionesco's work is his presentation
of bourgeois mores, manners and existence as fossilized and obsolete. Most of
his plays are situated therefore within bourgeois interiors, populated by
lower-middle-class characters who talk in clichés about utterly trivial
matters. Nowhere is this theme more apparent than in his play *Victims of
Duty* (1958). The play's 'hero', Monsieur Choubert, is spending the evening
at home with his wife Madeleine. Off-stage, someone is heard knocking at
the door of the concierge's apartment which is located in the same corridor
as the Chouberts'. Following timid knocks at his own door, Mr Choubert
opens it to a stranger, a detective, whereupon the following sequence of dialogue occurs:

[*The* DETECTIVE *is seen in the doorway. He is very young, with a brief-case under
one arm. He is wearing a beige overcoat and is hatless, a fair man, soft-spoken and
excessively shy.*]

DETECTIVE: [*in the doorway*] Good evening, Monsieur. [*Then to*
   MADELEINE, *who has also risen and moved to the door:*] Good evening, Madame.
CHOUBERT: Good evening. [*To* MADELEINE:] It's the detective.
DETECTIVE: [*taking one short timid step forward*] Forgive me, Madame,
   Monsieur, I wanted some information from the concierge, the concierge
   isn't there . . .

MADELEINE: Naturally.

DETECTIVE: . . . do you know where she is? Do you know if she'll soon be back? Oh, I'm so sorry, please forgive me, I . . .I'd never have knocked on your door, if I'd found the concierge, I wouldn't have dared to trouble you like this . . .

CHOUBERT: The concierge should soon be back, Monsieur. Theoretically she only goes out on Saturday nights. Goes dancing, you know, every Saturday night, since she married her daughter off. And as this is Tuesday night . . .

DETECTIVE: Thank you, Monsieur, thank you very much. I'll be going, Monsieur, I'll wait for her on the landing. You've really been very helpful. Glad to have had the privilege of making your acquaintance, Madame.

MADELEINE: [*to* CHOUBERT] What a polite young man! Such wonderful manners. Ask him what he wants to know. Perhaps you could help him.

(Ionesco 1958: 271)

The stage direction preceding the detective's entrance emphasizes that he is to be *excessively* polite and it is worth looking at the discourse strategies which Ionesco uses to develop this aspect of his character's behaviour. In spite of some acknowledged institutional authority, the detective's prodigious use of polite language suggests timidity and insecurity. In a more technical sense, he makes extensive use of a range of specific 'politeness strategies' (Brown and Levinson 1987) to mitigate his intrusion and to interactively 'soften up' his interlocutors. After a decorous greeting to his two addressees, garnished by the appropriate terms of address, he immediately offers an explanation of the reasons for his presence: 'I wanted some information from the concierge, the concierge isn't there'. Giving overwhelming reasons in this way is one means of redressing an imposition to an addressee. Another is to suggest that the speaker is not personally responsible for the infringement. This strategy is used, perhaps significantly, shortly after the Detective has broken off from a potentially threatening set of questions to the Chouberts: 'I'd never have knocked on your door, if I'd found the concierge, I wouldn't have dared to trouble you like this . . .' These politeness strategies are also interlaced with more obvious tactics, such as repeated apologies: 'Forgive me'; 'I'm so sorry, please forgive me'. Whereas it is assumed that speakers normally try to make the amount of linguistic politeness they use congruent with their imposition on an interlocutor, the inordinate amount of politeness on offer here seems somewhat out of kilter with the rather minimal imposition the detective is making on the Chouberts. The discoursal incongruity resides therefore in the mismatch between strategy and context at the level of character-to-character interaction, although it would be difficult to quantify precisely an appropriate number of politeness strategies for an exchange of this sort in the 'real' world. However, this is not in itself the key issue. Look at what happens a few lines later when the detective, at the behest of his hosts, takes another step into the room:

DETECTIVE: You are Monsieur and Madame Choubert, aren't you?
MADELEINE: Why yes, Monsieur.
DETECTIVE: [*to* CHOUBERT] It seems that you're fond of the theatre,
    Monsieur?
CHOUBERT: Er . . . er . . . yes . . . I take an interest in it.

(Ionesco 1958: 273)

In the light of what precedes it, this sequence marks an abrupt turn-around in
discourse strategies. The detective, seemingly confident and acting as if his
role is ratified by authority, now asks personal questions directly of his interlocutors, whose surprise at this is signalled in both of their responses. The
suggestion that the balance of power may be shifting towards the detective is
strongly endorsed a few lines later when, having advanced further into the
room and shown a photograph to Choubert, he initiates the following
sequence of exchanges:

DETECTIVE: Is this Mallot? I'm being very patient.
CHOUBERT: [*after a moment's silence*] You know, Monsieur Inspector, I . . .
DETECTIVE: Chief Inspector!
CHOUBERT: I'm sorry, you know, Monsieur Chief Inspector, I can't really
    tell [. . .] it certainly seems it *could* be him . . .
DETECTIVE: When did you know him and what did he talk to you about?
CHOUBERT: [*lowering himself on to a chair*] Forgive me, Monsieur Chief
    Inspector, I'm terribly tired! . . .
DETECTIVE: My question is: when did you know him and what did he talk to
    you about?
CHOUBERT: When did I know him? [. . .]
DETECTIVE: Answer!
CHOUBERT: What did he talk to me about? . . . What did he . . . But when on
    earth did I meet him? . . . When was the first time I saw him? When was
    the last time?
DETECTIVE: It's not my job to give the answers.

(Ionesco 1958: 276)

This is a cross-examination in the sense that a series of questions, without miti-
gation or redress, are directed to an addressee who has been stripped of their
right to initiate exchanges of their own. Choubert is now the hapless victim
of this cross-examination, floundering under a welter of questions from the
Detective which are supplemented by explicit comments on the now asymmetrical nature of their relationship. None of the politeness tactics that had
so characterized the detective's earlier talk remain. The politely reciprocal
term of address ('Monsieur') has collapsed into the non-reciprocal 'Monsieur
Chief Inspector'. The Detective also uses explicit metalanguage to shore up
the structural framework ('My question is: . . .') and to reinforce, in an
uncanny echo of the Magistrate's language in example 6 above, the seemingly
unwarranted gap in power that has suddenly opened up between the inter-

actants ('It's not my job to give the answers.'). The detective's questions, operating here as a mode of social control (Harris 1984), encode in language a total reversal in the interactive roles of the two participants.[4]

This is not to say that interactive roles cannot ever change in the course of interaction. Goffman (1969: 167) recounts an anecdote about an army general who, informally attired, goes for a recreational drive in a military jeep. He is stopped by military police who, assuming him to be an unauthorized civilian driver, subject him to some abusive cross-examination. When the general puts on his military cap, with its four stars clearly displayed, the initially rude behaviour of the police switches dramatically to deference and obsequiousness. New information about the personal dimension of a discourse context can radically alter discourse strategies, and it is easy to explain the abrupt change in linguistic behaviour in this episode. However, in the case of Ionesco and other absurdists, indices of social status are often ignored, or are patently at odds with the types of strategies assigned to dramatic characters. Moreover, even when some sort of discoursal pattern *is* established, as in the inordinately polite behaviour of the Detective, this may be transposed within a few lines of dialogue into its antithesis. Making sense out of mismatches between social roles and discourse strategies at the level of play, dialogue becomes a challenge to the communicative skills of the audience/reader. Indeed, the fact that absurdity is typified by unstable characterization and breakdowns in discourse has led critics to complain that it has 'no message' to offer (Hinchliffe 1969: 56). Yet the creation of incongruity, inconsistency and meaninglessness in language enacts the very futility of existence that the absurdists strive to represent in drama. Paradoxically, it is the drawing of attention to the absence of a message that becomes the message in itself.

Much is made in the critical literature of the comic nature of absurd drama. Esslin (1980: 411) suggests that the fact that the audience/reader fails to identify with any of its characters makes absurd drama essentially a comic theatre, even though its subject matter is often grotesque and violent. Incongruous dialogue and irrational actions help to construct characters who have no obvious points of reference outside the dramatic text, making them easier to laugh at than those developed within the compass of dramatic 'realism'. However, it was stressed early on in this chapter that the principle of linguistic incongruity transcends comic absurdism *per se* and extends into other humorous domains. The work of the Monty Python team is a case in point. During the 1970s, their sketches for BBC 2 television (entitled *Monty Python's Flying Circus*), were both radical and shockingly 'new' as a comic genre, although this form of surreal and frequently dark humour was often criticized for being in poor taste and was most certainly not universally popular. Nevertheless, it marked, along with the work of Spike Milligan of the Goons, a major shift in the linguistic and cultural fabric of verbal and non-verbal humour.

The sketch that follows, popularly referred to as 'Nudge nudge', bears all the 'Pythonesque' hallmarks, even if it is hopelessly politically incorrect and uncomfortably sexist. Subsequent to its initial broadcast in 1971, this routine, together with transcripts and stills, has been reproduced in various 'spin-off' books, audio-recordings and video collections.[5] Set in a plush English public house, the sketch opens with a man, carrying a full glass of beer, looking for a seat. The man (played by Eric Idle) is 'sportily' dressed: wearing a cravat and a crested blazer which suggests affiliation to a sports club or academic institution. He finds a seat beside a second man (played by Terry Jones) who is sitting alone drinking a pint of beer. The second man is similarly attired, in a blazer and what looks like an 'old school' tie. For ease of reference in the transcript that follows, the characters have been named metonymically, the first man as CRAVAT and the second as TIE. Throughout the interaction, CRAVAT embellishes each of his utterances with highly exaggerated non-verbal gestures that include nudging his interlocutor with his elbow at appropriate cues in his speech. CRAVAT also uses an exclusively sexual non-verbal gesture brought about by crossing his forearms and rapidly raising and lowering one fist. Here now are the first few lines of dialogue in the sketch:

CRAVAT: Is your wife a . . . goer . . . eh? Know what I mean? Know what I mean? Nudge nudge. Nudge nudge. Know what I mean? Say no more . . . know what I mean?

TIE: I beg your pardon?

CRAVAT: Your wife . . . does she, er, does she 'go'– eh? eh? eh? Know what I mean, know what I mean? Nudge nudge. Say no more.

TIE: She sometimes goes, yes.

CRAVAT: I bet she does. I bet she does. I bet she does. Know what I mean. Nudge nudge.

TIE: I'm sorry, I don't quite follow you.

CRAVAT: Follow me! *Follow* me! I like that. That's good. A nod's as good as a wink to a blind bat, eh?

TIE: Are you trying to sell something?

It is worth recalling first of all that this is an anonymous encounter in a public area in which a stranger moves into the physical space already occupied by another. Bearing in mind our earlier observations about the relationship between language and context, this is an odd interaction by any measurement. There are very strong interactive constraints on what can be said at the beginning of a conversation between two people who don't know each other. The sorts of discourse strategies which typify conversational openings – what linguists refer to as 'phatic communion' – are expected to be neutral and uncontroversial. Interactively 'safe' gambits in the context established in the sketch would include reference to the weather ('Nice day') or comments on the immediate physical environment ('About time someone cleared these glasses'). What is manifestly *not* cued by this context is the probing into the personal life of the interlocutor. The marital status of an addressee, for example, is their personal preserve, yet in this sketch it is mooted in CRAVAT's very first utterance ('Is *your wife* . . .'), thereby generating a presupposition which is ratified by TIE's reply. A more rigorous taboo again is placed on topics to do with sexual behaviour and it is this which makes outrageously incongruous CRAVAT's thinly veiled insinuations about TIE's wife's putative sexual voraciousness. As a phatic device this strategy is wildly at odds with the routinely polite behaviour demanded in anonymous social encounters of this sort. Moreover, in an echo of example 5 above, TIE's apparent bewilderment at CRAVAT's questions impacts on the development of the *structure* of exchanges. CRAVAT's initiations tend to be followed by requests for restarts from TIE which render the development of discourse structurally cyclical – a pattern that is sustained, incidentally, for thirty more lines of dialogue.

One way of interpreting this dialogue as a comic construct is to regard the viewer/reader in terms of what Goffman (1974) calls a 'non-ratified hearer'. Although not addressed directly by the interactants, the viewer/reader none the less occupies the position of a kind of discoursal 'onlooker'. The communicative competence that organizes everyday interaction for the onlooker acts as a frame for interpreting the incongruity of the displayed interaction. This permits different types of projection into the discourse and allows the interpretative perspective to shift between speaker and hearer as dialogue progresses. For example, as was suggested earlier, monitoring the hearer's responses to peculiar utterances offers one of the clearest indices of an 'absurd world'. This sketch endorses this point. Although CRAVAT's questions barely count as innuendo, TIE is perversely slow on the uptake. No rebuff is offered to CRAVAT nor does he make any attempt to distance himself physically from his interlocutor. It is only after thirty more lines of dialogue that TIE says: 'Look, are you insinuating something?' – a telling piece of metalanguage that functions as an emblem for the entire sketch.

In summary, the greater part of the outlandishness of this Python sketch arguably stems from the mismatch between character speech and the discourse context in which it is embedded within the text. Moreover, TIE's seeming inability to take up CRAVAT's thin innuendo creates an impasse which leads to repeated breaches in discourse structure. This is further compacted by CRAVAT's single-minded pursuit of innuendo beyond those phrases conventionally used as sexual *double entendres* ('*Follow* me! I like that'). In keeping with much of the Python genre, this sketch invites a satirical reading. Foregrounding odd talk implicitly draws attention to the canonical and the everyday in interaction and it is possible to read this text as a skit on the repressively mundane trivia that often passes for conversation. Both interactants are white, male and middle class and both speak with southern English accents, yet from CRAVAT's opening gambit onwards, the interactive diffidence that might be anticipated in social interaction between (particularly English?) middle-class strangers is shattered. To the extent that this fracture in cultural code is engendered by a fracture in discourse strategies, the sketch becomes language *about* language – a kind of 'meta-discourse'. It constitutes a form of humour where language itself forms the subject matter (Apte 1985: 211) and which relies for its decoding on the communicative competence and cultural attitudes of the interpreter; those very decoding strategies, in fact, which are brought into play in the interpretation of absurd drama dialogue.

CONCLUSIONS

This chapter has been about odd talk. Working from some basic assumptions about naturally occurring conversation, it has presented an informal model for studying incongruity in discourse. The core theoretical element of this model is the interface between utterance and discourse context. Speakers draw upon their communicative competence in order to align different types of utterance to different types of context. By extension, the concept of communicative competence becomes a valuable interpretative tool for accounting for any mismatches that occur between what a speaker says and what is anticipated by personal, physical and cognitive dimensions of context. Much of the dialogue found in absurd drama and in certain comic genres offers an excellent opportunity for studying this form of linguistic incongruity.

This is not the only form of linguistic incongruity, however. As Burton (1980) and Sherzer (1978), amongst others, have pointed out, discoursal mismatches can operate on a host of levels of language organization, ranging from the way characters tell stories to one another to the way sound patterns are used in their speech. It is also clearly the case that odd talk *per se* is neither the sole preserve of humour nor, as some critics have suggested, of absurdism. Esslin (1980) suggests that 'absurd dialogue' is exclusive to absurd drama, yet elsewhere he describes the language of Edward Albee's *The Zoo Story* as 'a clinically accurate study of schizophrenia' (1965: 22). This rather insensitive remark seems to contradict his argument for exclusivity. In a bona fide clinical study of schizophrenic discourse, Rochester and Martin (1979) do identify certain types of incoherence in the speech of thought-disordered patients, but as they cover aspects of language organization different from those studied here, definite parallels are difficult to draw. In any case, much more needs to be said about the circumstances under which each type of discourse is produced and interpreted; in short, the stage is a far cry from the psychiatric ward.

Raskin (1987: 13) argues, in my view correctly, that there is no such thing as a special category of 'linguistic humour'. In other words, no necessary and sufficient condition can be isolated which will guarantee that a text will have a humorous outcome. Odd talk, in particular, need not necessarily be funny. Its reception as comic discourse depends largely on the predisposition of the receiver. It is 'strategy-framed' (Paton 1988: 223) in that the text is geared towards humorous interpretation within an explicitly comic context of production. Linguistic incongruity, while undoubtedly laced with comic potential, is therefore not in itself a guarantor of laughter. In many respects, interpreting incongruity is as much to do with what interpreters are prepared to invest in the texts as with what is in the texts themselves. The precise mechanisms which underpin interpretation of this sort must be dealt with in another study at another time.

SUGGESTIONS FOR FURTHER WORK

1 There are many ways in which discoursal incongruity can be developed in dialogue. Here is a short 'recipe' for creating some odd talk of your own:

(a) Make a list of some 'terms of address' that speakers use to convey intimacy and social solidarity or to claim common ground with their hearer. If you are stuck, just imagine the sorts of terms that two close friends (or two lovers?) might use to each other during informal conversation.

(b) Examine the following transcript of courtroom dialogue between a Magistrate (M) and a Defendant (D). Try to identify any features of language which signal that there is a power differential between the interlocutors and that their interactive rights are not symmetrically distributed. Make a note of any terms of address that the Defendant uses to encode this power differential.

> M: You've still got uh twelve pounds to pay off and you haven't even paid off a thing yet
> D: That's correct your worship
> M: Yes – what are you going to do about it
> D: Well uh I would like to ask your worship if it would be all right if I had fourteen days to pay the three pounds – and uh – and still have to pay the fifty pence on the other your worship
> M: Why is it you've suddenly become flush with money
> D: Well as I say sir – uh – they've put me on an increase and uh – but I daren't draw out again till Monday
> M: How much money have you got on you
> D: I haven't got any on me your worship
> M: How'd you get here
> D: I uh got a lift – part way here

(adapted from Harris 1984: 20)

(c) Now replace the Defendant's terms of address with items from your own list of 'terms of endearment'. How does this affect the overall tenor of the dialogue? Are any sequences rendered especially incongruous? Are there any other discourse strategies which might be reversed in this way? For example, think again about conversation between two intimates. How would a request for a small financial payment (which is, after all, the substance of this courtroom encounter) be negotiated between close friends? And would the Magistrate's tactics be appropriate in this more intimate context?

2 This short exercise is based around a particularly common type of service encounter.

   (a) Think about the sort of interaction that typically takes place between customers and waiters in a restaurant or café. Make a note of any features of context which you think are relevant to the way restaurant 'discourse' is structured. In terms of cognitive context, for example, what sort of information do you expect waiters to have at their disposal (about booking a table, what is on the menu, etc.)? Or in terms of personal context, is there a perceived power differential between customer and waiter/waitress, and if so, will this impact on the sorts of discourse strategies which are used by the respective parties? For instance, are there any terms of address or politeness tactics which are associated with 'waiter-talk' but not with 'customer-talk'?

   (b) In the light of your predictions about the restaurant 'scenario', examine the following extract of play dialogue. It is the opening of Alan Ayckbourn's play *Between Mouthfuls*.

> [*A hotel dining room. The Waiter is finishing arranging his tables. At length Donald Pearce enters, a middle-aged businessman.*]
>
> WAITER: [*Approaching him*] Good evening, sir.
> PEARCE: Good evening. I have a table for two reserved in the name of Pearce.
> WAITER: Table for two sir. Did you make a reservation sir?
> PEARCE: Yes, I have just said I did.
> WAITER: Very good, sir. [*He consults the reservations book.*] What name was it sir?
> PEARCE: Pearce. I've just this minute said so.
> WAITER: Pearce – with a P, I presume? – ah, yes sir. [*Indicating the table nearer the door.*] Would this one over here suit you, sir?
> PEARCE: No, I don't think it would. I think I'd prefer this one over here.
> WAITER: Oh, just as you like, sir. [*The Waiter leads Pearce over to the table and holds the chair for Pearce, who sits, his back to the rest of the room.*]
> PEARCE: Thank you.
> WAITER: Just yourself is it sir?
> PEARCE: No.
> WAITER: Ah. Someone will be joining you, will they, sir?
> PEARCE: Yes indeed. That's really rather why I reserved a table for two.
> WAITER: Right sir.
>
> (Ayckbourn 1977: 26)

Is there anything about this dialogue which doesn't square with your predictions about restaurant discourse? Make a note of any anomalies.

Do you find this dialogue funny? If so, can you explain its humour in terms of discourse *structure*?

(c) Recall again your predictions about the restaurant scenario, especially about the sorts of politeness strategies which might be employed between waiter and customer. Now study the following two extracts from Steven Berkoff's play *Greek* (1983), making a note of any aspects of dialogue that 'violate' the restaurant scenario. (The extracts are separated by around forty lines of dialogue, which includes interaction between characters other than the two featured here.)

> [*Cafe. Chorus of kitchen cafe menu sounds and phrases.*]
> EDDY: One coffee please and croissant and butter.
> WAITRESS: Right. Cream?
> EDDY: Please.
>   [. . .]
> EDDY: Where's my fucking coffee? I've nearly finished this cheesecake and then my whole purpose in life at this particular moment will be lost. I'll be drinking hot coffee with nothing to wash it down with.
> WAITRESS: Here you are, sorry I forgot you!
> EDDY: About fucking time!
> WAITRESS: Oh shut your mouth, you complaining heap of rat's shit.
>   (Berkoff 1983: 35ff.)

Birch (1991: 68–73) offers an interesting interpretation of a longer sequence from Berkoff's play (in which these two extracts are included). He suggests that breaking the routines of innocuous service encounters serves to deconstruct established views of 'cosy co-operation' between people (71). Whereas Berkoff's dialogue may represent popular culture in 'non-standard' terms, Birch contends that it functions to foreground to a greater degree the conflictual nature of base culture, which is 'about people resisting, in one way or another, social control' (73). Do you agree that a dramatist's use of incongruous discourse can highlight the social conflict that is endemic in everyday culture?

NOTES

1 This is not an exhaustive list; other contenders for the title 'dramatist of the absurd' include Jean Genet, Fernando Arrabal and Arthur Adamov. Moreover, the status of some dramatists as 'absurdists' has become questionable as their work has developed over the years. Even in early studies of the genre, critics were ambivalent about Harold Pinter's inclusion in the category (see for example Hinchliffe 1969: 83) and the stylistic range of Edward Albee's drama – compare the 'absurdity' of *The American Dream* with the 'realism' of *Who's Afraid of Virginia Woolf* – has to some extent made his inclusion in the list provisional.

2 The communicative problems experienced in inter-lingual encounters, where one party only is a native speaker of the language used in the interaction, is the subject

of a paper by Gass and Varonis (1991: 125–6). They offer the following example of a problematic sequence of talk between NS (a native speaker of English) and NNS (a non-native speaker from Colombia):

NS: Who is the best player in Colombia?
NNS: Colombia?
NS: Does uh . . . who is *the* Colombian player?
NNS: Me?
NS: No, in Colombia.
NNS: In Colombia plays. Yah.
NS: No, on your team. On the Millionarios.
NNS: Ah yah, Millionarios.

Although writing in a different context entirely, Birch (1991) touches implicitly on inter-lingual communicative breakdowns in his short study of the situation comedy *Fawlty Towers* scripted by John Cleese and Connie Booth. Manuel, a Spanish waiter, is the butt of a great deal of humour, mostly because he is constructed as 'other', as 'inarticulate; unable to speak his own language "properly", let alone English' (Birch 1991: 122).

3 It is impossible to undertake here a scholarly survey of the various discourse models that are available for dealing with speakers' expectations about what constitutes well-formed discourse. Readers might find the following useful however: Goffman (1974), whose work is generally germane, proposes the concept of a 'frame' to account for how one's experience and knowledge of the world organizes expectations about language use. Tannen (1979) talks of 'structures of expectations' in a way that is linked to Goffman's ideas. Gumperz (1982) is an extended study of communicative competence and discourse strategies which contains much that is generally relevant to this chapter.

4 Unfortunately the politeness framework developed by Brown and Levinson cannot be presented in detail here, but in addition to their own extensive treatment of the subject, introductions to their model (in the context of dramatic dialogue) can be found in Simpson (1997: 155–64), Herman (1995: 190–2) and Short (1996: 212–17). Other stylistic studies of Ionesco's drama include Sherzer (1978), Burton (1980: 24–68) and Simpson (1989). The emphasis on politeness strategies in these passages from Ionesco is not meant to suggest that this is the only odd feature of this stretch of discourse. Politeness is reinforced by other incongruities. For instance, Choubert uses a definite article in his first reference to the detective ('It's *the* Detective') which presupposes among other things that he either knows the detective personally or at least expects that *some* detective will be calling. Yet this flies in the face of what has been presented to the audience/reader through stage directions and dialogue: the detective is a complete stranger and his arrival entirely coincidental. It seems then that the presupposition is at odds with what can be assumed about the *cognitive* context of the interaction. This oddity is further compounded when, in the second extract, the detective appears, perhaps ominously, both to know the Chouberts' names and the answers to the questions he puts to them. Other interesting features of the first extract include Choubert's response to the detective's query (over the concierge's whereabouts) which is bizarrely over-informative in the context of so straightforward a question. The act of saying more than is necessary often generates an 'implicature', which is a meaning that can be accessed without recourse to the literal reference of words spoken. Yet one would be hard pushed to unravel any implicature from Choubert's utterance (see Short 1996: 222–54 for more on implicature in relation to drama dialogue). Finally, the manner by which the Chouberts compliment the detective's politeness is odd indeed. They talk about him in the third person in his presence – a tactic which is

often considered rude because it suggests that the person referred to is incapable of speaking for themselves. It is no surprise that children are normally the recipients of the 'third person' treatment.

5　A reasonably accessible video collection which includes 'Nudge nudge' is *And Now for Something Completely Different* (RCA Columbia Video 1988). More recently, a selection of well-known Python sketches have been published as greetings cards, with a key still from the sketch on one side of the card and the transcript of the sketch on the other. I am grateful to Kate McNulty, a graduate of Queens University, for lending me her copy of the video of this sketch and for drawing my attention to the existence of the greeting card from which my transcript is taken.

5 Implicature, convention and *The Taming of the Shrew*

Marilyn M. Cooper

EDITORS' PREFACE

Marilyn Cooper's chapter considers how we understand dramatic texts. She argues that our interpretative strategies fall into two broad groups. The first consists of strategies that are based on knowledge of linguistic, literary and cultural conventions specific to a particular time; the second consists of more general strategies based on knowledge such as that of empirical laws. It is within this second group that Cooper places the work of the philosopher Paul Grice. Grice provides an interpretative model that explains *how* we draw inferences from conversation. However, Cooper points out that Grice's model does not explain *what* inferences are drawn. These issues are opened up in an analysis of Shakespeare's *The Taming of the Shrew*. This is a particularly suitable text for discussion, since literary critics have been engaged in hot debate over the interpretation of the roles of Kate and Petruchio. Cooper shows how we can reconstruct the inferential chains which lead us to a particular interpretation. In particular, she demonstrates how linguistic inferences, generated via Grice's model, interact with inferences based on the conventions of a particular genre (e.g. farce) and culture (e.g. courtship) to produce differing interpretations.

*

When, at the end of *The Taming of the Shrew*, Kate obeys Petruchio and admonishes wives saying that 'Thy husband is thy lord, thy life, thy keeper/ Thy head, thy sovereign' (V.ii.148–9), is she serious? Or is this comment, and her whole long speech, ironic, her way of demonstrating how completely she has duped Petruchio? Such puzzles are common in literary studies, and we delight in constructing evermore intricate arguments to support one conclusion or another. One important tool in constructing such arguments is the analysis of the conversational behaviour of the characters, which serves as a foundation on which to build interpretations. Interestingly, however, such analyses cannot by themselves tell us which interpretation is more correct.

As a test case of radically conflicting interpretations, let's look at Robert Heilman's and Coppélia Kahn's interpretations of the roles of Kate and Petruchio in *The Taming of the Shrew*. Heilman writes:

> As a tamer, Petruchio is a gay and witty and precocious artist and, beyond that, an affectionate man; and hence, a remarkable therapist. In Kate, Shakespeare has imagined, not merely a harridan who is incurable or a moral stepchild driven into misconduct by mistreatment, but a difficult woman – a shrew, indeed – who combines willfulness with feelings that elicit sympathy, with imagination, and with a latent co-operativeness that can bring this war of the sexes to an honorable settlement. To have started with farce, to have stuck to the main lines of farce, and yet to have got so much of the supra-farcical into farce – this is the achievement of *The Taming of the Shrew*, and the source of the pleasure it has always given.
>
> (Heilman 1972: 327)

Coppélia Kahn agrees with Heilman's characterization of the play as a farce, but disagrees on the meaning of the supra-farcical aspects of the play:

> The true focus of interest in *The Taming of the Shrew* is not Kate but Petruchio the tamer. Both characters and the taming action in which they participate are creations of that social habit called male dominance, but there is a crucial difference between Kate and Petruchio. He is a stereotype, animated like a puppet by the *idée fixe* of male dominance, while she is realistically and sympathetically portrayed as a woman trapped in the self-destructive role of shrew by her male guardians. Her form of violence is a desperate response to the prevailing system of female subjection; his represents the system itself, its basic mechanism displayed in exaggerated form.
>
> (Kahn 1977: 84)

Heilman argues that Petruchio 'develops a real warmth of feeling for Kate' (1972: 326) and plays the tamer only to bring out the best in her. Kahn argues that Kate 'quite possibly has fallen in love with her tamer' (1977: 97) and plays at being tamed only to authenticate him as a man in his own eyes and those of other men. Thus Heilman concludes that 'Kate's final long speech on the obligations and fitting style of wives we can think of as a more or less automatic statement of a generally held doctrine' (1972: 326), while Kahn concludes that 'Shakespeare finally . . . makes it clear to us, through the contextual irony of Kate's last speech, that her husband is deluded' (1977: 98).

Heilman and Kahn adduce evidence from Kate's final speech itself to support the interpretations, but both must finally rely on their reading of the rest of the play too. Thus Heilman argues that 'a careful reading of the lines will show that most of them have to be taken literally' and that 'forty-five lines of straight irony would be too much to be borne', but rests his interpretation on the argument that if Kate does triumph it's a poor triumph and an ending inconsistent with the rest of the play (1972: 326–7). And Kahn points out that the length of Kate's speech allows her to dominate the stage as Petruchio has until the last scene, and that the speech 'fairly shouts obedience, when a gentle murmur would suffice', but also notes that the action of the scene – a contest between males – is analogous to the action of the whole play and that Kate is merely turning the tables on Petruchio in her speech, aping the verbal dominance and moralistic stance he displayed earlier (1977: 98–9).

Neither Heilman nor Kahn say much about Kate and Petruchio's first encounter, but as with all other audiences of the play their conception of Kate and Petruchio's relationship depends heavily on how they interpret this scene. A linguistic analysis of Kate's and Petruchio's speech acts in Act II, scene i (lines 168–317), will reveal the basis of Heilman and Kahn's disagreement and at the same time will demonstrate how linguistic inferences interact with inferences based on genre and cultural conventions to produce an interpretation of a scene in a play.

Audiences use various kinds of knowledge to draw inferences about charac- ters in a play and about the meaning of a play. Some of what they know – facts and empirical laws – is much the same for all audiences, while other knowledge they bring to a play rests on conventions that may differ with time and culture – rules of language, cultural conventions such as those of courtship, and genre conventions such as those of farce. Commonly held cultural beliefs also vary over time, and strongly affect how an audience responds. Elizabethan audiences, for example, held particular beliefs about the importance of order and about the proper behaviour of wives that differ significantly from those of present-day audiences. E. M. W. Tillyard explains:

> To us 'chaos' means hardly more than confusion on a large scale; to an Elizabethan it meant the cosmic anarchy before creation and the wholesale dissolution that would result if the pressure of Providence relaxed and allowed the law of nature to cease functioning.
>
> (Tillyard 1963 [1943]: 26)

Thus, the progress of *The Taming of the Shrew* from the disorder in the Minola household depicted at the beginning to the order displayed in Kate's final speech, where she alludes to St Paul's dictum to wives as she equates hus- bands, sovereigns, and Christ as the head of the Church, would be a much more salient and significant theme to Elizabethan audiences than it is to present-day audiences. However, even noting the importance of order to Elizabethan audiences does not settle the question of whether we – or they – take seriously Kate's final speech in the play.[1]

The language philosopher Paul Grice explains one kind of general knowl- edge that all audiences share in his lectures on 'Logic and conversation', where he provides a model of how interpreters draw certain types of inferences from conversations.[2] Grice argues that conversation – as far as the exchange of information is concerned – is a co-operative endeavour and that what enables conversation to proceed is an underlying assumption that we as conversants have purposes for conversing and that we recognize these purposes are more likely to be fulfilled if we co-operate. These purposes can vary greatly, they can be mixed, and they are often not held in common by all participants in a conversation. But we nevertheless assume, unless there are indications to the contrary, that we have a shared purpose for conversing (or we struggle to make our purpose the shared purpose), and our actions reflect this assumption. Grice states the assumption as an imperative and calls it the 'Co-operative Principle': 'Make your conversational contribution such as is required, at the stage at which it occurs, by the accepted purpose or direction of the talk exchange in which you are engaged' (Grice 1975: 45). From the Co-operative Principle he derives a series of 'maxims':

Quantity
1 Make your contribution as informative as is required (for the current purposes of the exchange).
2 Do not make your contribution more informative than is required.

Quality
1 Do not say what you believe to be false.
2 Do not say that for which you lack adequate evidence.

Relation
1 Be relevant.

Manner
1 Avoid obscurity of expression.
2 Avoid ambiguity.
3 Be brief (avoid unnecessary prolixity).
4 Be orderly.

Although these maxims are also stated as imperatives, they do not rule conversation in any sense. We rarely fail to observe the maxims casually, for no reason, but we do fail to observe them intentionally for a variety of reasons. The most interesting reason for failing to observe a maxim is thereby to say something indirectly; Grice calls this way of generating meaning an 'implicature'. When we draw attention to our nonobservances – or *flout* maxims – we encourage our hearers to infer something about the reasons for our behaviour, something about our knowledge or beliefs, and what hearers are encouraged to infer is what we implicate. (Implicatures can also arise when maxims are not broken but are simply invoked – brought to the hearers' attention.) Other reasons for failing to observe maxims are: (1) to mislead, in which case the failure – or *violation* – will be hidden from hearers; (2) to *opt out* of a maxim or conversation in which we do not want to participate; and (3) to avoid clashes with another maxim. And we may unintentionally, through ineptitude, negligence, or absent-mindedness, *infringe* a maxim (cf. Grice 1981).

Audiences calculate implicatures made by characters in a play in the same way they do with real people in real conversations. They note failures to fulfil maxims, decide whether in the context of this particular genre of discourse and this particular time and culture the failures are significant, work out what has been implicated on the basis of what they know of the situation, and make further inferences about what kind of people they're dealing with on the basis of what has been said and implicated and what they know of the conventions operating in the situation.

But because analyses of the implicatures in dramatic conversations must themselves be interpreted, such analyses do not simply prove that one interpretation is correct and another incorrect. Kahn's observation that Kate's final speech 'exceeds expectations' marks her intuitive use of Grice's maxims; Kate flouts the second maxim of quantity ('Do not make your contribution more informative than is required') and thereby implicates that she doesn't believe a word of this fine lesson she's reciting. But such an analysis also rests on how the rest of the play is interpreted. Whether Kate's speech is significantly more than is required depends in part on whether we assume Kate has been tamed or not, and this decision depends on our interpretation of the previous conversations between Kate and Petruchio.

And even when audiences share knowledge of the same conventions, the conventions, which block some inferences and support others, may interact differently to produce different interpretations. Conventions block implicatures when a maxim is not observed, but the implicature that would result in normal circumstances (circumstances not governed by the convention in question) is neither intended by the speaker nor apprehended by the hearer; the speaker and hearer's knowledge of the relevant convention causes them to view the nonobservance as not significant. In plays, many implicatures are blocked by the conventions of the genre: for example, by speaking in iambic pentameter (which could be seen as a nonobservance of a maxim of manner) in *The Taming of the Shrew*, Kate and Petruchio are not implicating that they are poets. One might similarly argue that the length of Kate's final speech is merely due to a dramatic convention – a closing statement of the import of the play, much like Oberon's and Puck's speeches that conclude *A Midsummer Night's Dream* – and that this convention blocks any inferences about Kate's intentions, whether ironic or serious. But the fact that Kate's observations would have been so very conventional in Elizabethan times, along with the comment by Lucentio that "Tis a wonder . . . she will be tamèd so' (V.ii.191) that concludes the play, works against such an interpretation.

Petruchio announces his ostensible purpose in his first encounter with Kate – to 'woo her with some spirit when she comes' – before her entrance, and that he will indeed be 'rough and woo not like a babe' (II.i.137) is obvious in his first remark to her. He says:

(1) *Said*   Good morrow, Kate. (II.i.182)

   Reasoning[3]   Only her sister and her father have called her Kate (II.i.21, 167) and even her father usually refers to her as Katherina or Katherine (I.i.52, 100; II.i.44, 62). Everyone else has called her Katherina or Katherine – Hortensio (I.i. 98, 124, 127, 182), Grumio (I.ii.128), and even Petruchio (II.i.43). The shortened form of a name marks a close relationship and Petruchio makes use of it to conventionally implicate:[4]

   Implicated   I am on close terms with you.

The rest of his remark implicates something about his manner toward Kate.

(2) *Said*   For that's your name, I hear. (II.i.182)

   Reasoning   Petruchio knows that her name is Katherine, and Kate knows he knows. Petruchio flouts the first maxim of quality ('Do not say what you believe to be false') and conversationally implicates:

   Implicated   I will be forward with you.

What Kate says denies what Petruchio said and what she implicates denies what he implicated in the first part of his remark:

(3) *Said*   They call me Katherine that do talk of me. (II.i.184)

   Reasoning   Kate knows that Petruchio knows that she's called Katherine; she thus flouts the second quantity maxim ('Do not make your contribution more informative than is required') and conversationally implicates:

   Implicated   You are not on close terms with me.

This initial exchange sets the pattern for the rest of the conversation, in which Petruchio says and implicates something and Kate denies it on both levels.

In Petruchio's next speech virtually everything he says fails to fulfil the first quality maxim ('Do not say what you believe to be false'): Kate does not lie when she says she is called Katherine; she is not called plain Kate, bonny Kate, Kate the cursed (Hortensio's words were 'Katherine the curst,' I.ii.127), the prettiest Kate, and so forth; Petruchio has not heard her mildness praised, her virtues spoken of, and her beauty sounded. Petruchio does the same thing later, failing to fulfil the quality maxim to have adequate evidence for what you say when he says he finds Kate 'passing gentle', 'pleasant, gamesome, passing courteous', 'soft and affable', and so forth. Although Heilman would agree that the purpose of these compliments is primarily comic, he argues that the fact that Petruchio does 'praise her for her virtues (whether she has them or not)' (1972: 326) is also evidence of his warmth of feeling for her. If an audience agrees with him, they too will find that Petruchio implicates something in complimenting Kate:

(4) *Said*   Hearing thy mildness praised . . . (II.i.191)
              I find you passing gentle . . . (II.i.236)
     Reasoning Petruchio knows no one praises Kate for her mildness and has no evidence that she is passing gentle, but if Kate assumes he believes these things to be true he will be fulfilling the Co-operative Principle. And this is what he conversationally implicates when he flouts the quality maxims:
   Implicated I believe you have good qualities.

Kahn argues that these failures to uphold the Co-operative Principle are rendered meaningless by the conventions of courtship. Kate knows that marriages result from agreements between fathers and suitors and that court-ship is merely a matter of form. Petruchio 'dons the mask of the ardent lover' (1977: 96) in complimenting Kate, and in the context of courtship, failures to fulfil the quality maxims are more or less irrelevant, or even expected. If an audience agrees with Kahn, they too will find Petruchio's failures to fulfil the maxims not significant and that he implicates nothing – an implicature that might have occurred in another context is blocked in this context. These implicatures might also be seen to be blocked by a dramatic convention: Elizabethan audiences especially, for whom the shrew was a stock comic character, could interpret Petruchio's 'compliments' merely as Shakespeare's way of drawing attention to, and laughing at, Kate's shrewishness.

How the audience interprets the compliments (along with what they know has happened in the play up to this point) determines what inferences they draw from Petruchio's statement that she has not been highly enough praised ('not so deeply as to thee belongs') and from the generalized conversational implicature contained in lines 191–4:

(5) *Said*   Hearing thy mildness praised . . . /Myself am moved to woo thee for my wife.
     Reasoning What have her qualities to do with his intention? If a hearer believes they are the reason for his wooing, Petruchio can be assumed to be fulfilling the Co-operative Principle. Thus Petruchio invokes the relation maxim to implicate what anyone would normally implicate in saying such words:
   Implicated Because of your good qualities, I am moved to woo you.

Does he really believe Kate deserves praise? He might, for he has appeared to be a man who decides for himself what he believes. Is it really because of her good qualities that he intends to woo her? Not entirely if the audience believes what he said earlier – 'I come to wive it wealthily, in Padua;/If wealthily then happily in Padua' (I.ii.74–5) – and have found his discussion with Baptista over the dowry significant. But it could be an additional reason.

A further question is whether Kate believes him or not and whether she implicates anything in her response. Heilman dismisses the whole scene as a battle that 'hardly goes beyond verbal farce, in which words are mechanical jokes or blows' (1972: 326). He argues that 'the essential procedure of farce is to deal with people as if they lack, largely or totally, the physical, emotional, intellectual, and moral sensitivity that we think of as "normal"'. People in a farce, he says, 'are not really hurt, do not think much, are not much troubled by scruples' (1972: 324). Doubtless for him the conventions of farce act in this scene to block implicatures and inferences concerning the characters' feelings (except, inexplicably, Petruchio's warmth of feeling for Kate). Kahn agrees that the play is a farce, but as she sees two purposes of this farce – to portray and at the same time to mock a male fantasy (1977: 85, 99–100) – she must find the implicatures and inferences concerning the characters' feelings at least as significant as the verbal fun. She would argue that Kate puns on the word 'movable' in her answer to Petruchio's statement of his intention to woo but also implicates what she believes about his intention:[5]

(6)	*Said*	Moved! In good time, let him that moved you hither/Remove you hence. I knew you at the first/You were a movable. (II.i.195–7)
	Reasoning	She appears to fail to fulfil the quality maxim that you have evidence for what you say. But she knows that Baptista has made her marriage a condition for Bianca's, that Bianca has many suitors, and that she herself is not well-liked. If a hearer assumes that she thus has good evidence for the proposition that someone moved Petruchio to woo her, she will be seen as fulfilling the Co-operative Principle and the maxim too. Kate invokes the second maxim of quality to implicate:
	Implicated	Someone sent you to woo me (it wasn't your idea).

The conversation that follows ostensibly concerns furniture, asses, bees, buzzards, doves, heraldry, cocks, crabs, and such; but by assuming a relationship between what the characters say and the purpose of the conversation (courtship), Petruchio implicates a series of directives (requests or commands) and Kate implicates a series of refusals (and at the same time both make a series of bawdy puns). Some of Petruchio's directives are direct:

(7)	*Said*	Come sit on me. (II.i.198)
		Shall a buzzard take thee? (II.i.207)
		O, put me in thy books. (II.i.222)
	Reasoning	Hearers assume Petruchio's requests are related to the purpose of the conversation. Petruchio thus invokes the relevance maxim to conversationally implicate:
	Implicated	Marry me.

Others proceed indirectly: Petruchio implicates reasons for Kate to get married. For example:

(8) *Said*   Women are made to bear and so are you. (II.i.200)
   Reasoning By relation to the subject of the conversation (marriage)
                Petruchio conversationally implicates:
   Implicated Women should be married and you are no exception.

Similarly, Petruchio says 'Should – buzz!' (II.i.206) and implicates she should marry to avoid scandal, and he says, 'A combless cock, so Kate will be my hen' (II.i.224) and implicates he will be undemanding if Kate marries him (both implicatures operate via Petruchio invoking the relevance maxim). Normally a person who gives reasons for someone to do something will be taken to implicate that he wants the person to do it. Thus, by means of a generalized implicature, Petruchio also implicates in these statements that he wants Kate to marry him.

   Kate's refusals all proceed via a generalized implicature: she insults Petruchio, and insults in response to directives are normally taken to be refusals.

(9) *Said*   You're an ass, a jade, a swain, a buzzard, a man with a cox-
                comb for a crest, a craven, and a crab. (II.i.199-230)
   Reasoning By relation to what Petruchio has said, Kate's insults impli-
                cate refusals, a generalized implicature:
   Implicated No.

That she is refusing marriage is implicated by the assumed relation between her refusals and the purpose of the conversation. Even Heilman must agree that the conventions of farce do not block implicatures 7–9, but he and Kahn would disagree on what we infer about Kate from the implicatures. Heilman finds Kate wilful, and her six or so refusals of Petruchio's proposal could be considered proof of this. Elizabethan audiences in particular would note Kate's disobedience, but they might also conclude that Petruchio is not being particularly honest with her and interpret her actions as reasonable under the circumstances (in her final speech on the obedience wives owe husbands, Kate says that wives should be 'obedient to his honest will' [V.ii.160]). Present-day feminist audiences are more likely to agree with Kahn who argues that Kate's language is defensive (1977: 91), that she does not attack without provocation but merely refuses to obey directives.

   Two other exchanges in this conversation shed light on the reasons for Kate's refusals – she is angry with Petruchio. Petruchio twice complains that Kate is not responding correctly. He says, 'Come, come, you wasp, i' faith you are too angry' (II.i.209), and she replies with a warning (all the implicatures in 10–14 operate via the maxim of relation, so the reasoning for each is the same):

(10) *Said*   If I be waspish, best beware my sting. (II.i.210)
    Implicated If you find me too angry to woo, you had best give up.

   Petruchio has another solution:

(11) *Said*   My remedy is then to pluck it out. (II.i.211)
      Implicated   I'll allay your anger.

Kate replies:

(12) *Said*   Ay, if the fool could find it where it lies. (II.i.212)
      Implicated   Yes, if you could see the reason for my anger.

When Petruchio complains, 'Nay, come, Kate, come, you must not look so sour' (II.i.226), Kate replies:

(13) *Said*   It is my fashion when I see a crab. (II.i.227)
      Implicated   I look sour when I have a reason.

She implicates the reason when he asks her to show him the crab.

(14) *Said*   Had I a glass I would. (II.i.230)
      Implicated   You're the reason.

But what should the audience infer about Kate on the basis of these implicatures? Are Petruchio's actions sufficient to justify Kate's anger? Does she take his compliments to be ironic barbs, drawing attention to her shrewishness? Does she assume his wooing is *pro forma* and instigated by others and thus resent his insincerity? Or is she wilful, a shrew indeed in refusing his honorable proposal? Is she, as a farcical character, insensitive to such treatment, in which case her behaviour toward him is just a particular instance of her general shrewishness? Three conventions are involved in the decision: conventions of farce, conventions of courtship, and conventions governing gender role behaviour. If the scene is interpreted strictly as a farce, the conventions of farce will not allow an inference that she's hurt; thus, if it's a farce she's a shrew; if not, she's not. If Petruchio's wooing is interpreted as strictly conventional, if she sees him as insincere and perhaps deceptive, she has reason to be hurt; if not, she hasn't. If women are expected to defer to men under all circumstances, Kate's a shrew; if not, she's not.

An alternative description of Kate's responses might be that her refusals implicate that she is unwilling to co-operate in a conversation whose purpose is courtship (that she is opting out), but such a conclusion is unlikely because of her involvement in the verbal play. Only near the end of the scene, where she speaks directly, does she opt out of the Co-operative Principle: 'Let me go', 'Go, fool, and whom thou keep'st command' (II.i.235, 251).

However, Petruchio, in the speech that closes the conversation, retroactively opts out of the whole courtship conversation. Even though his statement that 'your father hath consented' (II.i.262) is at least partly a lie (Baptista did set a condition that Petruchio win Kate's love first), as are his statements to Baptista later that Kate loves him, his assertion of it robs the preceding conversation of its primary purpose: after trying for more than seventy-five lines to get her to say yes to his proposal he says that it doesn't matter anyway. And by saying, 'I will marry you', 'I am . . . born to tame you' (II.i.264, 269), he also robs the conversation of the other purpose it might have served: to maintain his own and Kate's face (a common purpose of indirect speech; cf. Brown and Levinson 1987). As long as he keeps up the pretence of playing at matching wits he can ignore Kate's refusals as mere jests. That Petruchio here states his meaning directly shows that he does not – and need not – care whether Kate is willing to marry him. In saying, 'Never make denial;/I must and will have Katherine to my wife' (II.i.272–3) he says what he earlier implicated in saying 'hear you, Kate, in sooth you scape not so' (II.i.234), that no matter what Kate says she will marry him.

Petruchio has done at least part of what he said he would do; he has manipulated Kate into playing a courtship scene with him and then showed her that she has been manipulated. Heilman and Kahn and all audiences will agree that this is so. What they disagree on is the significance of Petruchio's actions. Heilman argues that Kate is a willing participant in the game of matching wits, that the scene is merely a convention of farce anyway, and that even if Petruchio does manipulate her he does it for her own good. Kahn argues that Kate rightfully resents Petruchio's cold-blooded disregard for her feelings that he displays in this closing speech and that his conventional wooing does nothing to mitigate.

If both Heilman and Kahn were simply to describe Kate and Petruchio's courtship scene in terms of failures to fulfil Grice's conversational maxims, they would not disagree. Like all audiences – and all conversing people – they know when maxims have not been fulfilled; and this knowledge can be seen to be independent of the operation of conventions. What they disagree on is whether certain failures are significant or not and what inferences should be drawn from the implicatures that do result from the significant failures. But, like all of us, Heilman and Kahn build their arguments for their interpretations of Kate's and Petruchio's characters and intentions on their analyses of how the characters' failures to fulfil conversational maxims interact with the conventions operating in the play.

SUGGESTIONS FOR FURTHER WORK

1 In Act IV, scene v, of *The Taming of the Shrew*, Kate and Petruchio are married and are travelling back to Padua to attend the wedding of Kate's sister Bianca. On the road they get into an argument. Analyse the failures to observe maxims in this conversation between Kate and Petruchio. What conventions operate to condition how you interpret the maxim non-observances? How might Heilman and Kahn interpret the implicatures that arise? If your interpretation of the relationship between Kate and Petruchio differs from Heilman's or Kahn's explain how you would interpret the implicatures in this scene.

2 In *Much Ado about Nothing*, Beatrice and Benedict are nearly as contentious a romantic couple as are Kate and Petruchio, and there is much deception

involved in the courtship of both romantic couples in the play – Hero and Claudio and Beatrice and Benedict.

(a) At the end of Act II, scene iii, Benedict sees indirect meanings in Beatrice's statements that she does not intend. Explain what conversational maxims Benedict assumes she is flouting to signal her indirect meanings and explain the reasoning he follows to arrive at these meanings. What conventions does he assume are operating that help him arrive at these meanings?

(b) Both Claudio and Benedict are seemingly easily convinced by improbable things in this play: that Hero has been unfaithful and that Beatrice loves Benedict. Explain why you do, or do not, draw conclusions about their characters from their failure to have adequate evidence for what they say about Hero and Beatrice.

(c) Analyse the final conversation between Beatrice and Benedict in the play (V.iv.72-97). What conversational maxims do they fail to fulfil and what do they implicate by their failures? What conventions are operating in this scene, and how do they contribute to your interpretation of what the characters mean by their failures to observe the maxims? Explain the reasoning that connects their failures to observe maxims with your interpretation of their meaning.

(d) This scene, like all the scenes between Beatrice and Benedict, is full of indirectness. In contrast, Hero and Claudio's relationship is troubled by outright deception. Analyse the scenes in which the deception occurs and compare them to the scenes of indirection between Beatrice and Benedict. What inferences do you draw about this contrast between the two romantic couples, and how does it inform your interpretation of the play?

NOTES

1 I want to thank my colleague Charles Nelson for his insights on how Elizabethan audiences might have responded to *The Taming of the Shrew*.

2 Some have argued that Grice's theory of conversation is not universal; for refutations of this view, see Brown and Levinson 1987: 288–9, and Bach and Harnish 1979: 299–300.

3 In all implicatures described here, the reasoning is that which the speaker knows the hearer is able to and will work out; it is also the reasoning any audience will work out.

4 Grice distinguished several types of implicatures. Conventional implicatures result when the conventional meanings of the words used determine not only what is said but also what is implicated (see implicature 1, p. 59). Conversational implicatures are a subset of nonconventional implicatures and arise from flouts of conversational maxims. They are further divided into particularized conversational implicatures, which depend on special features of the context (see implicatures 4 (p. 60), 7 (p. 61) and 10–14 (pp. 62–3)), and generalized implicatures, which hold in the absence of special circumstances.

5 Here we have an example of 'layering' of implicatures. Puns, in that they mean two ways at once, could be said to fail to fulfil a manner maxim to avoid ambiguity or even the quality maxim to not say what you believe to be false. Kate knows that Petruchio is not a movable in the sense of being a piece of furniture, and her intentional failure to fulfil the quality maxim results in a punning insult. The puns are an important part of the scene and the interaction of the characters, but, at the same time, the two characters fail to observe other maxims and implicate more fundamentally how they feel about each other and their situation.

6 Accessing character through conversation

Tom Stoppard's *Professional Foul*[1]

Neil Bennison

EDITORS' PREFACE

How do readers of plays get from the words on the page to judgements concerning the 'personalities' of characters? Neil Bennison demonstrates how we can use frameworks from discourse analysis and pragmatics to analyse the conversational behaviours of characters and account for aspects of their character. He analyses the development of the character Anderson in Tom Stoppard's play *Professional Foul*, focusing on four prominent character traits. The first part of the analysis applies ideas from discourse analysis (including turn-length, turn-taking and topic-shift); the second part applies ideas from pragmatics (including Grice's Co-operative Principle and Politeness). Bennison shows how changes in Anderson's conversational behaviour may lead to inferences about changes in his character. He argues that the kind of analysis he undertakes is based on a relatively precise methodology, and that a plural approach to linguistic analysis involving many different linguistic frameworks is necessary if one is to capture the richness of character.

INTRODUCTION

When we go to the theatre, or read a play-text, the chances are that a significant part of this experience will be made up of our forming judgements about its characters. But how do we arrive at these judgements from the words of the play, whether in the text, or spoken in the performance? In this chapter I describe how we get from the words on the page to judgements concerning characters' 'personalities' by analysing their conversational behaviour and using the powerful interpretative apparatus of discourse analysis and pragmatics to this end. A number of linguistic critics working on characterization have already used these linguistic approaches to considerable effect.[2] The basic premise upon which much of this work is based is most succinctly expressed by William Downes:

> A real person is a theoretical entity for his interpreters, to which they assign those intentions that make sense of what he does. A character in drama is

an analogy of a person and is interpreted in the same way.

(Downes 1988: 253)

Although some critics would argue with Downes's treatment of characters as if they were 'real' people, his comments nevertheless provide us with a useful starting point. If, as he suggests, characterization 'involves the manifestation of inner states, desires, motives, intentions, beliefs through action, including speech acts' (1988: 226), then it follows that the methods of analysing conversational behaviour in the real world are also readily applicable to that of the dramatic work. In this chapter, I will be using these analytical techniques to consider a single character, in particular how he 'develops' as the play progresses. I will argue that this may be accounted for through the changes in his conversational strategies, from which we can infer changes in attitude.

The focus of my discussion is the character of Anderson, in Tom Stoppard's (1978 [1977]) television play, *Professional Foul*, and I will be focusing on the question of how it is that four prominent character traits are inferable from his conversational behaviour. The analysis begins with some approaches taken from discourse analysis; namely, an examination of conversational turn-length, turn-taking and topic-shift. In the second part of the discussion, I will be considering Anderson's behaviour from the viewpoint of pragmatic analysis – that is, in terms of the specific meaning of Anderson's utterances in their particular context. The implications of Anderson's statements are as significant as their surface meaning, and I will be examining these by referring mainly to three pragmatic frameworks: Grice's Co-operative Principle (1975), Brown and Levinson's model of politeness (1987) and Leech's Politeness Principle (1983). Firstly, I will give a very basic synopsis of the play in order to contextualize the analysis.

TOM STOPPARD'S *PROFESSIONAL FOUL*

Professional Foul is unlike many of Stoppard's more absurdist plays in that much of the action is centred on what we could broadly term a realistic character. Anderson, a professor of ethics, is invited to Prague to give a paper at a philosophy conference, but what really attracts him to this event is the chance of going to a World Cup qualifying match between England and Czechoslovakia. He doesn't, however, explain this to the play's other main character, McKendrick, another academic whom he meets on the plane. Things become more complicated for him when he is approached by his former student, Pavel Hollar, who tries to persuade him to smuggle his politically sensitive thesis out of the country. Anderson refuses, but, in response to Hollar's worries about being searched on leaving the hotel, he agrees to bring the document to Hollar's apartment the following day, on the way to the football match. Anderson attends part of the conference before leaving early to visit Hollar's apartment but he arrives to find it being searched by the Czechoslovakian police, Hollar having been arrested. In this pivotal scene (scene six), a confused Anderson attempts repeatedly to assert himself, but is detained for over an hour before he is finally permitted to leave. Shaken by the ordeal, he returns to the hotel where he finds out the result of the match – a heavy defeat for England – from two English sports journalists, Grayson and Chamberlain.

That evening, at a subdued dinner, Anderson argues with McKendrick about ethical problems before being approached by Hollar's wife, whom he had met at the searching of the apartment. At a park near the hotel, he promises Mrs Hollar that he will try to help her husband, and returns to the hotel, where he finds McKendrick drunkenly baiting some of the England team in Grayson's room. He borrows Grayson's typewriter, with which he rewrites the paper he is due to give the next day. His new lecture satirically comments on human rights under the Czechoslovakian constitution and irritates the Conference chairman, who brings the session to an abrupt end by staging a false fire alarm. At Prague airport, Anderson is searched for Hollar's thesis but nothing is found, the explanation being, as Anderson reveals to an indignant McKendrick once they have boarded the plane, that he has hidden it in McKendrick's briefcase.

INITIAL OBSERVATIONS ON THE CHARACTER OF ANDERSON

The play's initial stage directions provide us with some brief but significant descriptions of Anderson. He is an 'Oxbridge don' who gives a 'somewhat fastidious impression', a point which is almost immediately confirmed when he 'dabs at his mouth with his napkin and puts it down' (43). Both the comment and the action suggest a stereotypical old-fashioned academic figure, and to begin with Anderson is certainly quite absent-minded. Stoppard describes his 'manner' as being 'a little vague', and one function of pragmatic and discourse analysis here will be to identify more precisely how Anderson is 'vague' in conversation. Discourse analysis may also elucidate another area of Stoppard's characterization: Anderson's rather unpredictable tendency to be talkative in some scenes but not in others. Two other aspects of Anderson's character, his pomposity and his urbanity, can also be interpreted through discourse analysis, though we must also examine the complexity of his utterances and the level of formality he uses in particular speech situations if we are to establish the consistency of these traits. There are, I will argue, significant developments in Anderson's character which can be inferred from his changing conversational behaviour: he is not unaffected by his experiences, and emerges as a somewhat different character at the end of the play, where he appears more direct and less polite.

ANALYSIS

Turn-length

In discourse analysis, participants in conversation are said to take a 'turn' when they speak (see Vimala Herman's chapter in this volume), and a quantitative analysis of the length of these turns can provide useful initial clues to a character's behaviour – their relative power in the speech situation, or their interest in a particular conversational topic, for example – although the statistical evidence is not conclusive in isolation. Anderson's utterances are generally shorter in the later scenes in the play (from scenes seven to sixteen Anderson's average turn-length is 8.4 words/turn compared with 14.3 words/turn in scenes one to six). But what is likely to be more immediately conspicuous to the reader is that in a number of scenes he has by far the longest turn: in scenes one and three, for example, Anderson produces turns of over 100 words. Moreover, in scene four, Anderson has the longest turn (86 words compared with the next longest, McKendrick's 47), as he again does in the final scene (53 words against McKendrick's 14). If we discount Anderson's lecture in scenes eleven to fourteen on the grounds that he is reading from a prepared script, rather than speaking conversationally, this turn of 53 words is the longest turn taken by him after scene six. This suggests a change in Anderson's conversational behaviour, but it will require further linguistic evidence if it is to carry any weight, and we will thus return to this later.

In the context of the generally unremarkable figures for his average length of turn (except in scene five there are no scenes in which it exceeds 14.7), these large turns stand out sharply. Anderson is not consistently talkative, but he does occasionally produce lengthy utterances, which suggest the vagueness Stoppard describes in his initial stage direction. Anderson's occasional bursts of verbosity implicate a sudden urge to speak on a particular topic and this is very noticeable in the first scene, where his identification and development of a linguistic paradox generated by a photograph of Anderson in the Colloquium brochure (the photograph must be old because he appears young) precipitates his longest turn in the scene:

ANDERSON: The second glance is known as linguistic analysis. A lot of chaps pointing out that we don't always mean what we say, even when we manage to say what we mean. Personally I'm quite prepared to believe it. [*He finishes writing and closes the notebook. He glances uneasily out of the window.*] Have you noticed the way the wings keep *wagging*? I try to look away and think of something else but I am drawn back irresistibly . . . I wouldn't be nervous about flying if the wings didn't wag. Solid steel. Thick as a bank safe. Flexing like tree branches. It's not natural. There is a coldness around my heart as though I'd seen your cigarette smoke knock against the ceiling and break in two like a bread stick. By the way that is a non-smoking seat.

(Stoppard 1978: 45)

Even more important than the length of this utterance is its disorderly nature, and a consequence of Anderson's greater interest in certain topics of conversation is that sometimes it leads him, as it does here, to produce confusion, particularly in terms of the topic of conversation.

Topic-shift and topic-control

Anderson's identification of the linguistic paradox referred to above creates difficulties because, in doing so, he fails to return McKendrick's greeting:

ANDERSON: It must be an old photograph.
[McKENDRICK *gets up and comes to sit in the empty seat across the aisle from* ANDERSON]
McKENDRICK: [*Changing seats*] Bill McKendrick.
ANDERSON: How odd.
McKENDRICK: Is it?

(Stoppard 1978: 44)

By failing to return McKendrick's greeting, Anderson fails to provide the appropriate second pair-part of the adjacency pair (Schegloff and Sacks 1973) which constitutes a greeting. His long turn in the extract given above (from p. 45) amounts to an extreme example of what Brown and Yule describe as 'speaking on a topic', rather than 'speaking topically' (Brown and Yule 1983: 84), in that it ignores the previous speaker's utterance in order to develop a new topic. If we are not to infer from Anderson's failure to respond that he is deliberately being rude (unlikely, when McKendrick is, at this point, a complete stranger to him), then it is most likely to be seen as evidence of his vagueness and the fact that he is wrapped up in his own world.

This is also evident from the long turn quoted above, where Anderson also changes topic in a very disorderly way. In the same turn, he launches into a rhapsodic observation on the flexing motion of the aircraft's wings. This sudden topic-change and the change of register in the very lyrical statement about McKendrick's cigarette smoke, is partly explained by his fear of flying which is indicated just before the topic-change in Stoppard's stage directions – '*He glances uneasily out of the window*' (44) – but it is also a noteworthy example of his conversational meandering. This becomes more apparent later in the scene, as McKendrick draws Anderson's attention to Andrew Chetwyn, sleeping at the back of the plane. When McKendrick asks him, 'Do you know Prague?' (45), he fails to notice the obvious topic-shift and produces the absurdly irrelevant reply – 'Not personally. I know the name.' This is partially explained by the fact that the stage directions suggest he is still looking at Chetwyn, but we infer Anderson's absent-mindedness from his response because any confusion over the referent of the question is unlikely, assuming that Anderson, as a participant in the Colloquium (albeit an unenthusiastic one), knows that the venue is Prague.

Some of the clearest indications of Anderson's vagueness occur at the level of topic-control. When, in scene one, McKendrick tries to initiate a new topic by referring to the 'fictions problem' (46), Anderson fails to take it up because he doesn't realize that McKendrick is referring to Anderson's own conference paper. Significantly, when he does realize what the topic is, he implicates a lack of interest in it by changing the topic to that of his 'ulterior motive' in coming to Czechoslovakia. Anderson's behaviour appears even more extraordinary when, having initiated this topic, he immediately withdraws it. When asked to be more specific about his 'unethical' behaviour, Anderson is extremely uncooperative:

ANDERSON: I don't think I'm going to tell you. You see, if I tell you I make
  you a co-conspirator whether or not you wished to be one. Ethically I
  should give you the opportunity of choosing to be one or not.
McKENDRICK: Then why don't you give me the opportunity?
ANDERSON: I can't without telling you. An impasse.

(Stoppard 1978 [1977]: 47)

Anderson's conversational behaviour here repays our attention not only because it is a striking example of the problems he causes through his disorderly conversational behaviour but also because, like his earlier reference to the linguistic paradox, it suggests the character trait of urbanity – that Anderson enjoys 'playing' with language.

Turn-allocation and turn-taking

As Sacks *et al.* (1978) have demonstrated, conversation is in many ways governed by a system through which speakers offer spaces in which others may speak ('turn-allocation'), or elect to speak themselves at a relevant place in the flow of conversation ('self-selection'). We have already noted that Anderson is loquacious on certain topics, but that he also displays reluctance to talk in scene one. His vagueness is also implicated by the way he does not take up turns allocated to him enthusiastically, and his infrequent allocation of turns to McKendrick. In the first scene Anderson only allocates a turn clearly to McKendrick six times out of 43 turns (14 per cent). This contrasts with scene three where he allocates 28 turns to his former student, Hollar (mainly through direct questions), from 58 turns (48 per cent). To some extent this reflects the power relationship in scene three (they both act as if their former tutor/student relationship still exists), but it also indicates Anderson's greater interest in Hollar's news. By contrast, Anderson's growing hostility towards McKendrick is suggested, in the last scene, in the figures for his turn-allocation. The contempt which Anderson seems to have for McKendrick in scene sixteen (we shall see later that this is suggested by the level of politeness he uses) is strongly marked by the fact that he allocates no turns to him at all.

Hesitations and incomplete turns

Conversational hesitations are important indicators of a character's state of mind, in that they usually imply discomfort: unease, powerlessness or embarrassment, for example. Thus in scene three, when Anderson is faced with the predicament of not wishing to agree to Hollar's request to smuggle his politically charged thesis out of Czechoslovakia, but, at the same time, not wanting to jeopardize their friendship, his linguistic performance is noticeably flawed. Out of a total of 58 conversational turns, he hesitates 13 times and fails to complete an utterance on 3 occasions. Generally, in informal speech situations less importance is attached to linguistic non-fluency, but Anderson's frequent performance errors here suggest his unease at being placed in this position. In addition, since this is dramatic discourse, we know that his speech is written to be spoken and we are thus likely to infer greater significance for this non-fluency than we would in normal spoken interaction.

Similar discomfort afflicts Anderson in another extraordinary episode when he meets the two footballers in the lift. Dedicated football fan that he is, he attempts to give advice to Crisp and Broadbent in a long and excited utterance. However, his enthusiasm for the topic, implicated by the length of the turn (86 words), conflicts with the hesitancy he also displays.

ANDERSON: [*In a rush*] I realize it's none of my business – I mean you may think I'm an absolute ass, but [*Pause.*] Look, if Halas takes a corner he's going to make it short almost certainly – push it back to Deml or Kautsky, who pulls the defence out. Jirasek hangs about for the chip to the far post. They'll do the same thing from a set piece. Three or four times in the same match. *Really.* Short corners and free kicks. [*The lift stops at the third floor.* BROADBENT *and* CRISP *are staring at* ANDERSON. *Lamely.*] Anyway, that's why they've brought Jirasek back, in my opinion.

(Stoppard 1978 [1977]: 59)

Anderson's uncomfortable hesitancy is clearly marked in Stoppard's stage directions, particularly the last one, which suggests a lengthy and embarrassed silence and implicates the reason for his uncertainty. Throughout this turn he is waiting for a favourable reaction from the two footballers and he adopts a much less formal register in order not to alienate them. Earlier in the scene he corrected himself, when using the word 'Colloquium', replacing it with 'bunfight' (59), and now he speaks in short and simple sentences. The absence of any encouraging response from his interlocutors, however, indicates that his advice is falling on deaf ears.

Anderson's performance errors here reflect another conflict within him. The topic he is speaking on interests him greatly (much more so than his own lecture topic), but it is also one on which he is not recognized as an authoritative speaker. His advice, therefore, may be rejected as uninformed and undesirable by the footballers (even though events prove it to be correct). By self-selecting he risks losing what Brown and Levinson (1987) call 'positive face' (our wish to have our wants and conduct approved of by others), a fact which is reflected in the lack of assuredness in his utterance. What is remarkable here, then, is that Anderson chooses to give advice at all. The inference we can draw from it all is that his enthusiasm for the topic overrides his concern for his positive face, but that the conflict between these two concerns remains, and is visible in the nervous flaws in his linguistic performance.

Anderson's uneasiness here is of his own making, but in scene six it is the confusing and confrontational situation he finds himself in which unnerves him. Stoppard's authorial comments here make it explicit that Anderson is 'out of his depth' (66 and 73) and 'afraid' (73). Such statements are, of course, not available to the viewer of the television play, but Anderson's state of mind is inferable from his numerous hesitations (17 out of 52 turns, or 32.7 per cent, compared with the average number of hesitations in all scenes of 13.9 per cent), longer pauses (4 instances) and unfinished turns (5 instances). Three instances are especially worth noting. His initial unease is indicated in his hesitant reference to being on the way to an engagement (65), and his fear and powerlessness at the end of the scene reflects itself when he abandons his turn and 'decides abruptly to leave' (73). More significantly, Anderson's hesitancies undermine his attempts to assert himself. Midway through the scene, his anger at a policeman taking his wallet peters out timidly as 'MAN *3 gently pushes him back into the chair*' (67). The difference between Anderson's words and deeds here is a telling example of the emptiness of many pompous statements he makes in this scene.

Scene six is the point from which we can see a considerable change wrought in his character. Firstly, we may note the reduction in the number of performance errors he makes, and the data for scene seven onwards is very revealing here. Apart from scene nine, where Anderson, talking to Mrs Hollar and Sacha, displays occasional discomfort (4 hesitations), we find very few instances of hesitations or unfinished turns (no more than one instance of each in scenes seven, eight, ten and sixteen). Even taking into account scene nine, the quantitative difference between instances of hesitation in the first six scenes (43 instances) and the last six (5 instances) is 86 per cent, a figure which suggests that the difference would be perceptible to the reader or audience, suggesting a greater degree of conversational confidence on Anderson's part. The significance of the figures may, of course, be challenged on the grounds that both the number and length of turns taken by Anderson in the last six scenes is considerably smaller than in the earlier scenes, and we would therefore expect to see fewer performance errors. Nevertheless, the reduction in these figures is itself indicative of character development. Following his traumatic encounter with the Czech police, he becomes less prone to sporadic bouts of verbosity. Ironically, the most striking example occurs in scene ten, when Broadbent admits that Anderson's advice on the Czech team's tactics has proved correct:

BROADBENT: Here. That bloody Jirasek. Just like you said.
ANDERSON: Yes.
BROADBENT: They don't teach you nothing at that place then.
ANDERSON: No.

(Stoppard 1978 [1977]: 86)

Anderson's laconic replies implicate his loss of interest in the topic, even now that Broadbent actually shows interest in his earlier advice and allocates a turn to him twice. The difference in turn-lengths reveals a marked contrast between his weariness here and his uncontainable enthusiasm for the subject in scene four. It also suggests that he has been shocked out of his absent-mindedness and emerges as a more direct speaker. Support for this reading can also be seen in Anderson's interruptions of other speakers.

Interruptions

The degree to which characters in dramatic texts are prepared to interrupt others is an important indication of their power and confidence in a given speech situation. Thus in the first scene, where he has only marginally greater status than McKendrick (his university is more prestigious), but where McKendrick is a stranger, he does not risk threatening McKendrick's negative face (our desire not to have our freedom impinged upon by others: Brown and Levinson 1987) by encroaching on his conversational space through interrupting. The differential power relationship, however, between Anderson and Hollar in scene three, is visible in Anderson's three interruptions. When Hollar begins to apologize for intruding, Anderson is able to interrupt in order to minimize the threat to his negative face posed by Hollar's imposition on his time (51). Similarly, he upholds Leech's Politeness Principle (which, broadly stated, argues that politeness requires that we 'minimize the expression of impolite beliefs', or 'maximize the expression of polite beliefs' (Leech 1983: 81)) when he interrupts Hollar again (54), because he does so to affirm enthusiastically that he too remembers Peter Volansky, thus following Leech's maxim of agreement, 'maximize agreement between self and others' (Leech 1983: 132).

Only in his last interruption (56) is Anderson actually rude, and this reflects his priorities. Whilst he is generally careful to be polite, he wishes above all not to have his actions impeded. Thus when Hollar asks him to smuggle his thesis out of the country and proposes a solution to Anderson's ethical objections ('But if you didn't know you were smuggling it'), his determination to avoid troublesome obligations is demonstrated when he interrupts Hollar in order rigidly to assert the 'true' implications of Hollar's request at the expense of Leech's maxim of agreement ('smuggling implies knowledge' (56)). This uncooperative attitude is a far cry from that which Anderson displays in scene nine. Here, his unequivocal response to Mrs Hollar's pleas – 'Mrs. Hollar, I will do everything I can for him' (82) – is made more emphatic by the fact that he interrupts her in order to say it, and this affirms his commit-ment to help at the expense of any considerations for his negative face, a change in priorities which is central to his character development.

Although Anderson's attitudes towards his interlocutors may have changed in the example above, we find relatively few interruptions in the play because the speech situations dramatized in *Professional Foul* are generally co-operative. Scene six is the obvious exception, and its confrontational atmo-sphere is reflected in the nature of Anderson's interruptions of the Czech police captain. Two out of the three instances ('I don't believe any of that' (71) and 'How could I have told him that? I don't speak Czech' (72)) reverse the Politeness Principle by emphasizing his disagreement and carry with them the clear implication that he believes the captain to be lying. His inter-ruptions therefore coincide with his rejection of the principles of politeness to which he has hitherto adhered quite consistently.

POLITENESS

In examining politeness I will be drawing on Brown and Levinson's work on the Politeness Phenomenon (1987) and also Leech's Politeness Principle (1983). In the first scenes of the play Anderson tends to favour positive politeness strategies (paying attention to the addressee's positive face). In terms of Leech's Politeness Principle, Anderson's upholding of the approba-tion maxim ('maximise praise of others') is prominent: in scenes one and two he praises McKendrick's and Chetwyn's universities, and thus, by associa-tion, themselves. What is at question, though, is his sincerity. Anderson's praise of McKendrick through praising Stoke University is undermined by the fact that, only one turn before, he reveals that he does not know where McKendrick works, despite beginning as if he does ('And how are things at . . . er . . .', (47)). This suggests to the reader that his praise is superficial. Likewise we suspect, from the ignorance he displays in scene one of Chetwyn and his work, that his praise of Chetwyn's university, in the next scene, is also superficial politeness.

His praise of Hollar, in scene four, and Crisp, in scene five, appears more sincere. Anderson seems genuinely pleased to see Hollar when he appears outside his door (as indicated by his unequivocal directive to him to 'come in' (51)). He does remember Hollar from ten years ago and that he did get a good degree (52), and states his emphatic, repeated approbation – 'Of course you did. Well done, well done.' However, a telling indication of how greatly Anderson values his negative face is visible in his impolite-ness when Hollar asks him if he will smuggle his thesis out of the country. He threatens Hollar's positive face by interrupting him and peremptorily dis-missing as 'childish' (56) one of his answers to Anderson's 'ethical' objections. Anderson's fluctuating politeness behaviour here reflects his awareness of his greater power: he knows that he is not obliged to be polite, and he exploits this fact.

Anderson's praise of Crisp in scene four, however, suggests a different power relationship. Ironically, given the rude behaviour of the footballers in the lift, his attitude to Crisp appears to be one of awed nervousness, for he pauses once and then hesitates again before paying the compliment, 'I'm a great admirer of yours' (58). In addition, his approbation here is accompanied by his upholding of the modesty maxim ('maximize dispraise of oneself'). Before giving his information on the Czech team's tactics, he hedges twice ('I realize it's none of my business' and 'you may think I'm an absolute ass, but . . .'), apologizing in advance for giving them potentially bad advice and for threatening their negative face, whilst at the same time criticizing himself for doing so (59). He does this too in scene one when he fails to recognize McKendrick as a conference participant. Trying to repair the damage done to McKendrick's positive face, he asks to be excused for his own inadequacies:

ANDERSON: I *am* sorry. I'm sure I know your name. I don't read the philosophical journals as much as I should, and hardly ever go to these international bunfights. No time nowadays . . .

(Stoppard 1978 [1977]: 45)

Anderson's modesty is augmented by the emphasis he puts on the sincerity of his apology (the tonic syllable falling on 'am'), stressing that he is fulfilling the felicity conditions (Searle 1969) for that speech act. At this stage in the play, Anderson is concerned not to infringe the Politeness Principle, but in scene six he is forced into abandoning this attitude. Now his conversational behaviour is characterized by his inversion of the modesty maxim. He is at his most pompous as he repeatedly attempts to assert himself and this is noticeable in his regular use of metalinguistic directives demanding the attention of his interlocutors (for example, 'Now look here' (65) and 'now listen to me' (69)) and his emphatic use of what Searle terms 'illocutionary force indicating devices' (1969: 30) or IFIDs (as abbreviated by Levinson 1983). By making their status as speech acts clear, these statements are both more direct and more impolite. Anderson attempts a show of strength by using the performative IFIDs, 'I demand' five times and 'I insist' once, but his insecurity is also indicated by the fact that he supports his demands by referring to his social status. Anderson initially gives his academic position – 'I am the J. S. Mill Professor of Ethics at the University of Cambridge' – invoking both his personal status and Cambridge's prestige, but the pomposity of this reversal of the modesty maxim is absurd when his interlocutors speak little or no English. When, later, he addresses the English-speaking captain he again reverses the modesty maxim when stating, 'I am a guest of the Czechoslovakian government. I might almost say an honoured guest' (69), but these and further modesty maxim violations now function as statements of the felicity conditions for his threats:

ANDERSON: I speak the truth when I say that I am personally acquainted
with two members of the government, one of whom has been to my house,
and I assure you that unless I am allowed to leave this building immediately there is going to be a major incident about the way my liberty has
been impeded by your men . . .

(Stoppard 1978 [1977]: 69)

Anderson's insecurity is inferable from his emphasis of the closeness of his
connections with the government by the reference to having played host to
an MP, and his stressing of the sincerity conditions ('I speak the truth' and
'I assure you') for his threats. Their ineffectiveness has, however, already
been indicated by the captain's ironic question, 'Do you know the Queen'?
which punctures the professor's empty pomposity. Moreover, the fact that
Anderson fails to realize the ironic force of the question, and rushes into
affirming that he does know the Queen, demonstrates the extent to which he
has lost his composure.

By contrast, when giving his revised lecture in scene eleven, Anderson displays little pomposity when interrupted by the chairman, but he nevertheless
shows the most glaring disdain of politeness. His revision of his original lecture
is a major impingement on the negative face of the conference organizers
and his audience, yet he makes no attempt to mitigate the damage. His only
polite response to the chairman's objections is superficially to uphold the tact
maxim ('minimize the cost to others') by claiming that his paper is not a
'technical' one (88) and stating that he will 'speak a little slower'. Anderson
violates the agreement maxim, arguing that he 'wasn't invited to give a particular paper', and his reformulation of the chairman's description of his
action being a 'discourtesy' into being merely 'bad manners' implies his disagreement over the enormity of his transgression. Before, Anderson has
attached some seriousness to the question of 'bad manners', telling Hollar
that 'the history of human calumny is largely a series of breaches of good
manners'. But here his use of the expression is used to much more ironic
effect, a further implication of his antipathy for the Colloquium.

THE CO-OPERATIVE PRINCIPLE AND ANDERSON'S
LANGUAGE

H. P. Grice's 'Co-operative Principle' (1975) is summarized in Marilyn
Cooper's chapter in this volume. Briefly I want here to look at Anderson's
conversational behaviour through looking at where he does not seem to be
upholding Grice's Co-operative Principle, and his possible reasons for not
doing so. To begin with, Grice's maxims of quality and quantity are of
immediate concern to us here because, in scene eleven, Anderson fails to give
an adequate explanation for why he has chosen to give a new paper. The
only 'reason' – 'I changed my mind' (87) – clearly violates the maxim of
quantity in providing too little information, and his excuse, that he 'didn't

realize it mattered', violates the maxim of quality because, having been to a number of overseas conferences, he will be well aware of the procedures. As in scene six, Anderson withholds information, but there are important differences in his reasons for doing so here which implicate a major change of attitude. In scene six, he demonstrates his absent-mindedness when, talking to the captain, he unwittingly alludes to his primary motive for his visit to Czechoslovakia. His response to the captain's surprised question, 'So you came to Czechoslovakia to go to the football match, Professor?' (71) is, initially, to violate the maxim of quality ('Certainly not'), and then to imply that this is not entirely the case by violating the maxims of quantity and relevance when he provides three excuses for not attending all the sessions of the Colloquium instead of admitting the truth. In this instance, Anderson attempts to avoid divulging information which could compromise his academic credibility. Even in this tense and confrontational situation, he persists in protecting his positive face.

Another important point in relation to Anderson's infringement of the Co-operative Principle emerges from this argument. He occasionally reveals too much about his conversation with Hollar and this unwitting co-operation prompts the captain to spring awkward questions on him unexpectedly. Anderson's flustered reaction is to implicate his reluctance to co-operate any further by twice flouting the maxim of relation ('I believe you implied that I was free to go' and 'I insist on leaving now' (71)). On both occasions the flouting of the maxim asserts his wish, indirectly at first and then by a bald on-record demand, to leave the speech situation altogether, a fact which strongly implicates his insecurity in it. This contrasts sharply with Anderson's assuredness in scene eleven, and it indicates his preference for the formal speech event in which his utterances are prepared in advance and where, crucially, he has the greatest speaking rights. His exploitation of these rights enables him to achieve some success in making criticisms of the Czechoslovakian government. Also noticeable here is his awareness of the potential ambiguity of language, an awareness which reveals itself on a number of occasions in his urbane conversational behaviour.

This urbane character trait is frequently related to Anderson's flouting of the maxim of manner. We have already seen this in his aphoristic comments on the linguistic paradox produced by his and McKendrick's comments on Anderson's photograph. It is, though, more overtly apparent when he attempts to limit the damage to the conversation caused by McKendrick's accusation of his insincerity when praising Stoke university:

McKENDRICK: You know perfectly well you wouldn't be seen dead in it.
  [ANDERSON *considers this*]
ANDERSON: Even if that were true, my being seen dead in a place has never so far as I know been thought a condition of its excellence.

(Stoppard 1978 [1977]: 47)

Anderson's urbanity, displayed in many other scenes, is an amusing, though pretty negative feature of his character. We sense that beneath the linguistic competence which he displays in the early scenes, he is not actually committed to anything beyond language itself (with the exception of football). He occasionally uses his verbal felicity as a means of protecting his negative face, just as he does when he makes his ethical arguments for turning down Hollar's request deliberately complex. However, a significant development in his character is inferable when, in scene eleven, he uses his command of language to markedly different effect.

This change can best be described in terms of a shift away from the Interest Principle, as defined by Leech, towards the Irony Principle. Whereas earlier in the play Anderson fulfils the Interest Principle by merely 'saying what is unpredictable and hence interesting' (Leech 1983: 146), in his lecture he uses irony to implicate propositions which are too face-threatening to be made directly, since his aim is to criticize the human rights record of the Czechoslovakian regime. This also explains his failure to provide the chairman with a proper explanation for deciding to give a new paper. When he does produce his critique he does so through ironic positive politeness, more precisely through superficially observing the approbation maxim:

ANDERSON: The first Article of the American Constitution, guaranteeing freedom of religious observance, of expression, of the press, and of assembly, is closely echoed by Articles 28 and 32 of *the no less admirable* Constitution of Czechoslovakia, our *generous* hosts on this occasion . . .
(Stoppard 1978 [1977]: 88, emphasis added)

Anderson's irony here is relatively successful because he exploits the potential ambiguity of the academic discourse appropriate to a lecture. He conveys, through a single utterance, two very different propositions to his audience. His lecture is a good example of pragmatic 'ambivalence' (Leech 1983: 23–4), conveying, on one level, an academic argument which is appropriate to the speech event, but on another, a strongly political protest which is not. Although his lecture is curtailed by the fake fire alarm devised by the Czechoslovakian authorities (itself an indication that the ironic force of his lecture has been felt), Anderson's calmness (indicated by Stoppard in his stage directions, p. 91) as he gathers up his papers, not only contrasts sharply with his panic in scene six but indicates that he feels he has made an effective protest. That he has used his linguistic skills to make such a protest, where before he has been content merely with linguistic cleverness for its own sake, marks an important character development, and it leaves the reader with a distinctly more favourable impression of him at the end of the play than at the beginning.

CONCLUSION

In this chapter I have demonstrated that discourse analysis and pragmatics can give us important insights into Anderson's character, in particular how his various character traits are inferable from his linguistic performance in conversational situations. The analysis has also shown that the levels of formality and politeness used by a character in conversation with other characters may be a revealing area of study in determining a character's sense of his or her own power and confidence in a given conversational situation. Such analysis provides us with a relatively precise methodology for dealing with perceivable changes in character. Perhaps the most important thing to emerge from this analysis is the extent to which the study of dramatic characters allows, and indeed encourages, the application of many different areas of linguistic criticism – turn-taking, conversational implicature, politeness moves, for example – to a given character trait or specific dramatic episode. The wealth of information about character development which is revealed by this plural approach suggests the richness of characters' conversational behaviour as a basis for the study of characterization in dramatic texts.

SUGGESTIONS FOR FURTHER WORK

1 In the analysis above a single character has been isolated for discussion, and his development has been accounted for in terms of his own conversational behaviour with regard to other characters. The analysis does not, for example, consider the conversational behaviour of characters like McKendrick. What shortcomings might such an approach have? What other linguistic factors might we consider when we study the behaviour of dramatic characters?

2 Take an extract of two to three pages from a play you are familiar with where two very different characters are interacting. Summarize your intuitive assessments and their different personalities, and then analyse the text in detail to explore what features give rise to the contrasting qualities displayed.

3 One of the areas of Stoppard's play not covered in this analysis is the verbal comedy produced by Anderson's conversational behaviour. Dramatic comedy frequently depends on the violation or flouting of conversational norms. Monty Python sketches, for example, frequently flout the conversational maxims of Grice's Co-operative Principle. Select a comic extract from a dramatic text and consider which aspects of 'normal' conversation – turn-taking, politeness, the Co-operative Principle, etc. – are being flouted. What implications about the play's characters and their relationships are produced by these violations or floutings? How significant do you think these implications are for our experience of comedy?

NOTES

1 This chapter is an abridged version of an article entitled 'Discourse Analysis, Pragmatics and the Dramatic Character' (1993), in *Language in Literature* 2(2), 79–99. The complete version contains more statistical data and more examples.
2 For examples of this work see Geoffrey Leech's application of the Gricean Cooperative Principle and his own politeness maxims to examine the characters and relationships in Shaw's *You Never Can Tell* (Leech 1992). See also Mick Short's essay (1989) which uses discourse analysis to elucidate the role-reversal in Pinter's short sketch, 'Trouble in the Works'. Further work includes Paul Simpson's (1989) application of Brown and Levinson's politeness analysis to dramatic criticism in his examination of the power shift between pupil and teacher in Ionesco's *The Lesson*.

7   (Im)politeness in dramatic dialogue

Jonathan Culpeper

EDITORS' PREFACE

There has been quite a lot of work in linguistics to explain how speakers are polite to one another in what they say and do, and how they mitigate impolite behaviour linguistically in order to uphold social cohesion (think of the way, for example, that people will say 'I'm sorry' if they accidentally bump into someone else in a crowded street). In this chapter, Jonathan Culpeper explores the role of *impoliteness* in dramatic dialogue. He suggests that, in dramatic terms, impoliteness is particularly interesting because it generates the disharmony and conflict between characters which generates audience interest and often moves the plot forward. After outlining his theory in general terms, Culpeper goes on to analyse the relations between the two main characters, Charlie and the Colonel, in the film *Scent of a Woman*. He does this by analysing three short extracts from the dialogue, showing the Colonel to be an interestingly complex personality, and also how the characterization of Charlie develops during the film.

INTRODUCTION

A number of studies have shown that frameworks of linguistic politeness can be used to shed light on literary critical issues (c.g. Leech 1992; Simpson 1989; Bennison this volume). Why is politeness so useful in the study of drama? Broadly speaking, politeness is about the strategic manipulation of language, about expediting our conversational goals by saying what is socially appropriate. A framework that brings together *face* (an emotionally sensitized concept about the self) and sociological variables (such as power and social distance) and relates them to motivated linguistic strategies is going to be particularly useful in helping us understand (1) how characters position themselves relative to other characters, (2) how they manipulate others in pursuit of their goals and (3) how the plot is pushed forward. Such a framework will allow us to describe systematically, for example, how one character might ingratiate themselves with another or how one character might offend another. A stumbling block, however, is that pragmatic theories, particularly politeness theories, have tended to concentrate on how communicative strategies maintain or promote social harmony. In the case of drama, the key 'dramatic' points often occur at times of interactional conflict. Thus, one of the tasks of this chapter is to begin to investigate *impoliteness* strategies: strategies that are designed to cause offence and social disruption.

In the second section of this chapter I will approach impoliteness by first outlining a framework of linguistic politeness, and in the third section I will briefly consider why it is that the study of impoliteness is important for drama, particularly recent twentieth-century drama. In the fourth section I conduct an extended discussion of dialogue extracts from the film *Scent of a Woman* (1992), focusing, in particular, on how (im)politeness relates to characterization. Then I conclude the main body of the chapter, and finally introduce a number of exercises involving extracts from recent twentieth-century plays.

FROM POLITENESS TO IMPOLITENESS

Politeness

Brown and Levinson (1987) explain politeness with reference to the notion of *face*. In the everyday sense of the word, face is involved in notions such as reputation, prestige and self-esteem. Brown and Levinson (1987) suggested that face consists of two basic socio-psychological wants. *Positive face* is the want to be approved of. For example, I may assume that you want me to acknowledge your existence, approve of your opinions, or express admiration of you and what you say. *Negative face* is the want to be unimpeded. For example, I may assume that you want me to let you attend to what you want, do what you want, and say what you want. Life would be wonderful if our faces remained unassailed. However, even in relatively mundane interactions our actions often threaten the other person's face. For example, requests typically threaten negative face; criticism typically threatens positive face. Acts such as these are called *Face Threatening Acts* (FTAs).

How face threatening any particular act is depends upon a number of factors, but in particular (a) the relationship between the participants and (b) the size of the imposition involved in the act to be performed. If I have been slaving away in my office for hours and I am desperate for a cup of tea, it is going to be easier for me to ask a long-standing colleague than a new one. That is because in terms of *social distance* I am closer to the colleague I have known for ages than the one I have only known for a few days. If the head of my department happened to be in my office at the time, it would be more difficult to ask him than to ask my new colleague. That is because he is more *powerful* than I am, whereas my new colleague would be more or less equal with me in terms of power. If I popped in after work to visit a friend and was asked if I would like a drink, asking for a glass of water would be less face threatening than asking for a glass of vintage port. Brown and Levinson suggest that it is possible to *rank* acts according to size of imposition.

What has politeness got to do with all this? Politeness comes about when one indicates concern to support someone else's face. For example, if I request someone to help me operate my computer, my FTA would threaten negative face in causing inconvenience. Rather than just say 'Help me with my computer', I could say 'Would you mind helping me with my computer?' On the surface, I am asking a question about whether the addressee would mind helping me; only indirectly does my utterance carry the speech act force of a request.[1] By displaying concern not to impose – in other words, concern for face – I maintain social harmony (and probably stand a greater chance of being helped). Of course, there are many different politeness strategies that we may use in the performance of an FTA. Which politeness strategy, or which combination of politeness strategies, is selected would depend – other things being equal – on one's assessment of how face threatening a particular act is going to be. For reasons of space, I am unable to describe these strategies in any kind of systematic detail, but will introduce them as and where relevant.[2]

Impoliteness

So far I have considered issues to do with politeness: how we use linguistic strategies to maintain or promote harmonious social relations. However, there are times when people use linguistic strategies to attack face – to *strengthen* the face threat of an act. I will used the label 'impoliteness' to describe this kind of linguistic strategy. To illustrate what I mean, imagine the different ways in which the face threatening act of criticism might be conveyed in, say, criticism of an essay you have written:

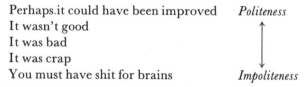

Here we have a scale varying from very polite to very impolite. At one end of the scale, the utterance 'Perhaps it could have been improved' could be interpreted as polite, given a suitable context, for two reasons: (1) the hedge 'perhaps' reduces the force of the speaker's criticism, and (2) 'it could have been improved' is an oblique way of expressing the criticism. The speaker flouts Grice's Maxim of Manner (see Marilyn Cooper's contribution to this volume for a description of Grice's Co-operative Principle (1975)), and conveys the criticism in an implicature. This is an example of what Brown and Levinson (1987) would call 'an off-record strategy'. At the other end of the scale, the utterance 'You must have shit for brains' could be interpreted as extreme positive impoliteness, given a suitable context, for several reasons:

(1) 'shit' is a taboo word (more so than 'crap'), and (2) the criticism is personalized through the use of 'you', and (3) the speaker flouts Grice's Maxim of Quality in order to implicate the impolite belief that the writer has absolutely no intelligence. What about the utterance 'It was bad' in the middle of the scale? Whether one interprets this as polite or impolite would depend very much on the context. For example, if it were not part of someone's role (as a tutor, say) to make the criticism, and if it were known that the addressee was particularly sensitive to criticism, then 'It was bad' would seem to be impolite. It should be noted that the key difference between politeness and impoliteness is a matter of (the hearer's understanding of) *intention*: whether it is the speaker's intention to support face (politeness) or to attack it (impoliteness). Of course, there are a number of other types of rudeness. For example, a speaker might unintentionally cause offence or might use *mock* impoliteness (banter), perhaps to reinforce social solidarity. These would not constitute cases of 'genuine' impoliteness, as I have defined it here.[3]

IMPOLITENESS AND DRAMA

Why is impoliteness important for the study of drama? Impoliteness is a type of aggression, and aggression has been a source of entertainment for thousands of years. It is made intriguing by the fact that generally it is – thankfully – fairly rare and by the fact that it is socially outlawed (the compulsive desire of children to do what they have been told not to is evidence of how what is forbidden attracts interest). Moreover, it is from a position of relative safety and comfort that theatre audiences can watch violent conflict. Lucretius, writing in the first century BC, noted the positive feelings that can arise when one in safety watches others in danger:

> It is pleasant, when on the great sea the winds are agitating the waters,
> to look from the land on another's great struggle;
> not because it is a delectable joy that anyone be distressed,
> but because it is pleasant to see what ills you yourself are free from.[4]
>
> (*De Rerum Natura*, Book II, 1–4)

In the case of drama, this aggression often takes place in dialogue. It is not surprising that the courtroom has provided the basis for so many plays, films and television dramas. Here prosecutors are licensed to aggravate a witness's face. The courtroom provides a socially respectable and legitimate form of verbal aggression.

In drama, impoliteness is not thrown in haphazardly for audience entertainment: it serves other purposes. Conflict in interaction appears either as a symptom, or as a cause of, social disharmony, and where there are tensions between characters we are more likely to see developments in character and plot. Let's first consider characterization. It is important to note here that our interpretative assumptions about (im)politeness behaviours in fictional texts differ somewhat from those which we have for 'real life'. In a fictional context, there are two reasons why any character behaviour is assumed to carry more interpretative significance than would the same behaviour in real life. Firstly, we know that we have the *complete* set of behaviours that constitute a particular character or characters. This is, of course, never possible in real life. Secondly, and perhaps more importantly, we know that any character behaviour is not just determined by the fictional personality that gave rise to it, but is also the *motivated choice* of the writer. In real life, impoliteness, because of its rarity and social restrictions, is often perceived as unexpected or fore-grounded behaviour, and such behaviour will trigger an attributional search: we want to know why something odd happened, what the special circumstances were for someone to break the social norm. We might look for a cause in the person's mood or personality, or in the situation, or simply dismiss it as unintentional. In fiction, however, we are more likely to interpret such behaviour as a message from the author about an aspect of the fictional world which will be of future consequence.

With regard to plot, analysts, such as Bremond (1966, 1973), have described plot development in terms of a movement from a situation of equilibrium, through a situation of disequilibrium, to the re-establishment of equilibrium. Consider the plot of the limerick below:

> There once were two cats of Kilkenny,
> Each thought there was one cat too many.
> So they fought and they fit,
> And they scratched and they bit,
> Till excepting their nails and the tips of their tails,
> Instead of two cats, there weren't any.
>
> (Edward Lear, 'The Cats of Kilkenny')

The plot moves from a state of equilibrium (there being two cats in Kilkenny), through to a state of disequilibrium (the fight), and finally to the re-establishment of an ironic equilibrium (there being no cats in Kilkenny). Just as the violence in the limerick is symptomatic of the state of disequilibrium, so verbal conflict can be a symptom of disequilibrium in dramatic dialogue. Furthermore, matters of characterization often move in tandem with plot developments. Conflict frequently leads to a shift of character in its resolution. Thus, the predatory character of the cats induces a state of conflict, and this is resolved – rather dramatically – when the cats, along with their characters, annihilate each other.

Given the value of impoliteness in plays, why in the history of theatre has there not been more of it? The fact that all the extracts I have chosen to analyse come from the twentieth century is not in any way incidental: verbal violence is a characteristic of recent twentieth-century drama and film. It is beyond the scope of this chapter to discuss the cultural changes that may have led to this situation. However, it is worth noting that in Britain theatrical censorship has played a part. Beginning in the reign of Henry VIII, censorship had been reinforced through successive legislation (notably in 1737 and

1843) up to the twentieth century, though there was a period of relative freedom from 1600 to 1700. Initially, censorship had a largely religious and political agenda, but by the nineteenth century social propriety had become a key issue. Remember that this is the century that saw the arrival of the eponymous Thomas Bowdler's *Family Shakespeare*, a cleaned-up version of Shakespeare's plays fit for the Victorian family. According to Findlater (1967: 112), the Joint Select Committee of 1909 recommended that the Lord Chamberlain refuse a licence to any play which could be reasonably held:

(a) to be indecent,
(b) to contain offensive personalities,
(c) to represent on the stage in an invidious manner a living person or any person recently dead,
(d) to do violence to the sentiment of religious reverence,
(e) to be calculated to conduce to crime or vice,
(f) to be calculated to impair friendly relations with any foreign power,
(g) to be calculated to cause a breach of the peace.

This list is, of course, fairly broad. The British Board of Film Censors, set up in 1912, worked to a similar list (see Findlater 1967: 123). In practice, any language which was construed as anti-social was liable to be prohibited. Obvious targets throughout the history of censorship have been oaths, swearing and four-letter words. Theatrical censorship in Britain was finally relaxed in 1965 and abolished in 1968.[5]

(IM)POLITENESS AND CHARACTERIZATION IN THE FILM *SCENT OF A WOMAN*

Nowadays, people mostly experience fictional dialogue when watching films. Going to the theatre is a minority activity and reading plays is almost exclusively the provenance of school and university courses. It thus seems pertinent to consider in this chapter dialogue from a film. Of course, films are not plays, but the differences relate primarily to the nature of the medium not the dynamics of the dialogue. Short (this volume) points out that a film embodies one particular performance; it lacks the variation of different stage performances. Also, film allows greater possibilities for the creation of realism or special effects, and it allows the exploitation of camera techniques for the manipulation of point of view, for instance.

Scent of a Woman (1992), directed by Martin Brest, is a remake of the 1974 Italian film *Profumo di Donna* and is the film which finally won Al Pacino an Oscar for best actor. Set in America, it revolves around two characters, Charlie and the Colonel. Charlie is a student at a prestigious private school, but he is not rich and is supported by student aid. In order to make ends meet, rather than go home for Thanksgiving, he responds to an advertisement asking for somebody to act as a carer for their blind relative – the Colonel.

The dialogue below is the first encounter between Charlie and the Colonel (Charlie = CH, Colonel = COL).

(1) CH: Sir?

(2) COL: Don't call me sir.

(3) CH: I'm sorry, I mean mister, sir.

(4) COL: Uh – ooh, we've got a moron here, is that it?

(5) CH: No mister ... I ... er ... that is ... er ... lieutenant, yes sir, lieu –

(6) COL: Lieutenant-Colonel. Twenty-six years on the line, nobody ever busted me four grades before. Get in here, you idiot. [*Pause*] Come a little closer, I want to get a better look at you. How's your skin, son?

(7) CH: My skin, sir?

(8) COL: Ah, for Christ's sake!

(9) CH: I'm sorry, I don't –

(10) COL: Just call me Frank. Call me Mr. Slade. Call me Colonel, if you must. Just don't call me sir.

(11) CH: Alright, Colonel.

(12) COL: Simms, Charles, a senior. You on student aid, Simms?

(13) CH: Ah, yes I am.

(14) COL: For student aid read crook. Your father peddles card telephones at a three hundred per cent mark-up; your mother works on heavy commission in a camera store, graduated to it from expresso machines. Ha, ha! What are you ... dying of some wasting disease?

(15) CH: No ... I'm right here.

(16) COL: I know exactly where your body is. What I'm looking for is some indication of a brain.

The Colonel's conversational behaviour comes as something of a surprise. We might have expected much politer behaviour, given that he and Charlie are complete strangers. Furthermore, it is likely that our prior knowledge of the role relationship between Charlie and the Colonel – that of 'carer' and 'cared for' – would have given rise to other expectations about their relationship and thus their behaviour. For example, we might have expected that the balance of power, at least in some respects, lay with Charlie. From the outset, the Colonel's conversational behaviour is contrary to expectations. His first utterance is oddly brusque. We might have expected reciprocal greetings, phatic activity of some kind; instead, in turn 2 the Colonel uses an imperative to command Charlie not to use 'Sir'. Thus, the deference encoded in Charlie's first utterance receives something of a slap in the face – negative face, in this case. The Colonel proceeds in his next turn (4) to refer to Charlie as a 'moron'. Clearly, this is threatening to Charlie's positive face, as is the Colonel's term of address 'you idiot' in turn 6. In the same turn, the Colonel's imperative command 'Get in here' is particularly face threatening. The Colonel's question 'You on student aid, Simms?' (turn 12) transgresses social rules. It is taboo in Western culture for strangers to ask someone about their income. Moreover, earlier in the film we have been made aware that being on student aid is stigmatized. Charlie's response, the filled pause 'Ah', suggests that he is taken aback. In the following turn, the Colonel presents an offensive account of Charlie's parents' professions. Moreover, the Colonel has no evidence for this account: he flouts Grice's Maxim of Quality in order to implicate an impolite belief about Charlie's parents. One should note here that face is not confined to the self, but is invested in other things related to the self, including other people. Thus, an attack on Charlie's parents is an attack on Charlie's extended positive face. In the same turn (14), the Colonel asks 'What are you . . . dying of some wasting disease?' Obviously, Charlie is not dying of a wasting disease. The Colonel flouts the Maxim of Quality and implicates the impolite belief that Charlie acts as if he were moribund. Similarly, the Colonel's utterance 'What I'm looking for is some indication of a brain' (turn 16) flouts the Maxim of Quality, since there is no evidence that Charlie lacks intelligence, and implicates the impolite belief that Charlie exhibits no intelligence.

Charlie's contribution to this dialogue is restricted. He speaks much less than the Colonel – 32 words compared with 136 words – and, moreover, is interrupted twice (turns 5 and 9). The Colonel controls the dialogue, impeding Charlie's contributions and thus damaging his negative face. What Charlie does say is always polite. His use of 'sir' as a deferential term of address backfires, since the Colonel has some peculiar objection to it. This leads to two apologies from Charlie (turns 3 and 9) – a politeness strategy addressed to the Colonel's negative face. In addition, Charlie always attempts to comply with the Colonel's requests to do something (e.g. turn 3) or his requests for information (e.g. turn 13). Charlie's responses are 'preferred', that is to say, they are structurally unmarked (see Levinson 1983: 332ff. on 'preference organization'). The key point to note about Charlie's politeness and the Colonel's impoliteness is the interaction – or rather the lack of inter-action – between them: Charlie is polite in spite of the Colonel's impoliteness, and the Colonel is impolite in spite of Charlie's politeness. Each type of behaviour is made more salient in the context of the other.

The fact that the Colonel's behaviour is unexpected, consistently breaking social norms, invites explanation, much in the same way that foregrounding through linguistic deviation invites interpretation (Leech 1985: 47). A strong possibility is to attribute his behaviour to his character: the Colonel is an embittered man, a man with a warped personality, a misanthropist. But we should also note that the Colonel is no mindless anti-social being. His impoliteness is achieved through a range of strategies, some of them quite sophisticated, even a touch humorous. Charlie also exhibits a pattern of con-sistent and unexpected behaviour, given the unpleasant reception he receives from the Colonel. Again, we can attribute this to his character: Charlie seems to be the prototypical 'nice guy'. Perhaps he might also be thought to be rather shy, even passive or spineless, since he does nothing to counter the abuse. Clearly, Charlie and the Colonel are contrasting characters. As is often the case in drama, a system of contrasts helps in defining character. We shall see that these early impressions of the Colonel and Charlie develop as the film proceeds.

The Colonel takes Charlie to New York for, as he puts it, 'a final tour of the field'. He plans to enjoy himself and then kill himself. In what is probably the most famous scene in the film, the Colonel and Charlie are ensconced in a high-class restaurant, when the Colonel smells the scent of a woman. Charlie describes the woman to the Colonel, and seems to find her attractive himself. The Colonel determines that they should introduce themselves to the woman, Donna, and initiates the conversation below (Colonel = COL, Donna = DON).

(1) COL: Excuse me, *señorita*, do you mind if we join you? I'm feeling you're being neglected.

(2) DON: Well, I'm expecting somebody.

(3) COL: Instantly?

(4) DON: No, but any minute now.

(5) COL: Some people live a lifetime in a minute. What are you doing right now?

(6) DON: I'm waiting for him.

(7) COL: Well, would you mind if we waited with you? Just to keep the womanizers from bothering you.

(8) DON: No, I don't mind.

(9) COL: Thank you.

As in the previous extract, this is the Colonel's first conversation with a particular stranger, but here his conversational behaviour is dramatically different. He opens the conversation with the apology 'Excuse me', a negative politeness strategy. His request for permission to join her, 'do you mind if we join you?', is indirect: it is couched as a question about whether she minds, not whether they can do it. He supports her positive face in expressing apparent concern for her: 'I'm feeling you're being neglected.' When Donna fails to invite them to join her, the Colonel in turn 7 reiterates the request and increases the politeness: 'would you mind if we waited with you?' The possibility that they might wait with her is further distanced – and thus made more indirect – by the fact that it is set in a hypothetical context indicated by the modal conditional 'would' and the use of the past tense. The Colonel also provides a reason why they should wait with her: 'Just to keep the womanizers from bothering you.' Ostensibly, the Colonel is offering to do her a favour, a negative politeness strategy. Of course, there is also a touch of humour here in that the Colonel and Charlie themselves appear to be the womanizers. Donna agrees to their request, and the Colonel expresses gratitude, 'Thank you', a negative politeness strategy.

Thus, impoliteness is not the sole behaviour of the Colonel; he is capable of a far wider range. Moreover, we see that the Colonel can produce context-sensitive behaviour: if he wants to produce face-supporting behaviour in order to pursue particular goals in a particular context, he can do. Flat characters tend to exhibit the same behaviour regardless of context. Our impression of the Colonel's character is likely to develop, but to what? Earlier we had an apparently embittered man taking gratuitous verbal pot-shots at Charlie; now we have someone laying on the linguistic honey, partly, so it seems, to help Charlie meet Donna. This contradiction forces us to pay more attention to the Colonel's character – one cannot easily conceptualize him as one particular type of person. In fact, later in the film we discover that the cause of the Colonel's bitterness does not lie in his personality, but in the circumstances which led to his blindness.

Charlie's character remains fairly flat for the bulk of the film. He is the predictably polite Charlie in all contexts. However, in a tense scene three-quarters of the way through the film, Charlie's character develops suddenly and dramatically. The Colonel, in his hotel bedroom, is preparing to kill himself with a pistol. Charlie has been trying to persuade the Colonel to give him the gun, and has, characteristically, relied on politeness strategies. For example, in 'Colonel, why don't you just give me the gun . . . alright?' he (1) uses a deferential term of address (and one approved by the Colonel!), (2) performs the request indirectly by asking a question about why the Colonel should not give him the gun, (3) uses the hedge 'just' to minimize the imposition of the request, and (4) adds the tag question 'alright?' which softens the presumptuousness involved in making the request. But Charlie fails to get the gun. At the point when the Colonel looks as if he is going to pull the trigger, Charlie grapples for the gun, and the Colonel threatens him with it in order to get him out of the room. The following dialogue ensues:

(1) COL: Get out of here.
(2) CH: I'm staying right here.
(3) COL: Get out of here.
(4) CH: I'm staying right here.
(5) COL: I'll blow your fucking head off.
(6) CH: Do it. You want to do it, do it. Let's go. [*Pause*]
(7) COL: Get out of here.
(8) CH: Look, you fucked up, alright, so what? So everybody does it. Get on with your life would you.
(9) COL: What life? I got no life. I'm in the dark here, you understand? I'm in the dark.
(10) CH: So give up. You want to give up, give up. Because I'm giving up too. You say I'm through, you're right, I'm through. We're both through. It's all over. So let's get on with it, let's fucking do it. Let's fucking . . . pull the trigger . . . you miserable blind motherfucker. [*Pause*] Pull the trigger.

Charlie's conversational behaviour is suddenly very different from what we have seen. This is the first time he directly defies the Colonel's commands (turns 2 and 4). This is also the first time he uses taboo words (turns 8 and 10). Clearly, in this kind of extreme situation, such verbal behaviour is not inappropriate. However, more strikingly, this is the first time he is impolite – 'you miserable blind motherfucker' (turn 10). This 'name-calling' strategy seems calculated to cause maximum positive face damage to the Colonel.

Charlie deviates dramatically from his usual pattern of behaviour. Of course, how we interpret Charlie's behaviour depends on the context. There is no necessary equation such that impolite behaviour results from a nasty personality. Charlie's goal seems to be to call the Colonel's bluff (note how Charlie handles the Colonel's violent threat in turn 5) and to shock him out of his present course of action. Charlie's attack on the Colonel's face is a short-term goal designed to bring long-term benefit to the Colonel. Thus, we might infer that Charlie is not simply a 'nice guy', but somebody who has determination and bravery, somebody who is prepared to employ whatever means are necessary to achieve what he believes in, somebody who – as the Colonel puts it – has 'integrity'.

CONCLUSION

Any analysis of dialogue needs to be sensitive to the social dynamics of inter-action. A politeness analysis attempts to describe how participants manipu-late their messages in order to support or give face. Even in 'real life' there are situations of conflict – such as politics, the courtroom or heated arguments in private conversation – where we also need to consider how participants manipulate their messages in order to attack face. In the case of the dramatic dialogue of plays or films, writers, particularly in recent years, have exploited the full range of the politeness/impoliteness spectrum for literary purposes. Conflict in dialogue not only has the general potential to be entertaining, but, more importantly, can play a key role in furthering characterization and plot.

In *Scent of a Woman* (im)politeness is crucial to the construction of character. Thus, at the beginning of *Scent of a Woman* the extreme impoliteness of the Colonel and the extreme politeness of Charlie is likely to result in strong inter-pretative assumptions about their respective characters. The polarization in their (im)politeness behaviour works in tandem with the polarization or con-trast of character. Later in the film, in episodes like that of the second extract, the relationship between Charlie and the Colonel becomes more complex, as a result of changes in the Colonel's behaviour and, as a consequence, a shift in our impression of his character. In the third extract above this contrast between the characters begins finally to be resolved. Charlie changes from exclusively polite behaviour and from this we understand a shift in his charac-ter. In fact, the change in Charlie is also a catalyst for change in the Colonel. Charlie's impoliteness is more than an attempt to get the Colonel's gun. He tackles the causes of the Colonel's embitterment and his consequent drive towards suicide: his self-blame for his blindness (caused by playing with a grenade) and his self-pity for his blindness (see turn 9 in the third extract above). Moreover, Charlie is successful: he gets the gun and brings about a change in the Colonel. Needless to say, the Colonel uses no more impoliteness towards Charlie for the rest of the film.

SUGGESTIONS FOR FURTHER WORK

1 Conflict plays a key role in the development of both plot and character in Harold Pinter's *The Birthday Party*. Stanley Webber, once a sea-side pianist, has been staying at a boarding-house. He is rather perturbed by the arrival of two other guests – Goldberg and McCann – who have 'a job' to do. They subject him to a rather strange interrogation. The following day, Stanley is transformed: he appears wearing a sober suit and is inarticulate. Goldberg and McCann take him away with them for 'special treatment'. The plot, as outlined above, moves from a situation of equilibrium to dis-equilibrium and back again to equilibrium. As for characterization, it is the interrogation that acts as the catalyst for the transformation in Stanley. Below is a small part of that interrogation (in total it runs to more than 150 turns). Describe the impoliteness phenomena in detail. Also, consider in what ways it is like a 'real' interrogation and in what ways is it not. [N.B. 'Drogheda' is an Irish town whose inhabitants were massacred at the instigation of Cromwell in 1649.]

GOLDBERG: Why did the chicken cross the road?
STANLEY: He wanted . . .
MCCANN: He doesn't know. He doesn't know which came first!
GOLDBERG: Which came first?
MCCANN: Chicken? Egg? Which came first?
GOLDBERG and MCCANN: Which came first? Which came first? Which came first?
STANLEY [*screams*]
GOLDBERG: He doesn't know. Do you know your own face?
MCCANN: Wake him up. Stick a needle in his eye.
GOLDBERG: You're a plague, Webber. You're an overthrow.
MCCANN: You're what's left!
GOLDBERG: But we've got the answer to you. We can sterilise you.
MCCANN: What about Drogheda?
GOLDBERG: Your bite is dead. Only your pong is left.
MCCANN: You betrayed our land.
GOLDBERG: You betray our breed.
MCCANN: Who are you, Webber?
GOLDBERG: What makes you think you exist?
MCCANN: You're dead.
GOLDBERG: You're dead. You can't live, you can't think, you can't love. You're dead. You're a plague gone bad. There's no juice in you. You're nothing but an odour!

(Pinter 1981 [1959]: Act II)

2 I made the point earlier that politeness can be used to expedite our goals. What happens if you take politeness away? Clearly, we are less likely to achieve our goals. If I want to borrow fifty pounds from you and I ask you directly (or even swear at you), you would be unlikely to give me the money. Some dramatists have created a world stripped of politeness, a world of self-destruction, a world from which there is no escape. Edward Bond is one such dramatist. Take one of his plays (e.g. *Saved*) and explain how (im)politeness is used to create the anti-social world of the characters.

3 Paul Simpson (this volume) uses an extract from Steven Berkoff's play *Greek*. Consider this extract – and indeed the whole play – specifically in terms of (im)politeness. How is the breakdown in co-operation achieved and what are the dramatic effects?

NOTES

1 See Searle (1975b) for a discussion of indirect speech acts, and for briefer comments see Toolan and Lowe in this volume.

2 Brief introductions to Brown and Levinson's model appear in Short (1996: 211–17) and Simpson (1997: 155–64).

3 A more comprehensive description of linguistic impoliteness appears in Culpeper (1996).

4 Suave, mari magno turbantibus aequora ventis,
e terra magnum alterius spectare laborem;
non quia vexari quemquamst iucunda voluptas,
sed quibus ipse malis careas quia cernere suave est.

5 Of course, it is not now the case that 'anything goes'. There are, for example, still British laws governing what you can do in a public place (thus the indecent or pornographic could be banned) and there are laws covering blasphemy (though only in relation to Christianity, as the famous Salman Rushdie case reminds us).

8 'Catch[ing] the nearest way'

Macbeth and cognitive metaphor

Donald C. Freeman

EDITORS' PREFACE

In this chapter, Donald C. Freeman applies the theory of cognitive metaphor to Shakespeare's *Macbeth*. Cognitive metaphor theorists argue that many of our basic metaphors are formed on the basis of a set of very basic experiential cognitive factors, and can be grouped together in relation to these factors. So, for example, good is often portrayed metaphorically as up, and bad as down (e.g. we go up to heaven and down to hell), and the future is usually portrayed as being in front of us metaphorically, whereas the past is behind. Freeman argues that different Shakespeare plays are based on different sets of cognitive metaphors. He suggests that *Macbeth* is based on the PATH and CONTAINER schemata. So, for Macbeth, life is a journey, and success is reaching the end of the path. The play also contains a profusion of CONTAINER metaphors (Macbeth's castle is a container and Duncan's body is a container which Macbeth has breached by stabbing him). Besides showing that the PATH and CONTAINER metaphors are dominant in *Macbeth*, Freeman goes on to show how the two schemas interact in the play to create a four-dimensional image of Macbeth's downfall.

*

> To understand how the body emphasis works in [*Macbeth*], we need to step back for a moment and ask, what are the most basic things we do with our bodies? We wash them, we feed them, we commit them to sleep and its restorative powers. We clothe them. What we take into them that they don't need, we eliminate. We fear for their health and sense their vulnerability. When the blood that is supposed to stay inside them comes out we are frightened and even nauseated. And of course we use our bodies to engender, bear, and nurse children.
>
> (Young 1990: 106)

In an important recent book about Shakespeare's dramatic language, David Young epitomizes the significance of cognitive metaphor in the study of Macbeth. This shortest and most intense of Shakespeare's plays is dominated from beginning to end by metaphors arising from two deeply entrenched image-schemata, the CONTAINER and the PATH.[1] These embodied imaginative understandings move out from the play's language to dominate its characterizations, its depictions of events, and what we might loosely call its structure – the relationship of its component parts to one another. The critical tradition – including those who write against the grain of that tradition – has for the last two centuries understood *Macbeth* in terms of the CONTAINER and PATH schemata, from which derive the metaphors in which they write about the play.[2] Small wonder, then, that nearly everyone who has ever written about *Macbeth* agrees on the play's unity and focus. These arise directly from the almost unbearable intensity with which Shakespeare concentrates our understanding of this play through these two central schemata. I want to sketch these out briefly, and then examine how Shakespeare uses them to create our understanding of several of the play's most important scenes.

> A CONTAINER schema, on a standard cognitive-science account, consist[s] of a boundary distinguishing an *interior* from an *exterior*. The CONTAINER schema defines the most basic distinction between IN and OUT. We understand our own bodies as containers – perhaps the most basic things we do are ingest and excrete, take air into our lungs and breathe it out.
>
> (Lakoff 1987: 271)

We abstract from our earliest bodily experiences the elements of the container and it becomes, on this theory, an image-schema by which we organize and extend our perceptions, and from which as a source domain we project structure onto target domains to create metaphors.

A PATH schema, on the other hand, consists of four major elements: a source point, a terminal point, a vector that traces a 'sequence of contiguous locations'[3] connecting the points, and a trajector, the entity that moves along the path. The experiential basis of the PATH schema resides in our very first primitive movements toward our physical goals; as a result, we tend to project the schema of this experience into a great many of our more abstract experiences. The PATH schema partakes of a number of other defining features of prototypical paths: they have side boundaries, often not well defined (our attention can 'wander'); temporality is mapped into them ('in the course of time'); they have end boundaries so intimately wrapped up with purpose that it is virtually impossible to understand the idea of purpose in terms other than the PURPOSES ARE PHYSICAL GOALS metaphor that arises from the PATH schema ('We have nearly arrived at an agreement').

The CONTAINER schema dominates the metaphors of Lady Macbeth's very first appearance on stage, in which she conceptualizes both her husband and herself as containers. Macbeth, for his wife, is a container made of nature whose contents are a liquid, milk, that is the medium, in turn, for Macbeth's 'human kindness', both the essential quality of his humanity and of his goodness:

Yet I do fear thy nature:
It is too full o' th' milk of human kindness
To catch the nearest way.

(I.v.16–18)

Macbeth's 'human kindness' is an abstraction, a character trait. By having Lady Macbeth characterize this trait in terms of the prototypically nourishing and nurturing liquid of milk, and Macbeth's body as a container overfull of that liquid, Shakespeare anticipates Lady Macbeth's constant derogation of her husband's manhood (I.vii., III.iv.59ff.), and Macbeth's own concern for his progeneration (see especially the Witches' dumb show of the royal succession, IV.i.112ff.). The prototypical container of the liquid of one sort of human (nurturing) kindness is the woman who is a nursing mother – both roles that Lady Macbeth will reject in the same metaphorical terms (see discussion below, p. 99). The container of the liquid of another sort of human (qualitatively defining) kindness is the human body, whose violability is highlighted when its very highest, kingly, representation is pierced ('Yet who would have thought the old man [Duncan] to have had so much blood in him?': V.i.37–8).

The 'nourishment' slot of this source domain reverberates through the play, to the nourishment that feasts prototypically provide, but which Macbeth's feast (where the guest–host relationship is so inverted that the event is known to literary history as *Banquo*'s feast) denies; to the horrors of which Macbeth, by Act V, has 'supped full'; to Macbeth's characterization of the sleep that is denied him as 'great Nature's second course,/Chief nourisher in life's feast –' (II.ii.38–9).

The nurturing 'milk of human kindness' that presently fills her husband's body Lady Macbeth would, by implication, drain out; she would refill that container with the liquid of her 'spirits':[4]

Hie thee hither,
That I may pour my spirits in thine ear,
And chastise with the valour of my tongue
All that impedes thee from the golden round . . .

(I.v.25–8)

She likewise conceives of her own body as a container of her human kindness, and of her sexuality as the liquid that fills that container. Lady Macbeth's body-container must, like her husband's, be emptied so that it can be refilled with a similarly abstracted liquid that is not responsive to her 'nature', her humanity, that same 'nature' that she so fears in Macbeth:

Come you Spirits
That tend on mortal thoughts, unsex me here,
And fill me, from the crown to the toe, top-full
Of direst cruelty! make thick my blood,

Stop up th'access and passage to remorse;
That no compunctious visitings of Nature
Shake my fell purpose, nor keep peace between
Th'effect and it!

(I.v.40–7)

Lady Macbeth asks that she be made, in effect, a watertight container, proof against just the kind of influence she proposes to have upon her husband. She would close all the orifices of her body-container, in particular the orifice that, open, implicates both her gender – her kindness, her soft-heartedness, her prototypical woman's weakness – and her sexuality, the blood that she would now 'make thick', like the night and light later in the play, the potentiality of sexual penetration, and the possibility of that penetration's natural consequence, the child that is the ultimate sign of her gender and her sexuality.[5] Lady Macbeth barely hints at the childbirth motif that will become crucial when Macbeth learns that Macduff has been 'untimely ripped' from the container of his mother's womb.

Thus altered, the liquid contents of Lady Macbeth's body will cause her to produce anti-nourishment – milk that is not human kindness, but gall – like the anti-feast after Banquo's murder contained in Macbeth's castle, and the anti-medicine compounded in the container of the witches' cauldron:

Come to my woman's breasts
And take my milk for gall, you murth'ring ministers,
Wherever in your sightless substances,
You wait on Nature's mischief!

(I.v.47–50)

Lady Macbeth invokes this curse upon her own motherhood knowingly; having 'given suck', she knows – has bodily experience of – what it means to be the container of that nourishment and human kindness that she would now transmute to cruelty and poison:

I have given suck, and know
How tender 'tis to love the babe that milks me:
I would, while it was smiling in my face,
Have pluck'd my nipple from his boneless gums,
And dash'd the brains out, had I so sworn
As you have done to this.

(I.vii.54–9)

Even the anonymous babe is metaphorized as a container of brains that Lady Macbeth would slaughter by spilling its contents, a formulation anticipating Macbeth's realization that the physical death of Banquo, emptying the container of his head, is not enough:

> ... the time has been,
> That, when the brains were out, the man would die,
> And there an end;
>
> (III.iv.77–9)

At one time or another nearly every character in the play – Fleance, Macduff's son, Banquo, Malcolm, Duncan – is metaphorically portrayed as a container. Duncan, in particular, is surrounded by CONTAINER metaphors, especially when his murder is announced by Macduff:

> Most sacrilegious Murther hath broke ope
> The Lord's anointed Temple, and stole thence
> The life o' th' building!
>
> (II.iii.66–68)

Macduff understands murder as a burglar who has violated the outer boundary, the precincts of a sacred building, the body of a king. The loot the burglar has removed from that container's interior is the spirit that gives life to Duncan and legitimacy to his kingdom, upon which the CONTAINER schema projects the life that religious faith gives to a temple and the structure of belief that temple provides to the human community that worships within it.

Macbeth, in turn, characterizes Duncan's body first as a fountain, containing under pressure a fluid that gives life as water gives life (invoking the metaphor LIFE IS A FLUID, which we are to see once more near the play's end), and later as an Edenic natural refuge protecting its interior from the danger outside it:

> The spring, the head, the fountain of your blood
> Is stopp'd; the very source of it is stopp'd.
>
> [. . .]
>
> Here lay Duncan,
> His silver skin lac'd with his golden blood;
> And his gash'd stabs look'd like a breach in nature
> For ruin's wasteful entrance . . .
>
> (II.iii.96–7, 109–12)

Once again the exterior of the human body, its boundary as a container, and, in the case of Duncan, the divine protection that hedges about a king, are metaphorized as 'nature', the natural order. Recall that Macbeth's exterior, the boundary of his body-as-container, already has been characterized, by Lady Macbeth, as 'nature' that 'is too full o' th' milk of human kindness'. Just as Lady Macbeth breaches that exterior of human nature to empty her husband of the milk of human kindness, so does Macbeth, once emptied of that humanity, breach the exterior of Duncan's nature to empty him of his blood, his spirit, and the order of the kingdom that he embodies.

Duncan's body-container is itself contained within the larger container of Inverness Castle, an avatar for the structure of taboos that should serve Duncan as an exterior protecting structure, as Macbeth points out:

> He's here in double trust:
> First, as I am his kinsman and his subject,
> Strong both against the deed; then, as his host,
> Who should against his murtherer shut the door,
> Not bear the knife myself.
>> (I.vii.12–16)

The boundary of the castle-as-container, that physical and cultural structure which should protect its royal contents, King Duncan, from what lies beyond its exterior, provides the structure for Macbeth's conception of his ancient duty to his guest, his kinsman, and his king. Each of these three duties forbids Macbeth to do injury to Duncan within that boundary. The container of Macbeth's castle contains another container, Duncan's sleeping-room, with a door that Macbeth has himself characterized as representing his duty of protection and loyalty, a duty further highlighted in the stage action:

> I'll bring you to him.
>
> [...]
>
> This is the door.
>> (II.iii.46, 49)

Within the twice-contained container of Duncan's sleeping-room lies the container of his kingly body, the 'anointed temple', 'the building', the 'fountain of [Donalbain's and Malcolm's] blood', the 'nature' that Macbeth's knife has 'breach'd'.

This central metaphor of Macbeth's castle as container is reinforced in the assembly of the Murderers and in the famous Porter scene. When Macbeth commissions Banquo's murder, he is at pains to stress the wide border that must be established – a key element of the CONTAINER schema – to separate himself from the deed. In effect, the murder must be committed outside the physical limit of the palace and the moral container of Macbeth's existence:

> for 't must be done to-night,
> And something from the palace; always thought,
> That I require a clearness ...
>> (III.i.130–2)

This 'clearness' that Macbeth requires curiously echoes Lady Macbeth's remark after Duncan's murder: 'A little water clears us of this deed' (II.ii.66). The castle's nearly mile-wide *Sperrzone* is re-emphasized by the third Murderer:

FIRST MURDERER: His [Banquo's] horses go about.
THIRD MURDERER: Almost a mile; but he does usually,
  So all men do, from hence to the palace gate
  Make it their walk.

(III.iii.11–14)

In the Porter scene (II.iii.1–21), the CONTAINER metaphor is presented less in the play's language than in its staging. Since at least the time of the Romantic critic Thomas De Quincey,[6] *Macbeth* criticism has held that this scene marks the play's turning point, as the forces of retribution represented in Macduff enter the drama. The action of this intensely compressed play stops, as the Porter is at pains to emphasize the physical and moral separateness of Macbeth's castle from the world outside it. Macduff and Lennox can gain entry only after five knocks and four challenges from the drunken Porter, and only after he has defined the world inside the door, the boundary circumscribing his master's castle, as a hell, the 'everlasting bonfire' that is the end point of life's path, the 'primrose way'. Within the container bounded by the door that the Porter guards are the murdered Duncan, himself an 'anointed temple' and a container of blood who is contained within the room where his murder is shortly to be discovered.

The container of Macbeth's castle also is a thing contained, for it exists within a Scotland that has become a container for the blood that Macbeth has spilled, a Scotland that is no longer a mother, a benign container of generations,[7] but, like the murdered Duncan, a breached container of blood, a grave containing the end of human progeneration:

MALCOLM: I think our country sinks beneath the yoke;
  It weeps, it bleeds; and each new day a gash
  Is added to her wounds . . .

(IV.iii.39–41)

ROSSE: Alas, poor country!
  Almost afraid to know itself. It cannot
  Be call'd our mother but our grave . . .

(IV.iii.164–6)

And this Scotland-as-container is in turn contained within an earthly atmosphere of fog and filthy air explicitly represented as a container, one where 'light thickens' into Lady Macbeth's 'thick night,' or in Ross's words, 'darkness does the face of earth entomb' (II.iv.9).

When Lady Macbeth despairs of her husband as being 'too full o' th' milk of human kindness/To catch the nearest way', she conceives of him as a container. But she understands 'the way' (for Macbeth to achieve his ambitions) in terms of a second skeletalized bodily experience, the PATH schema, from which stem many of the play's most crucial metaphors, particularly those involving Macbeth's career.

From the play's outset, Macbeth himself conceives of his career as a spatially represented path:

> Glamis, and Thane of Cawdor:
> The greatest is behind.
>
> (I.iii.116–17)

In the source domain of CAREERS ARE PATHS (a related metaphorical projection, which grows more important as the play proceeds) is LIFE IS A JOURNEY; in order to get from the start of the path to its end, the trajector, Macbeth,[8] must pass all of its intermediate points. Notice that the metaphor even specifies the forward-facing position of the trajector. Because Macbeth understands his career as a path, he sees himself, now that he has received the news from Duncan of his promotion from his first thanedom to a larger and more prestigious one, as having progressed beyond these points.

Once Glamis and Cawdor are 'behind' Macbeth on the path of his career, he turns his attention to what is ahead. When Duncan names Malcolm as his successor, Macbeth sees the next obstacle in the path of his career, which is now becoming such a steep upward climb[9] that he reconceptualizes it as a staircase. Now he must risk an all-or-nothing leap, a metaphor derived from the path schema, DIFFICULTIES ARE OBSTACLES:

> The Prince of Cumberland! – That is a step
> On which I must fall down, or else o'erleap,
> For in my way it lies.
>
> (I.iv.48–50)

As Macbeth contemplates Duncan's murder, in his momentary indecision he at first conceives of his intention as a horse, a more rapid trajector than a human, which he as rider must spur in order to progress along the path toward achievement of that intention. But the vision of the speeding horseman collapses[10] as Macbeth both recalls his earlier use of the SUCCESS IS UP spatial orientation metaphor, and predicts its opposite:

> I have no spur
> To prick the sides of my intent, but only
> Vaulting ambition, which o'erleaps itself
> And falls on th'other –
>
> (I.vii.25–8)

As the forces of retribution gather head, Macbeth begins to see that the end of the path along which his life has travelled is near, and fuses with the LIFE IS A JOURNEY metaphor those of A LIFETIME IS A YEAR, LIFE IS A FLUID, SUCCESS IS UP, and FAILURE IS DOWN, in which the stages of the seasons are projected onto the stages of life, here metaphorized as a fall, and his approaching death is understood as increasing dryness, loss of fluid:

> . . . my way of life
> Is fall'n into the sere, the yellow leaf;
> And that which should accompany old age,
> As honour, love, obedience, troops of friends,
> I must not look to have . . .
>
> (V.iii.22–6)

Macbeth now understands his life as a journey in which he has descended along a path from a fertile, watered upland of success into the aridity of a land unnourished by the fluid of life,[11] which in turn is metaphorized as a year in which the 'way of [his] life,' his passage through time, has descended into the time of autumn. Through this metaphor Macbeth also stresses his solitude, as he lacks the companions toward the end of life's journey that men customarily have – a wife and family ('honour', 'love', and 'obedience' are the elements of the wife's vow in the traditional wedding ceremony) and companions (here metaphorized as troops marching along the path of a parade).

Finally, when Macbeth is at bay, at the end of his life's path (an end very far from that 'nearest way' that Lady Macbeth was so obsessed that he 'catch'), he must make an about turn to face what has pursued him ever more closely on that path, the play's retributive forces personified in Macduff:

> MACDUFF: Turn, Hellhound, turn!
> MACBETH: Of all men else I have avoided thee:
>   But get thee back!
>
> (V.viii.3–5)

Macbeth's final turning marks an end to a career path that until then has successfully negotiated a series of macabre, water-like obstacles created by the shattering of containers: the royal blood that he has spilled by violating the container of Duncan's royal body; and the blood both literal and figurative of Macduff's wife and son, his progeneration, that Macbeth sheds and demolishes in violating the containers of Macduff's castle and family. The path of Macbeth's sanguinary career is crossed and recrossed by another path-like entity, a river of blood: at its source is the shattered packaging of Inverness Castle, Duncan's sleeping-room, and Duncan's 'silver skin lac'd with his golden blood'.

The path of Macbeth's career requires him to ford that bloody stream, horrifically parodying the river that in many cultures must be crossed at the BEGINNING and the END of life's journey (see note 15):

> I am in blood
> Stepp'd in so far, that, should I wade no more,
> Returning were as tedious as go o'er.
>
> (III.iv.135–7)

Although Macbeth laments that he has 'stepp'd in' as far as the middle of this river, our enculturated knowledge of the LIFE IS A JOURNEY metaphor tells us that he could not return even if he wished. He must continue 'stepping' on his journey, wading through the river of blood to what awaits him on its far bank: human and divine retribution.

This river that is itself a path and that is now an obstacle in Macbeth's path consists of the same blood that is elsewhere understood as a fluid contained in the bodies of Macbeth's victims. The play's PATH and CONTAINER metaphors interact even more clearly and synergistically in many more of the play's major speeches:

> If it were done, when 'tis done, then 'twere well
> It were done quickly: if th'assassination
> Could trammel up the consequence, and catch
> With his surcease, success; that but this blow
> Might be the be-all and the end-all – here,
> But here, upon this bank and shoal of time,
> We'd jump the life to come.
>
> (I.vii.1–7)

Macbeth hopes that his assassination of Duncan can contain the consequences within a trapper's or fisherman's net, containing in addition to Duncan's death or 'surcease' his succession,[12] the line or path which, we have already seen, necessarily implicates time,[13] because successors succeed only over time. If Macbeth fails to 'trammel up' in one container Duncan's corpse and the succession, time will instead 'stretch out' as a 'line . . . to th' crack of doom' (IV.i.132). But if Macbeth *can* net both Duncan's corpse and his succession, if the blow Macbeth is about to strike makes Duncan the last king in the line of that succession ('be-all') and annihilates any possible retribution on Macbeth ('end-all'), he will be in full and final control of time and the path of the succession that it implies.

Thus Macbeth, uniquely, will be able to travel from, say, Point E to Point G in the journey of his life without passing through Point F either topologically or chronologically. He will stand on the bank of the river that emblematizes the death as a point through which every journey of life must lead, and will 'jump' it[14] just as he sought to 'o'erleap' Malcolm, to immortality and kingship gained solely by his own efforts, not by divine grace or blood succession. The 'life to come', what is ahead of him on life's journey, if he overleaps nothing, if he 'fall[s] down', is his own death and the death of his line (he has sired no children, no legitimate successor of his own). If he can 'jump' the river that mortals must cross to get to heaven or hell,[15] the only conventional existence beyond the 'life to come' (if he can murder Duncan, control the succession, and get away with it), Macbeth can become immortal without dying, he can become king without travelling the path that one must travel, passing the points that one must pass in order to become a king.

This ambition, like all of Macbeth's ambitions, fails. Macbeth cannot 'jump the life to come'. He must wade through the river of blood. He cannot control the succession. He cannot control time. The journey of Macbeth's life takes him through the isolation of the 'sere, the yellow leaf', the time, importantly, of the autumn of life's year, to the play's final articulation of time as a necessary sequence of events. Macbeth, who once 'o'erleaped' and then 'stepp'd', can now only creep or walk or strut.

> To-morrow, and to-morrow, and to-morrow,
> Creeps in this petty pace[16] from day to day,
> To the last syllable of recorded time;
> And all our yesterdays have lighted fools
> The way to dusty death. Out, out, brief candle!
> Life's but a walking shadow; a poor player,
> That struts and frets his hour upon the stage,
> And then is heard no more: it is a tale
> Told by an idiot, full of sound and fury,
> Signifying nothing.
>
> (V.v.19–28)

Now time, 'the life to come', 'to-morrow', is not something that Macbeth can 'o'erleap'. The path along which time travels so freely for Macbeth at the outset has become 'trammelled' within the container of a 'petty pace'. Time, and with it, Macbeth, marches in measured steps along each point, each day, of the 'way to dusty death', as inevitable an end to that path and that journey as the pen of a civil servant recording each syllable of a legal document.

Two vague measures of time that are, in cognitive-linguistic terms, continuous and unbounded, become discrete and bounded[17] (both 'tomorrow' and 'yesterday' are pluralized and reified). As they light 'fools/The way to dusty death', our yesterdays (the source point) illuminate a path forward that is now constrained by a clearly visible terminal point. The path has become a shrinking container, and the metaphors LIFE IS LIGHT and LIFE IS A JOURNEY become fused. This precise horizontal spatial representation now is rotated 90 degrees, from a horizontal path to a vertical one. The path now has as its source point the flame of the candle where the light of 'all our yesterdays' was located, and the brief distance from the fools to the now-visible 'dusty death' has become the distance from the candle's wick to the terminal point of its base. As candles burn down (and if GOOD IS UP, then BAD IS DOWN), they flicker; we become more conscious of the shadows cast by what they illuminate, and less sure of the size of those objects. The light, hence the life, of the LIFE IS LIGHT metaphor now is reduced to a shadow, and the steps of that shadow are constrained to the very short distance that an actor can 'strut' (itself a very short step) upon a stage, and for a very short time (now less than the one-day minimum implied by 'to-morrow' and 'our yesterdays').

Macbeth finally invokes the common LIFE IS A STORY metaphor, describing life as a 'tale', one of the shortest prose literary forms, prototypically a straightforward narrative without flashbacks or subplots. But this is a 'tale/ Told by an idiot', and tales told by idiots lack a coherent time scheme – they are journeys without coherent beginnings and ends, and they tend to wander a lot. So Macbeth's mature career is, finally, a deranged narrative, a meaninglessly contorted and convoluted path, in which what should have come at the end ('honour, love, obedience, troops of friends' (V.iii.25)) came at the beginning, at a time when we think the natural movement is upward from where we are. Such a state of affairs leaves nothing for 'the life to come' except unanchored 'vaulting ambition' and its perils, or tedium, decay, aridity, and death. Now the path of Macbeth's career becomes itself contained, ironically echoing his own effort to contain the paths of succession and time in the same net as Duncan's death.

Taken together, the CONTAINER and PATH schemata interact in this speech to create a four-dimensional image of Macbeth's downfall: the path of his career becomes a container that constrains him in height (he can only 'creep' and 'strut', he can no longer 'o'erleap'), in width (the 'syllables' of time are recorded – and limited – horizontally; the actor-trajector in life's drama can 'strut' over no wider an area than the stage), in depth (the 'dusty death' of his end is now clearly lit and visible), and in time (his yesterdays become trajectors impelling Macbeth toward a now enumerable, finite set of 'tomorrows').

The interacting PATH and CONTAINER schemata explain elements of the plot as well. We have already seen Macbeth's career conventionally metaphorized as a journey along a path. But the beginning of Macbeth's final downfall also invokes the PATH schema. Birnam Wood travels a path toward its terminal point, Dunsinane. Lady Macbeth sleepwalks – like that 'tale/ Told by an idiot,' the path of her journey is random: it has no coherent beginning or end. And Macduff as the avatar of retribution brings the CONTAINER and PATH schemata full circle, as he finally forces Macbeth to reverse direction on the path of his career. In having been born by Caesarean section, Macduff leaves the container of his mother's womb by 'o'erleaping' the conventional path (what today we call 'the birth canal') when he begins the journey of his life. That path is the necessary condition for his ability – not his literal ability, but, far more important, his metaphorical ability – to stop Macbeth in his tracks.

We understand *Macbeth* – its language, its characters, its settings, its events, its plot – in terms of these two central bodily based image-schemata. Even where they disagree in what they conclude about the play, critics who have written about *Macbeth* have always used critical language betraying an understanding of the play in these terms precisely because the bodily experiences implicated by these image-schemata are so universally and deeply entrenched. The unity of the language of and about *Macbeth*, as well as the unity of opinion about *Macbeth*'s unity, arises directly and consequentially from this embodied imaginative human understanding.

SUGGESTIONS FOR FURTHER WORK

1 A frequently noted conundrum in *Macbeth* is the strained, wary conversation between Macduff and Malcolm in Act IV, Scene iii, lines 1–140. Analyse and trace the development of CONTAINER metaphors through this strange scene, customarily interpreted as each man seeking to establish the bona fides of the other. For each container metaphor you find, what is the containing periphery? Who or what is contained within – or excluded by – that periphery? How does the pattern you find support the scene's traditional interpretation – or perhaps a very different one?

2 Another metaphorical schema often used by Shakespeare is that of VERTICALITY: in its most frequent form, GOOD IS UP and BAD IS DOWN. Trace Shakespeare's variations on the VERTICALITY schema in Sonnet 29 below. How does the GOOD IS UP and BAD IS DOWN pair interact with the CONTAINER schema?

> When, in disgrace with Fortune and men's eyes,
> I all alone beweep my outcast state,
> And trouble deaf heaven with my bootless cries,
> And look upon myself and curse my fate,
> Wishing me like to one more rich in hope,   5
> Featured like him, like him with friends possessed,
> Desiring this man's art, and that man's scope,
> With what I most enjoy contented least;
> Yet in these thoughts myself almost despising,
> Haply I think on thee, and then my state,   10
> Like to the lark at break of day arising
> From sullen earth, sings hymns at heaven's gate;
> For thy sweet love rememb'red such wealth brings,
> That then I scorn to change my state with kings.

3 This chapter has argued for Shakespeare's synthesis of the LIFE IS LIGHT and LIFE IS A JOURNEY metaphors in Macbeth's famous 'To-morrow and to-morrow . . .' speech. How would you compare that synthesis with Othello's use of the LIFE IS LIGHT metaphor in the following speech as, candle in hand, he contemplates the sleeping Desdemona, whom he is about to strangle?

> Put out the light, and then put out the light:
> If I quench thee, thou flaming minister,
> I can again thy former light restore,
> Should I repent me; but once put out thine,
> Thou cunning pattern of excelling nature,

I know not where is that Promethean heat
That can thy light relume.
(Othello, V.ii.7–13)

4 Critics of the cognitive approach to metaphor have argued that literary analysis and interpretation based on projection from schematized bodily experience constitute mere algorithms, mechanical discovery procedures whose meaning and validity are guaranteed in advance. Like Shakespeare, the American poet Emily Dickinson used metaphors based on the path and container schemata. In the light of the claims made in this chapter and your analysis of the following Dickinson poem, how would you compare Dickinson's and Shakespeare's use of these metaphors?

The Brain, within its Groove
Runs evenly – and true –
But let a Splinter swerve,
'Twere easier for You –

To put a Current back –
When Floods have slit the Hills –
And scooped a Turnpike for Themselves –
And trodden out the Mills –

The holograph manuscript of this poem (reproduced in Franklin 1981: 634) shows that one variant phrase that Dickinson considered and rejected as a substitute for 'a Current' in line 5 was 'the Waters'. How does a cognitive analysis of these alternatives explain Dickinson's final choice?

NOTES

1 This chapter is a revised version of an article that appeared in *Journal of Pragmatics*, 24 (1995), 689–708. A longer version will appear as a chapter of my *Shakespearean Metaphor: A Cognitive Approach* (in preparation). My quotations from *Macbeth* are based on Muir (1984). The theory of metaphor upon which this study depends was first articulated in Lakoff and Johnson (1980). The present analysis depends for its theoretical framework largely on Johnson (1987) and Turner (1991). For a study along similar lines of metaphors derived from BALANCE and LINKS schemata in *King Lear*, I.i., see Freeman (1993).
2 Some brief examples: Macbeth 'blindly rush[es] forward on the objects of his ambition' (Hazlitt 1939 [1817]: 14); he 'strides from crime to crime' (Bradley 1904: 353); 'the highway of [Macbeth's] intense progress' (Low 1983: 826); 'each step taken [by Macbeth] undoes what he has won' (Eagleton 1967: 132); Macbeth's 'linear course into winter' (Watson 1984: 112).
3 Johnson (1987: 113).
4 The term itself is metaphorical. Alcoholic drinks called 'spirits' have their organic content progressively distilled away. Lady Macbeth would substitute for her husband's 'milk of human kindness' a distilled liquor whose humanity has been refined away.
5 See La Belle (1980), for an interesting discussion of how Lady Macbeth can be said literally to want her menstrual processes stopped.

6 See De Quincey (1897 [1823]: 393).

7 See Turner (1987: 38–40).

8 For discussion of the trajector as an element of the PATH schema, see Lakoff (1987: 419).

9 The upward orientation of Macbeth's path invokes the orientational metaphors THE FUTURE IS UP and GOOD IS UP. See Lakoff and Johnson (1980: 22).

10 Cognitive-metaphoric analysis is also useful as a diagnostic tool for problems whose solutions remain elusive. If we project into Macbeth's situation each element of the speeding horseman scenario, his 'intent' is the horse; Macbeth himself is the horseman; the kingship is the implied endpoint of the journey whose speed will be increased by the 'spur'. But into what abstraction is the 'spur' projected (another way of asking 'for what does the spur stand?')? The conventional reading says that the only spur Macbeth-as-horseman has is 'vaulting ambition'. But how can Macbeth's 'ambition' be the 'spur' when it 'o'erleaps itself/And falls on th' other'? If, adopting the approach of Turner (1996), we consider this passage as the projection of a spatial story, we can at least provisionally resolve this difficulty. A horseman spurs his mount in order to reach his goal more quickly for a purpose. The spur is a catalyst for reaching the goal – and, more importantly, for accomplishing the purpose. Macbeth undermines his own story. Embedded in its own proper narrative, ambition is a desire to rise in the scheme of things in order to accomplish a purpose. By itself, however, ambition is neither a goal nor a purpose. Macbeth has no articulated purpose beyond rising; he has no programme other than becoming king. Purposeless ambition, an abstraction stripped of its contextualizing narrative, cannot vault into the saddle and guide Macbeth's intent, because Macbeth's sole intent is that ambition itself. Like Malcolm's nomination as Duncan's successor, which Macbeth sees as the step on which he 'must fall down or else o'erleap', Macbeth's ambition, having vaulted (a word prominently associated with a rider's quick leap into the saddle, see *OED*, *s.v.* vault, v2, 2a), has nowhere to seat itself and must fall. As is so often the case, we find residues of this spatial story in proverbs: What goes up must come down. It isn't what you want to be, it's what you want to do.

11 This passage does not refer directly back to the fillings and emptyings of fluids earlier in the play: the milk(s) of human kindness, nourishment, and concord; Lady Macbeth's gall; Duncan's and Banquo's blood. But the underlying metaphor is the same: LIFE IS A FLUID. Analysis by the cognitive method thus can tease out a coherence that otherwise might be missed.

12 See Everett (1989), to which much of the subsequent discussion is indebted.

13 When Duncan names Malcolm as his successor, the two paths intersect briefly. Malcolm occupies one point on the path of the legitimate succession while he is simultaneously an obstacle in the path of Macbeth's career, whose end-point is to 'trammel up' that succession and take over its path.

14 I believe that the standard interpretation of 'jump' here as 'risk' is too limited. Brooke's reading (1990: 118) preserves both senses: 'leap over (from the horse sense of "trammel"), hazard'. The scenario at this point – of a riverbank – appears to strengthen the 'leap over' sense, the *OED*'s entry (which cites only 'risk' for this sense and cites this passage as its sole source) to the contrary notwithstanding.

15 In the Christian tradition, the Jordan; in various classical traditions, the Styx, or Acheron (the very river later chosen by Hecate as the place where the Witches will meet for their last confrontation with Macbeth: see III.v.15).

16 Brooke (1990: 204) has an interesting reading of this passage that deepens the nexus between CONTAINER and PATH metaphors I am arguing for here. He reads 'pace' as 'a narrow passage – "pace" in the early seventeenth century was used for

a narrow passage, pass, or strait, which would make sense here and explain the use of "in" rather than "at" '.

17 See Talmy (1988), especially pp. 174–82. The theory of metaphor upon which this study depends was first articulated in Lakoff and Johnson (1980). The present analysis depends for its theoretical framework largely on Johnson (1987) and Turner (1991). For a study along similar lines of metaphors derived from BALANCE and LINKS schemata in *King Lear*, I.i., see Freeman (1993).

9 Three models of power in David Mamet's *Oleanna*

Jean Jacques Weber

EDITORS' PREFACE

The analysis in Weber's chapter has a much broader compass than many of the other chapters in this book. Weber moves beyond the linguistic strategy, the exchange and the pattern of turns to focus on the social context (power relations) and the cognitive context (conceived as 'schemata'), and how the two interact. He shows how we construct the cognitive worlds of the characters and how our interpretations of the dialogue are affected by our own assumptions. Weber's discussion centres on David Mamet's *Oleanna*, a particularly suitable choice, since the play is about a university tutor and a student, and their changing power relationships. It evokes a situation familiar to many readers of this book, and is thus a good basis for discussing the application of background knowledge, as well as being a situation with complex power dynamics. Weber argues that the text attempts to seduce the reader with one particular conception of power, but that a 'resisting' reader will rethink the very assumptions upon which that conception is based.

INTRODUCTION

Oleanna is David Mamet's recent and highly controversial intervention in the political correctness debate. It stages a confrontation between a male professor, John, and his female student, Carol. John is about to be granted tenure and, on the strength of this promotion, has started negotiations to buy a new house for his family. Carol is a rather shy and confused student who is afraid that John will fail her, and John treats her with a mixture of surface concern and underlying condescension. He asserts that he likes her and promises her a grade 'A' if she comes back to his office to talk about the course. When Act II opens, it turns out that Carol has accused John of sexual harassment. Her newly gained self-confidence contrasts with John's gradual loss of confidence, as he fears that he may not be granted tenure, that he may not be able to buy the house and that he may even lose his job. In Act III, Carol offers to withdraw her complaint to the tenure committee on one condition: he must sign a list of banned books, including his own.

John indignantly rejects what he sees as an attack against academic freedom and when, in the final climactic scene, he finds out that Carol has lodged criminal charges of battery and attempted rape against him, he physically assaults and verbally abuses her, thus committing the very acts of which she had previously accused him.

The play is divided into three acts, each of which consists of an office-hour interaction between the professor and his student. These literary representations of office-hour interactions have greater complexity than real-life office-hour interactions in terms of what is usually referred to as discourse layering:[1]

level 1: author–reader/audience discourse
level 2: inter-character discourse

In other words, the inter-character discourse in the play between John and Carol is embedded within the discourse between the dramatist David Mamet and his readers or audience. And if we look at the play as performance, we also have to allow for the interpretative contributions of the production director and the actors.

In the analysis that follows, I will largely focus on the inter-character discourse layer and consider the dynamics of the office-hour interaction in an educational institution such as a university. I trust that many readers – to the extent that they themselves are either students or academics – have taken part in such encounters and will therefore have certain expectations about them. For example, we assume that the main roles are played by a lecturer and a student (or more than one student). The former is the more powerful participant, whose authority relies on, first, his expert knowledge and pedagogic expertise and, second, on the external, social legitimation of his role as a lecturer. The student, on the other hand, is the less powerful participant, because she is the novice possessing less knowledge of the subject area that she is studying. I refer to the professor as 'he' and the student as 'she' because this accords with the gender distribution in Mamet's play.

Another plausible expectation that we may have about the office-hour interaction is that the dominant discourse-type associated with it is academic discourse, although the impersonal academic discourse may at times shade into a more caring, more personal type of discourse. This is what happens in Act I, where John makes up for Carol's insufficient socialization into academic discourse by trying to establish a positive affect bond between them. In Acts II and III, on the other hand, the dominant status of academic discourse is threatened or even subverted by Carol's increasing use of legal discourse. A particular genre such as the office-hour interaction can thus be seen to draw upon a range of discourses, or even become a site of conflict between institutionally and ideologically diverse discourse-types.[2]

The main point that we are concerned with here is how the characters manage these discourse conflicts, and how the reader and the audience interpretatively (re)construct the discourse processes attributed to the characters by the author. A narrow and exclusive focus on the text will not take us very far here; I shall try to show that we need to bring in aspects of the social and cognitive context. It is to these contextual matters that we turn in the next two sections.

THE SOCIAL CONTEXT: POWER

Power can be defined as the ability of people and institutions to influence or control the behaviour and material lives of others.[3] Though 'control' has more negative connotations, 'influence' suggests that power can be exerted both in a positive and a negative way. In the positive sense, power is something that can be given to marginalized groups (e.g. women in patriarchal society, or students in an educational context) so that they are empowered. But power can also be used to constrain, oppress, disempower, and marginalize certain people or groups of people. Note that there is a continuum between the two extremes, so that power often has good and bad aspects, in the sense that, for example, giving power to one person may imply not giving it to, or taking it away from, somebody else. Hence there is a first important distinction to be made between power as enablement and empowerment versus power as domination and oppression.

The other important distinction that I want to make is between institutionally or socially legitimated power and discursively constructed power. Perhaps a good way of approaching it is via West and Zimmerman's (1985: 116) concept of 'participant identities'. They distinguish between three types of participant identities:

1 'master identities', which crosscut all occasions of discourse: these are our more permanent identities such as age, sex, social class; on all these dimensions, John has power over Carol, who is young, female and lower class;
2 'situated identities', which inhabit particular social settings: these are less permanent identities such as professor and student; on this dimension, too, John has power over Carol;
3 'discourse identities', which constantly shift between discourse participants: these are ephemeral identities created by the verbal activities that we engage in; for example, in many social situations, apologizing is a self-threatening act, whereby we put ourselves in the position of the powerless discourse participant; uttering a command, on the other hand, is an act which threatens our interlocutor's face or self-image, and puts us in the position of the powerful discourse participant (though it all depends on whether our command is taken up or ignored or rejected).

It is our master and situated identities which invest us with social and institutional power, a power which, as we have seen, has not a single source but multiple sources: age, sex, class, job status, etc. But social power is not completely stable; it constantly has to be renegotiated. The renegotiation is done through our discourse identities which provide us with discursive power so that, to some extent at least, power has to be seen as an effect of discourse.[4]

This means that any power relation is inevitably dynamic: it is possible for socially powerless participants to temporarily gain discursive power over socially powerful participants in particular discursive encounters. The powerful participants may tolerate or even encourage this as long as they do not feel threatened in their own superior social power. In that case, the powerless participants may be lulled into a false sense of being taken seriously and having a say in things, or they may become aware of this paradoxical state of affairs and experience the seemingly emancipatory moves as oppressive ones.

This, in fact, is the way Carol reacts to John's moves in *Oleanna*: she feels that rather than trying to empower her, he is really only interested in upholding his own institutional power and hence in oppressing her. One of the questions we shall address in the analysis below is why this should be so. I shall argue that it is largely due to the nature of Carol's background assumptions about teaching and power. In the remainder of this chapter I will try to uncover this underlying conflict in what Carol's background assumptions are, what John's are, and to what extent they clash with each other. But first of all I have to explain more clearly the role played by background assumptions in interpretative processes.

THE COGNITIVE CONTEXT: SCHEMATA

According to Durant and Fabb (1990: Ch. 7), the creation of meaning is an inferential process, which combines new information with information already stored in memory. The information in the mind is stored not individually but in chunks, sets of beliefs, assumptions and expectations; and it is these sets that I refer to as 'cognitive models' or 'schemata'.[5] If the speaker's schemata are highly similar to the hearer's, with many shared assumptions, they will find it easy to communicate and understand each other. In this case, speaker and hearer can be said to belong to the same interpretative or discourse community, all the members of which use highly similar assumptions in their inferential processing of discourse. Such a set of shared presuppositions, assumptions, beliefs, values and cultural practices constitutes a world-view, a version of reality which comes to be accepted as 'common sense' within that particular community. If, on the other hand, speaker and hearer belong to different discourse communities and hold differing worldviews, they will nevertheless understand each other to the extent that they share at least some interpretative assumptions. If their background schemata are widely divergent, then the result is likely to be misunderstanding or even a breakdown in communication. In this case, we can say that the discourse participants are locked in a situation of schematic or presuppositional conflict.

In Act I of *Oleanna*, Carol and John use very different interpretative schemata, and therefore find communication extremely difficult. The conflict can be seen as that between an elaborated code and a restricted code (Bernstein 1971), with the latter being associated with disempowerment, marginalization and inarticulacy. Carol is the restricted-code speaker, who has to acquire a new 'language' – namely, academic discourse. Indeed, John frequently provides ordinary-language synonyms for the more specialized lexical items that he uses (e.g. *pointer* for *index* (24), *liking* for *predilection* (31), *model* for *paradigm* (45), *bill of particulars* for *indictment* (63), *happen* for *transpire* (66)). But using a new language also means taking on a new identity (as a member of the academic discourse community) and acquiring a new belief-system, a new world-view. It is this process of socialization, as we shall see, that Carol seems to resist.

The important theoretical point is that our belief-systems, and the cognitive schemata in which they are enshrined, are not fixed and static, but are highly dynamic structures which are constructed in and through discourse, and are constantly revised and updated. Schemata, as Cook (1994: 188) says, 'are used in processing, but also changed by processing'. So there is constant flux and change. For example, our schemata for teacher and student are influenced by our self-image (if we ourselves happen to occupy either of these social roles) and by our real-life encounters with particular teachers and students. But they are also influenced by the representations of teachers and students in the verbal and visual texts that we come across in our daily lives, particularly if a large number of texts use similar ways of representing them. In other words, our cognitive schemata are socially, culturally, discursively and intertextually constituted.

But the very fact that certain representations tend to dominate in a particular culture also works against change. These dominant representations are naturalized and become part of the culture's 'common sense'. We do not question them any longer, and the prejudiced beliefs or stereotyped images that they may include become almost invisible. At one stage in the play, John reminds Carol that the minimum common ground that is needed for communication to take place at all is to look upon the other person as human (53). But cognitive schemata – precisely because of their stereotypical simplifications and overgeneralizations – encourage a depersonalization of the Other. Therefore it is important to be aware of the way in which our schemata are constituted. A critical awareness is the precondition for positive cognitive change, for identifying and deconstructing the more pernicious aspects of schemata, and helping towards the construction of alternative, more positive ones.

In *Oleanna*, we witness a schema change in Carol, but it is a negative one, towards greater stereotypicality and depersonalization: she moves from an early view of John as an empowering tutor to a later view of him as oppressor, male predator and obstacle to her empowerment who has to be ruthlessly removed. Why and how she shifts from the early to the later model is a basic question to which, in the rest of this chapter, I will try to provide an answer. In order to do this, we shall attempt to (re)construct the putative cognitive processes of the characters, to uncover the cognitive models and assumptions underlying Carol's and John's verbal exchanges. The relevant assumptions that we shall look at in the next section are those concerning the nature of teaching, power and the roles into which the two protagonists cast each other.

DAVID MAMET'S *OLEANNA*

Mamet's play thus presents us with an inherently unequal power relation situated within the institutional context of higher education: Carol goes to see her professor in his office in order to talk about her coursework. There is a big difference for students between having a casual chat with a lecturer and being in a tutorial. In the latter case, there are a wide range of assumptions and expectations, which both lecturer and student rely on as mutual knowledge. They include, first of all, the assumption that the student will go to the lecturer's office (rather than the lecturer going to the student's room). Some lecturers might require students to make an appointment. For instance, in *Oleanna* John points out to Carol that 'this was not a previously scheduled meeting' (13). Next, we assume that the student goes to the lecturer's office because the former wants to talk to the latter about a specific topic, a topic which usually will be connected in some way with a particular course that the lecturer is teaching. In other words, the student does not go to the lecturer for a general chat; on the contrary, there is a constraint on topic relevance that the student will have to observe. Consequently their verbal interaction will not be unfocused conversation, but goal-orientated, instrumental discourse. In this way, we can gradually build up a general teaching schema for the office-hour interaction, which is widely taken for granted within the academic community and which contains the following assumptions amongst many others:

1 the lecturer possesses some piece of information, knowledge or advice that the student needs in order to get on with her work;
2 the lecturer is both willing and able to pass on that information to the student.

These assumptions presuppose the lecturer's competence and pedagogic expertise, neither of which would be expected in a general conversation, where the above assumptions would not be in force and there would be fewer constraints on topic selection. In *Oleanna*, for example, when John is talking on the phone to his wife, Carol overhears him using the expression 'term of art' and questions him about it. John, however, assumes that she has come to talk about her essay, and is so intent on introducing this delicate topic that he fails to see the point of her question:

CAROL: [*Pause*] What is a 'term of art'?
JOHN: [*Pause*] I'm sorry . . .?
CAROL: [*Pause*] What is a 'term of art'?
JOHN: Is that what you want to talk about?

CAROL: . . . to talk about . . . ?

JOHN: Let's take the mysticism out of it, shall we?
    Carol? [*Pause*] Don't you think? I'll tell you: when you have some 'thing'.
    Which must be broached. [*Pause*] Don't you think . . . ? [*Pause*]

(Mamet 1993 [1992]: 2–3)

What is going on here is that Carol is still operating within a conversational
schema, in which she can develop whatever topic comes up, whereas John
already operates within a teaching schema, presupposing that there is something specific and relevant to the course that Carol 'want[s] to talk about',
that there is some ' "thing" [w]hich must be broached'.

    However, John eventually realizes that he has been too brusque; he apolo-
gizes and proceeds to answer Carol's question:

JOHN: It seems to mean a *term*, which has come, through its use, to mean
    something *more specific* than the words would, to someone *not acquainted* with
    them . . . indicate. That, I believe, is what a 'term of art', would mean.
    [*Pause*]
CAROL: You don't know what it means . . . ?
JOHN: I'm not sure that I know what it means. It's one of those things, per-
    haps you've had them, that, you look them up, or have someone explain
    them to you, and you say 'aha', and, you immediately *forget* what . . .
CAROL: You don't do that.
JOHN: I . . . ?
CAROL: You don't do . . .
JOHN: I don't, what . . . ?
CAROL: for . . .
JOHN: I don't for . . .
CAROL: no . . .
JOHN: forget things? Everybody does that.
CAROL: No, they don't.

(Mamet 1993 [1992]: 3–4)

The fragmented nature of the two interlocutors' turns points to a major dys-
functionality in the interaction. Carol is shocked that John does not know for
sure or has forgotten what 'term of art' means. She seems to make a confusion
here between a conversational schema and a teaching schema, by applying
the presuppositions of the latter to the former. She expects John to be able to
supply an exact definition of the concept 'term of art', although this information is not relevant to the course that John is teaching and in which he
alone is normally expected to have the necessary expertise.

    So is Carol simply guilty of a conversational *faux pas* here? Or could the
fact that Carol expects expertise from John in this area, too, be a first indication that she is operating in a teaching schema of her own, the assumptions
of which differ significantly from the office-hour interaction teaching schema
set out above? If so, we would be witnessing a schematic conflict, with Carol

expecting a much more wide-ranging expertise from John than would usually be the case.

In the next extract, Carol again tries to raise a general conversational topic, but this time John does not follow up her topic and instead imposes his own:

CAROL: Oh, oh. You're buying a new house!
JOHN: No, let's get on with it.

(Mamet 1993 [1992]: 5)

From here on, John is in the dominant position and in control of the topic, whereas Carol is reduced to a submissive position. She is almost inarticulate, unable to talk about her work, and is finally reduced to a barren enumeration of the physical actions that she has undertaken in her fruitless attempts at socialization into the specialist academic discourse which is so alien to her:

JOHN: I know how . . . *believe me.* I know how . . . potentially *humiliating* these . . . I have no desire to . . . I have no desire other than to help you. But: [*He picks up some papers on his desk.*] I won't even say 'but'. I'll say that as I go back over the . . .
CAROL: I'm just, I'm just trying to . . .
JOHN: . . . no, it will not do.
CAROL: . . . what? What will . . .?
JOHN: No, I see, I see what you, it . . . [*He gestures to the papers.*] but your work . . .
CAROL: I'm just: I sit in class I . . . [*She holds up her notebook.*] I take notes . . .
JOHN: [*simultaneously with 'notes'*]: Yes, I understand. What I am trying to *tell* you is that some, some basic . . .
CAROL: I . . .
JOHN: . . . one moment: some basic missed communi . . .
CAROL: I'm doing what I'm told. I bought your book, I read your . . .
JOHN: No, I'm sure you . . .

(Mamet 1993 [1992]: 5–6)

Researchers such as Erickson *et al.* (1978) distinguish between a 'powerful' and a 'powerless' speech style. Whereas the former is marked by disaffiliating, non-supportive interruptions, the latter is marked by hesitations, repetitions and uncompleted turns. Could John be seen as using a powerful speech style and Carol a powerless one in the above passage? After all, John frequently interrupts Carol or his turns overlap with Carol's, which might indicate his power; and Carol uses many hesitations, repetitions and uncompleted turns, which might indicate her lack of power. But, if we look more closely at the dialogue, we find that many of Carol's turns also interrupt, or overlap with, John's; and John, too, has hesitations, repetitions and uncompleted turns. It thus becomes extremely problematic to identify certain linguistic features as reflexes of a powerful speech style and others as reflexes of a powerless one. A more promising route might be to look at the differing functions that one and the same linguistic form can have in context: whereas Carol's hesitations and repetitions indicate her lack of power, John's can be interpreted as instruments of power, aiming to lessen or soften the anticipated antithetical emotional reaction that Carol may have to him.

John's evaluations of Carol's work are quite negative here: he repeats 'no' three times ('no, it will not do'; 'No. I see, I see what you, it . . . but your work'; 'No, I'm sure you'). But he mitigates these negative evaluations by using a variety of redressive strategies to minimize the threat to Carol's face or self-esteem. Buck and Austin (1995: 65), relying on Brown and Levinson's (1987) politeness model, describe three different types of redressive strategies:[6]

negative face strategies: choosing more polite forms;
positive face strategies: emphasizing one's high regard for the hearer;
off-record strategies: performing the face-threatening act in an indirect way.

Significantly, John uses all three types: in the dialogue that immediately precedes the quoted passage, his language is almost exaggeratedly polite ('You paid me the compliment, or the "obeisance" – all right – of coming in here.' (5)), he emphasizes his feelings of empathy for Carol ('I know how . . . potentially *humiliating* these . . .'), his basic solidarity with her ('I have no desire other than to help you.') and his high regard for her (in the dialogue immediately following the quoted passage, he refers to her as 'an incredibly bright girl' (7)); and he employs linguistic indirectness in order to avoid a direct assignment of blame. Instead of telling her how bad her essay is, he prefers to talk about 'some basic missed communi[cation]' between them. When he eventually gets round to discussing Carol's essay, he uses a series of questions which on the surface are requests for information and only function as accusations in an indirect way:

JOHN: [*Picks up paper.*] Here: Please: Sit down. [*Pause*] Sit down. [*Reads from her paper.*] 'I think that the ideas contained in this work express the author's feelings in a way that he intended, based on his results.' What can that mean? Do you see? What . . .

(Mamet 1993 [1992]: 8)

Carol's unexpectedly forceful reaction to this indirect attack allows us to glimpse hidden potentialities in her which will not be fully revealed until Acts II and III:

CAROL: I did what you told me. I did, I did everything that, I read your book, you told me to buy your *book* and read it. Everything you *say* I . . . [*She gestures to her notebook.*] [*The phone rings.*] I do . . . Ev . . .
JOHN: . . . look:
CAROL: . . . everything I'm told . . .
JOHN: Look. Look. I'm not your *father*. [*Pause*]
CAROL: What?

JOHN: I'm.
CAROL: Did I say you were my father?
JOHN: . . . no . . .
CAROL: Why did you say that . . .?
JOHN: I . . .
CAROL: . . . why . . .?

(Mamet 1993 [1992]: 9–10)

John feels that Carol would like him to be more like a father than a lecturer; he feels that she moves out of the teaching schema into a family schema, where parents support their children. Carol's reaction, however, shows that there is a basic misunderstanding here: she was still operating within the assumptions of the teaching schema, not a family schema. It gradually dawns on us that all along Carol has been operating in a teaching schema which is significantly different from John's. In other words, the conflict between them is a presuppositional one, a clash of schemata, which explains their incapacity to reach some form of common ground.

For Carol, assumptions like 'doing whatever you are told by the lecturer' (9) belong to the teaching schema. According to her, the lecturer has to 'teach' (11) the students, in the sense of passing some information or facts on to the students, who then also 'know something they didn't *know*' (12). If the students have difficulty in understanding, the lecturer has to provide support for them: 'You have to help me' (10). Her teaching schema is a highly specific and also highly traditional extension of the office-hour interaction teaching schema that we encountered above:

Carol's teaching schema:

1 the lecturer possesses knowledge and expertise in all areas;
2 the student lacks knowledge and expertise in all areas;
3 the student does whatever she is told by the lecturer (e.g. to read a particular book);
4 if the student understands, then she has acquired knowledge;
5 if the student is unable to understand, then the lecturer has to 'help' her;
6 the lecturer knows how to help the student.

John, on the other hand, feels that Carol is treating him as if he were her father. His teaching schema is also an extension of the office-hour interaction teaching schema, but includes more innovative and critical assumptions such as the following:

John's teaching schema:

1 the lecturer tries to 'awake' the students' interest (26);
2 the lecturer teaches the students how to think for themselves: 'What do you think? . . . What do you think, though?' (29);
3 the lecturer tries to 'provoke' the students (32);

4 the students are expected to be independent and critical, to 'question' things (33);

5 the lecturer can tell the students what he thinks, and then the students 'decide' (53);

6 the lecturer does not try to 'fix' the students (54).

We are faced here with a clash between two opposed teaching schemata, which I shall refer to as (Carol's) 'power of' model and (John's) 'power to' model. Carol sees power as the acquisition and possession of knowledge, with the lecturer possessing power because he possesses knowledge, and the student acquiring power by acquiring knowledge. She has a naive view of empowerment as a passive process of transfer. John, on the other hand, sees empowerment as an active process in which the lecturer gives the students the power to achieve their own goals. And this is to be arrived at not so much by the students acquiring knowledge but through their developing critical skills which open up new horizons of understanding.

John's schematic or background beliefs also lead him to treat Carol sensitively as a person. He shifts repeatedly from an impersonal academic discourse towards a more caring, more personal type of discourse, in which he and Carol play the roles of mentor and *protégée* rather than lecturer and student.[7] In his attempt to make Carol feel better, John now tells her that he himself used to be considered stupid. Carol, however, is shocked by John's revelations: 'People said that you were stupid . . . ?' (Mamet 1993 [1992]: 17). The point is that John unwittingly destroys some of Carol's assumptions about education: the lecturer possesses expert knowledge and passes it on to the novice, the powerless student, and then the student comes to possess expert knowledge and gains power, too. John also tells Carol that he has problems with his work (21–2); again, this does not fit into Carol's 'power of' model, which stipulates that:

- the student has problems with work;
- the student goes to see the lecturer;
- and the lecturer solves the student's problems.

Finally, John tells Carol that tests 'were designed, in the most part, for idiots. *By* idiots' (23). All that Carol can offer in reply to this is a shocked 'no' (23). After all, in her model, exams have a clearly defined function: they test whether the student has acquired the necessary expert knowledge.

In this way, John destroys the main assumptions of Carol's 'power of' model. Will she now, as a consequence of the collapse of her own model, embrace John's 'power to' model? We might have expected that she would have experienced the 'power to' model as a truly liberating one; but what she experiences instead is a contradiction between theory and practice inherent in the 'power to' model:

CAROL: . . . that it is prejudice that we should go to school?
JOHN: Exactly. [*Pause*]

CAROL: How can you say that? How . . .

JOHN: Good. Good. *Good.* That's right! Speak up! What is a prejudice? An unreasoned belief. We are all subject to it. None of us is not. When it is threatened, or opposed, we feel anger, and feel, do we not? As you do now. Do you not? Good.

CAROL: . . . but how can you . . .

JOHN: . . . let us examine. Good.

CAROL: How . . .

JOHN: Good. Good. When . . .

CAROL: I'M SPEAKING . . . [*Pause*]

(Mamet 1993 [1992]: 30)

Again and again John interrupts Carol, inhibiting her discourse and imposing his own meanings. This abuse of power contradicts his stated conviction that students should be taught to think for themselves. John's interruptions are seemingly supportive and co-operative, but in fact Carol experiences them as devices for maintaining power.

Thus a deep-seated hypocrisy is revealed within John's 'power to' model. And a fundamental emptiness has been revealed within Carol's 'power of' model. The result is a moral vacuum which is filled by yet another teaching model, which I shall refer to as the 'power over' model. For the two models of empowerment, Carol now substitutes a model of disempowerment and oppression, in which education is seen as an arbitrary relation of dominance and submission, which can be reversed.

And this is exactly what we find in Acts II and III: the normal roles have been inverted. Here, the lecturer has asked the student to come to his office (46, 59). Moreover, it is the lecturer who has a problem, who needs something that the student can provide him with. In Act II, Carol asks: 'What do you want of me?' (45), and in Act III: 'What is it you want?' (61). John still tries to pretend that Carol has a problem which he can help her solve: 'Look, I'm trying to *save* you . . .' (57), but Carol has already turned the tables on him. She has publicly accused him of politically incorrect behaviour, and therefore she now has power over him. He needs her to drop her charges; she, on the other hand, does not need his help any longer: 'I don't think I need anything you have' (49). On the contrary, she is the one now who decides what words and actions mean, who has the power of imposing her own meanings:

CAROL: My charges are not trivial. You see that in the haste, I think, with which they were accepted. A *joke* you have told, with a sexist tinge . . . To lay a hand on someone's shoulder.

JOHN: It was devoid of sexual content.

CAROL: I say it was not. I SAY IT WAS NOT. Don't you begin to *see* . . .? Don't you begin to understand? IT'S NOT FOR YOU TO SAY.

(Mamet 1993 [1992]: 70)

And John is the one who does not understand any longer, who in his worries about losing his job is reduced to virtual inarticulacy, e.g. 'Well, I . . . I . . . I . . . You know I, as I said. I . . . think I am not too old to *learn*, and I *can* learn, I . . .' (Mamet 1993 [1992]: 71).

Even the basic teaching situation has been inverted here, with John 'learning' and Carol taking over the role of the teacher: 'I came here to instruct you' (67). What she reveals to him is that the lecturer–student relation is an accuser–accused relation, that the 'power to' ideal with its attendant beliefs in free thought and free speech is illusory and impossible to realize in the oppressive reality of a 'power over' institution:

> CAROL: Why do you hate me? Because you think me wrong? No. Because I have, you think, *power* over you. Listen to me. Listen to me, Professor. [*Pause*] It is the power that you hate. So deeply that, that any atmosphere of free discussion is impossible. It's not 'unlikely'. It's *impossible*. Isn't it?
>
> (Mamet 1993 [1992]: 68–9)

The roles have been inverted. The student has become the powerful accuser and the lecturer the powerless accused – and the dominant discourse-type has shifted from academic to legal discourse, which allows Carol to gain discursive power over John:

> CAROL: Do you hold yourself harmless from the charge of sexual exploitativeness . . .? [*Pause*]
> JOHN: Well, I . . . I . . . I . . . You know I, as I said. I . . . think I am not too old to *learn*, and I *can* learn, I . . .
> CAROL: Do you hold yourself innocent of the charge of . . .
> JOHN: . . . wait, wait, wait . . .
>
> (Mamet 1993 [1992]: 71)

Carol's accusations followed by John's hesitant replies enact the prototypical question and answer structure of courtroom discourse. But Carol goes further than this. By formally accusing John of rape, and thus moving her case out of the educational setting and into a legal one, she gains not only discursive but also (in the terminology of West and Zimmerman) 'situated' power over him. In all these ways, Carol appropriates power for herself. However – and this is what is so negative about it – she is not trying to change the system which she experiences as an oppressive one into an empowering and emancipatory one, but simply appropriates as much power as possible for herself within the existing system, which ultimately of course only serves to uphold and reinforce it.

CONCLUSION

What I hope to have shown in this chapter is that it is not possible to interpret a text produced by a particular speaker as mere text, but that interpreting involves (re)constructing relevant portions of that speaker's social and cognitive context. In other words, understanding Mamet's play is not just understanding the text but also understanding the social context (power relations) and the cognitive context (background schemata), and the extent to which the two are enmeshed. Paradoxically, however, such a (re)construction of the cognitive 'worlds' of the characters and, by implication, of the author, can only be achieved through the reader's own socio-cultural schemata. And since you as a reader will doubtlessly use different assumptions from mine in your cognitive processing of the text, you may well come up with a different interpretation.

In this way, we cannot but use our schemata to process discourse; but we must not forget that this is a two-way interaction and that our schemata are also changed in response to the discourses that we process. More specifically, particular textual representations either harden the stereotypical elements contained within our schemata, or they have the opposite effect of breaking up their stereotypicality, forcing us to look at the world in defamiliarizing ways.[8] I should like to suggest that Mamet's play has both these effects on its audience and readers: an effect of gender polarization and one of cognitive defamiliarization. On the one hand, it seduces us into a brutal 'power over' model by tempting us to empathize with John's final actions. Indeed, several reviewers and critics have commented on theatre audiences being elated or roaring with approval as John begins to assault Carol.[9] In our support of John's stance towards academic freedom, and our opposition to Carol's fanatic and repressive attitude of political correctness, we are seduced into an equally fanatic wholesale rejection of political correctness. In the words of Kureishi (1995: 111), we could ask: 'So who's the fanatic now?' Is it Carol, or John assaulting Carol, or Mamet tempting his audience into supporting John's assault, or the audience who allow themselves to be seduced into supporting John's assault?

The critical reader or spectator will resist this textual seduction and be more concerned with *Oleanna*'s ambiguities and its effects of cognitive defamiliarization. This is what I have attempted to do in the above critical discussion, using schema theory in order to sharpen our awareness of the ways in which the play forces us to rethink our assumptions about teaching and power. Whatever model of power in education we may have, it is bound to be shaken up by this play in which the 'power of' model is deconstructed and ridiculed right from the beginning, the 'power to' model is upheld and yet also discredited in more subtle ways, the 'power over' model wins and yet is also revealed in its full brutality and inhumanity. By exposing the different types of power relations inherent in the process of education, Mamet leads us to realize that education is not *either* a 'power of' *or* a 'power to' *or* a 'power over' process but *all* of them at the same time; that there is a dynamic tension between social and discursive power, as well as between power as domination and power as enablement; and that this precarious balance can easily be abused, from both sides, by the more powerful as well as the less powerful participants.[10]

SUGGESTIONS FOR FURTHER WORK

1 David Mamet: *Oleanna*. Using schema theory, explain as clearly as possible what John means when he says to Carol, 'We can only interpret the behavior of others through the screen we . . . create' (19–20).

2 Caryl Churchill: *Top Girls*. The following is a brief extract, illustrating Caryl Churchill's technique of overlapping dialogue:

> NIJO: It's a literary allusion to a tenth-century epic,/His Majesty was very cultured.
>
> ISABELLA: This is the Emperor of Japan?/I once met the Emperor of Morocco.
>
> NIJO: In fact he was the ex-Emperor.
>
> MARLENE: But he wasn't old?/Did you, Isabella?
>
> NIJO: Twenty-nine.
>
> ISABELLA: Oh it's a long story.
>
> MARLENE: Twenty-nine's an excellent age.
>
> (Churchill 1991 [1984]: 5)

The slashes mark the points of interruption where one character starts speaking before another has finished. Are the interruptions supportive or non-supportive? According to Wandor (1987: 123), Churchill's technique suggests 'a sharing of experiences, and the interruptions give a sense of bubbling excitement, but also suggests (depending on the nature of the production) the ways in which the women can chatter on and on without necessarily listening to one another'. Do you agree with Wandor's assessment, on the basis of the above extract? Are the interruptions in *Oleanna* used for similar purposes?

3 David Hare: *The Secret Rapture*. In this extract, Isobel comes back to the office unexpectedly and finds her boyfriend there with another woman, Rhonda:

> ISOBEL: Look, all right . . . [*She is suddenly vehement as if finally accepting that she cannot avoid this argument.*] I don't understand. What do you *want* from me? Like for instance tonight. I come in. What's in the air? A smell of cheap sex . . .
>
> IRWIN: No!
>
> ISOBEL: And I think, oh yes, I see, I know what this is for. This is to make me into the one who's responsible. There is no purpose to this except to make me feel awful. Because I'm the girl who can't be giving this man all the love he needs.
>
> IRWIN: I never said that.
>
> ISOBEL: You didn't need to. All I had to do was walk in the door and I was handed a role. My role is: the woman betrayed. Well, Irwin, I don't want to play it. I've no interest in playing it. Because it's humiliating. All I get to do is make catty remarks.
>
> (Hare 1988: 54)

Analyse Isobel's conversational strategies in the above extract in order to determine how successful she is in transcending the stereotypical role of 'the woman betrayed'.

NOTES

1 See, for example, Bruce (1981) or Leech and Short (1981: 257–72).
2 I follow Fairclough (1995: 14) here, who distinguishes between genre as 'a socially ratified way of using language in connection with a particular type of social activity (e.g. interview, narrative, exposition)' and discourse as 'a way of signifying a particular domain of social practice from a particular perspective'.
3 This definition is based on Fowler (1985: 61).
4 For a similar argument, and an application to E. M. Forster's *Howards End*, see Buck and Austin (1995).
5 Readers interested in schema-theoretic approaches should refer to Bartlett (1932), Rumelhart (1975, 1980), Tannen (1993a); and for applications of schema theory to literature, Cook (1990, 1994) and Semino (1995, 1997).
6 According to Buck and Austin (1995: 65), *negative face* refers to the desire to be able to act freely and to avoid having one's privacy violated, and *positive face* to one's aspiration to be respected and liked.
7 See Hubert-Leibler (1992: 75) on the nature of the mentor–protégé relationship, where 'the exercise of power is mitigated by feelings of solicitude and love, and a real concern for the other's well-being'. The two nouns, 'solicitude' and 'love', bring out the dangerous potential ambiguity of this relationship, with John later claiming that he was motivated by pure solicitude, whereas Carol interprets his behaviour as a form of 'rape' (1992: 67).
8 For an argument associating literary texts with the 'defamiliarizing' effect and non-literary texts with the 'hardening' effect, see Cook (1994).
9 See Csicsila (1995: 6) and Piette (1995: 185). It is, I think, this seductive effect of the play that Showalter (1992: 17) has in mind when she accuses Mamet of playing a rigged game.
10 I should like to thank Clara Calvo, Marion Colas-Blaise and the editors of this volume for their most perceptive comments on an earlier version of this chapter. I have not always followed their advice, so all remaining errors are mine.

10 'Unhappy' confessions in *The Crucible*

A pragmatic explanation

Valerie Lowe

EDITORS' PREFACE

An approach to the study of pragmatics which has been very influential in language study over the last twenty years is the theory of speech acts associated with the work of J. L. Austin and John Searle. In this article, Valerie Lowe outlines the approaches of Austin and Searle, and applies them, in connection with other pragmatic approaches, to the scene in Arthur Miller's *The Crucible* where the black slave Tituba confesses to witchcraft. Lowe uses the speech–act distinctions between an utterance's illocutionary force and its intended and actual perlocutionary effects to show in various ways how Tituba's confession is 'unhappy'. She apparently confesses, but her 'confession' has a number of attributes which render it void, including the fact that she does not believe herself to be a witch. Tituba's position as a slave means that she is powerless to deny her guilt, and indeed her 'confession' enables her to escape execution. A white woman, Rebecca Nurse, refuses to confess because she does not want to be damned eternally by God for lying, and is executed. Lowe's analysis shows how the irony in the play works as a consequence of the fact that the speech acts of Tituba and Rebecca are interpreted differently by the other characters on the one hand and the reader/audience on the other.

INTRODUCTION

In many respects, the conversation in which characters in dramatic texts take part is similar to that found in naturally occurring conversation, and lends itself readily to similar kinds of analysis.[1] One of the advantages that fictional dialogue has over natural conversation, however, is that we often have access to information that is denied to us in real-life situations; for example, an awareness of the truth or falsity of characters' utterances often allows us to judge their integrity with greater accuracy than that of our real life co-conversationalists. Arthur Miller's play *The Crucible* is a particularly useful vehicle for illustrating this point, and for demonstrating the power of

language, since the conversational performances of the characters largely
determines their fate.

The Crucible was written in the 1950s, and was intended to draw compari-
sons between the rise of McCarthyism during this period and the Salem
witch hunts of the seventeenth century.[2] Miller implies that an accusation of
being politically 'Left' in America at his time of writing could be compared
to an accusation of witchcraft in earlier times, resulting in fear for the
'accused' in both instances. This arises, in Miller's opinion, from our tendency
to justify the 'rightness' of our own beliefs by condemning as 'wrong' those
who hold alternative views, resulting, in extreme cases, in an assumption
that 'certain ideas and emotions and actions are of God, and their opposites
are of Lucifer (Miller 1986: 37), an idea which can be extended to include
the realm of politics: 'A political policy is equated with moral right, and opposition to it with diabolical malevolence' (Miller 1986: 38).

Although expressly intended to draw parallels between the McCarthy
'witch hunt' and the Salem witch hunt, the ideas expressed in Miller's play
are not limited to these two eras, and we can use the 'witch hunt' analogy to
explain the way in which society excludes *any* element which is perceived as
different, unwelcome or 'wrong' in some way, since 'all organisation is and
must be grounded on the idea of exclusion and prohibition, just as two objects
cannot occupy the same space' (Miller 1986: 16). Being accused of something
which is seen as 'wrong' (or 'diabolical') is sufficient to ensure a loss of
reputation at least, and sometimes even worse, as is illustrated by the fate of
the characters in *The Crucible*.

At the beginning of the play we learn that four white girls, Abigail, Betty,
Mercy and Mary, have been caught dancing naked in the woods at night by
Abigail's uncle, the Reverend Parris. Dancing or any form of entertainment
is banned in Salem and is punished by whipping, and the shock of discovery
is so great that Betty falls into an apparent coma, adding fuel to speculation
by the other characters that the girls are possessed by witchcraft. The reader
or member of the audience *knows* that the girls were not just dancing: a conversation between Abigail, Mercy and Mary makes it apparent that previously Abigail had asked Parris's black female slave, Tituba, to give her a
'charm' to kill Elizabeth Proctor, the wife of John Proctor, Abigail's ex-lover
(Act I, p. 26). If this fact is discovered, the girls can definitely be accused of
witchcraft, an unenviable situation, since those so accused are faced with a
desperate choice: (1) they can 'confess' to the charge (regardless of whether
or not the accusation is true) and be imprisoned, losing their reputation and
any land which they may own, or (2) they can deny the charge, in which
case they will be hanged. Faced with this dilemma, Abigail deflects attention
from herself and the other girls by claiming that Tituba 'made' them take
part in witchcraft, intimating that they are the innocent victims of Tituba's
power, and thereby diverting blame from herself onto the slave. The accusation of witchcraft is thereby transferred from Abigail to Tituba, whose
increasing fear and confusion, and her relatively powerless status in the

community, cause her to produce ineffectual conversational contributions which are interpreted by her accusers as a confession, and result in her imprisonment.

What Miller's play demonstrates is the potentially destructive power of words. Pragmatics offers us a way of explaining systematically *how* this destructive process is set in motion. It provides us with a framework enabling us to explain the misunderstandings which may arise as a result of the gap between what a speaker intends to say and what the hearer perceives him or her as saying. This potential for misunderstanding is often exploited in literary works, and can become a source of entertainment and enjoyment, or sadness, as in this play, when the reader is placed in the privileged position of being able to judge what a speaker means, and to witness the reaction of those who listen.

The play illustrates powerfully the way in which, in extreme circumstances, (mis)interpretation of utterances can lead to tragedy. The characters in the play are trapped in a situation where what they *say* and what they intend to mean is less important than the *significance* attributed to their words by others. Those characters who are unfortunate enough to be accused of witchcraft are faced with a situation whereby a denial of the charge is seen as evidence of the truth of the accusation, regardless of whether the accused is guilty or innocent. However, although a confession of guilt means that characters may lose their reputations, they at least avoid being hanged. Therefore an act of confession is not just a matter of saying something, it is also a way of performing an act – in this case, the act of saving one's own life. This potential for language to bring about a change of state is something which is explored by J. L. Austin and J. R. Searle in a theory of language use commonly referred to as 'speech act theory'.

AUSTIN AND SPEECH ACTS

In *How to Do Things with Words* (1962: 6) J. L. Austin discusses utterances which have the kind of 'performative' function that I have suggested is true of a confession, thus: 'the issuing of the utterance is the performing of an action – it is not normally thought of as just saying something'. Austin cites as examples the following, which are not only statements but have the simultaneous effect of performing an action:

- I do (take this woman to be my lawful wedded wife).
- I name this ship the *Queen Elizabeth*.
- I give and bequeath my watch to my brother.
- I bet you sixpence it will rain tomorrow.

In all of these examples, the uttering of the words has specific consequences: the person concerned is married, the ship is named, the watch is bequeathed and the bet is made. However, Austin notes that the *circumstances* must also be appropriate. For example, in order to marry someone it is not enough simply to say 'I do', it is necessary also that the person uttering the words 'should not be already married with a wife living, sane and undivorced' (Austin 1962: 8).

In addition, Austin notes that there is usually an 'accepted conventional procedure having a certain conventional effect' (Austin 1962: 8) which includes 'the uttering of certain words by certain persons in certain circumstances' (Austin 1962: 8), and that those participants and circumstances must be appropriate. Further, the procedure must be executed 'correctly' and 'completely' in order to be successful or 'happy'. If any aspect of the procedure is not adhered to, then the performative act is not achieved and is termed a 'misfire'.

Austin also suggests that it is sometimes necessary for certain *mental* processes to be involved, that 'a person participating in and so invoking the procedure must in fact have those thoughts and feelings' (Austin 1962: 15); otherwise, although the act is still achieved, the lack of requisite thoughts and feelings constitutes an *abuse* of the procedure. For example, the act of 'apologizing' usually includes an assumption that the apologizer 'repents' (Austin 1962: 83). However, saying 'I apologize' does not necessarily entail having appropriate feelings of remorse, merely that the person performs the act of apologizing. This kind of performative is 'self-referential'; that is, it only refers to what the speaker is doing, without providing any indication as to whether or not she or he is sincere.[3] Austin suggests that we could ask the question, 'But did he *really*?' (Austin 1962: 84), to which we can only confirm that he or she performed the act of apologizing, but not that the person was *really* sorry. Similarly, it is not automatic that the person apologized *to* will necessarily accept the apology, even if it is sincere, thereby illustrating the gap between the *intentions* of the speaker and the *reaction* of the hearer, something which we will consider below. Austin suggests therefore that certain conditions must be fulfilled in order to produce what he termed 'happy' performatives. Those characters in *The Crucible* who confess while believing themselves to be innocent produce 'unhappy' confessions.

To complicate matters further, Austin excludes those performatives which are 'done under duress': these 'come under the heading of "extenuating circumstances" or of "factors reducing the agent's responsibility"' (Austin 1962: 21). The threat of being hanged for refusing to confess is evidence of the duress to which the characters are subjected, and is sufficient to explain why some should choose to abuse the procedure in this way. We would be rightly suspicious of any confession elicited in such circumstances.

Tituba's case is more complicated, since it is not clear that her utterances should even be classed as a confession. There is no explicit performative. We need to consider whether it is a misfire. In order to discuss this, it is necessary to look at some examples from the text. The extract below begins when Abigail deflects the accusation from herself onto Tituba, and ends with Tituba's 'confession'.

[MRS PUTNAM *enters with* TITUBA, *and instantly* ABIGAIL *points at* TITUBA.]

(1) ABIGAIL: She made me do it! She made Betty do it!

(2) TITUBA: [*shocked and angry*] Abby!

(3) ABIGAIL: She makes me drink blood!

(4) PARRIS: Blood!!

(5) MRS PUTNAM: My baby's blood?

(6) TITUBA: No, no, chicken blood. I give she chicken blood!

(7) HALE: Woman, have you enlisted these children for the Devil?

(8) TITUBA: No, no sir, I don't truck with no Devil!

(9) HALE: Why can she not wake? Are you silencing this child?

(10) TITUBA: I love me Betty!

(11) HALE: You have sent your spirit out upon this child, have you not? Are you gathering souls for the Devil?

(12) ABIGAIL: She sends her spirit on me in church; she makes me laugh at prayer!

(13) PARRIS: She have often laughed at prayer!

(14) ABIGAIL: She comes to me every night to go and drink blood!

(15) TITUBA: You beg *me* to conjure! She beg *me* make charm –

(16) ABIGAIL: Don't lie! [*To* HALE:] She comes to me while I sleep; she's always making me dream corruptions!

(17) TITUBA: Why you say that, Abby?

(18) ABIGAIL: Sometimes I wake and find myself standing in the open door way and not a stitch on my body! I always hear her laughing in my sleep. I hear her singing her Barbados songs and tempting me with –

(19) TITUBA: Mister Reverend, I never –

(20) HALE: [*resolved now*] Tituba, I want you to wake this child.

(21) TITUBA: I have no power on this child, sir.

(22) HALE: You most certainly do, and you will free her from it now! When did you compact with the Devil?

(23) TITUBA: I don't compact with no Devil!

(24) PARRIS: You will confess yourself or I will take you out and whip you to your death, Tituba!

(25) PUTNAM: This woman must be hanged! She must be taken and hanged!

(26) TITUBA: [*terrified, falls to her knees*] No, no, don't hang Tituba! I tell him I don't desire to work for him, sir.

(27) PARRIS: The Devil?

(28) HALE: Then you saw him! [TITUBA *weeps.*] Now Tituba, I know that when we bind ourselves to Hell it is very hard to break with it. We are going to help you tear yourself free –

(29) TITUBA: [*frightened by the coming process*] Mister Reverend, I do believe somebody else be witchin' these children.

(30) HALE: Who?

(31) TITUBA: I don't know, sir, but the Devil got him numerous witches.

(32) HALE: Does he! [*It is a clue.*] Tituba, look into my eyes. Come, look into
me. [*She raises her eyes to his fearfully.*] You would be a good Christian
woman, would you not, Tituba?

(33) TITUBA: Aye, sir, a good Christian woman.

(34) HALE: And you love these little children?

(35) TITUBA: Oh, yes, sir, I don't desire to hurt little children.

(36) HALE: And you love God, Tituba?

(37) TITUBA: I love God with all my bein'.

(38) HALE: Now in God's holy name –

(39) TITUBA: Bless him. Bless Him. [*She is rocking on her knees, sobbing in
terror.*]

(40) HALE: And to His glory –

(41) TITUBA: Eternal glory. Bless Him – bless God . . .

(42) HALE: Open yourself, Tituba – open yourself and let God's holy light
shine on you.

(43) TITUBA: Oh, bless the Lord.

(44) HALE: When the Devil comes to you does he ever come – with another
person? [*She stares up into his face.*] Perhaps another person in the
village? Someone you know.

(45) PARRIS: Who came with him?

(46) PUTNAM: Sarah Good? Did you ever see Sarah Good with him?
Or Osburn?

(47) PARRIS: Was it man or woman came with him?

(48) TITUBA: Man or woman. Was – was woman.

(49) PARRIS: What woman? A woman, you said. What woman?

(50) TITUBA: It was black dark, and I –

(51) PARRIS: You could see him, why could you not see her?

(52) TITUBA: Well, they was always talking; they was always runnin' round
and carryin' on –

(53) PARRIS: You mean out of Salem? Salem witches?

(54) TITUBA: I believe so, yes, sir. [*Now* HALE *takes her hand. She is surprised.*]

(55) HALE: Tituba. You must have no fear to tell us who they are, do you
understand? We will protect you. The Devil can never overcome a
minister. You know that, do you not?

(56) TITUBA: [*kisses* HALE's *hand*] Aye, sir, oh, I do.

(57) HALE: You have confessed yourself to witchcraft, and that speaks a
wish to come to Heaven's side. And we will bless you, Tituba.

(58) TITUBA: [*deeply relieved*] Oh, God bless you, Mr Hale.

(Miller 1986: 45–8)[4]

The sense of unease which we may experience at Hale's interpretation of
Tituba's utterances as a confession (turn 57) can be investigated textually.
Examining the characters' words in detail enables us to identify those features
which lead us to feel that there is something 'not quite right' about Hale's
declaration 'You have confessed yourself to witchcraft'. This concerns our

expectations of what constitutes a confession; namely, that a person who is accused of some action can only confess by admitting, in words, that he or she did, in fact, perform that action.[5] First we need to establish the rules by which we judge whether or not a person can be said to have 'happily' (in Austin's sense of the term) confessed. Speech act theory can help us to explain how people 'do things with words', and what happens when things 'go wrong'.

Austin discusses the potential gap between what the words *mean* and what they *do*, and suggests that it is possible to distinguish among three types of speech acts; namely, 'locutionary', 'illocutionary' and 'perlocutionary' acts.

A locutionary act refers to the *meaning* of the words spoken:

> in saying something we perform a locutionary act which is roughly equiva-
> lent to uttering a certain sentence with a certain sense and reference,
> which again is roughly equivalent to 'meaning' in the traditional sense.
>
> (Austin 1962: 109)

This is distinguished from the *illocutionary force* of the utterance. Austin uses the example, 'He said to me "Shoot her!"' where the meaning 'shoot her' (the locutionary act) has an underlying *force* (the illocutionary act) with which the speaker intends to 'urge', 'advise', or 'order' the hearer to comply (the illocutionary act). The locutionary act and the illocutionary act are performed simultaneously: in saying 'shoot her!' the speaker intends to 'urge' the hearer to 'shoot her!'

For an illocutionary act to be performed 'happily' depends on 'uptake'; that is, the hearer must act in accordance with the intentions of the speaker for the successful achievement of the illoctionary act. In our example, the intended uptake will be secured if the hearer does what is asked – that is, shoot the person to whom the speaker refers. This third dimension is termed the 'perlocutionary' effect of an utterance. It may be simpler to think of the different acts as follows:

```
LOCUTIONARY act      = meaning
ILLOCUTIONARY act    = force
PERLOCUTIONARY act   = achievement of certain effects
```
(Austin 1962: 120)

The notion of locutionary, illocutionary and perlocutionary acts is particularly effective in describing the plot of *The Crucible*. An accusation (illocution) has an intended force of inducing a guilty person to confess, but also has unforeseen perlocutionary consequences – most significantly, the confession of those who are innocent. Austin accounts for these unforeseen effects by claiming that a 'perlocutionary act may be either the achievement of a perlocutionary object or the production of a perlocutionary sequel' (Austin 1962: 118). The 'object' is that which is intended by the speaker, whereas the 'sequel' is an unforeseen or unintentional result arising from the hearer's (mis)interpretation of the speaker's meaning. Thus in our earlier example, rather than being persuaded to shoot someone (the perlocutionary object), the hearer may in fact be 'alarmed', 'surprised', or even deterred from shooting – an unintended perlocutionary sequel which indicates that the speaker has not been successful in securing 'uptake'.

In Miller's play, the perlocutionary *object* is achieved if those characters who confess are, in fact, guilty of performing witchcraft. However, the persuasion of those to 'confess' who believe themselves to be innocent is an unintended perlocutionary *sequel*. The accusations do not always 'happily' realize an admission of guilt, since at least some of those who confess are lying. The 'confessions' of Abigail and Betty may be seen as falling into this category (Act I, p. 49) as they claim that they are able to name those that they have seen 'with the Devil', something which Betty later admits is not true (Act III, p. 92). We can now also recall that Austin includes in his criteria for 'happy performatives' the involvement of certain 'mental processes', and we can observe that these are absent in the case of a false confession, since it is not possible to confess truthfully to something one has not done. A false confession therefore constitutes an abuse of the procedure.

To sum up, in Salem, an accusation of witchcraft is *intended* to elicit a *true* confession from the accused, the production of which is seen as evidence that the person has renounced witchcraft. As a consequence, his or her life is spared and the character can be deemed to have been *persuaded* to confess. In this instance, the accuser has achieved his or her perlocutionary *object*. However, a *false* 'confession' is an unintended perlocutionary *sequel*. In both cases, the 'confessor' is saved, since the accusers have no real way of knowing whether a confession is true or false. Unfortunately, this is also true in the case of a denial, since the accusers cannot assume that someone who denies the charge is telling the truth. A denial can therefore be seen as an unintended perlocutionary *sequel* to an accusation.

Returning to Tituba's 'confession', we can claim that in fact she does not confess according to Austin's conditions for 'happy' performatives, for the following reasons:

1 She does not use an explicit performative admitting her guilt *in words* (e.g. 'I confess').
2 The 'circumstances' of the confession are inappropriate since it is extorted under duress.
3 We have no evidence at this stage of Tituba's 'mental processes' (i.e. that she believes herself to be guilty of 'witchcraft').

Even if Tituba had admitted her guilt in words and said 'I confess' (which she does not) the 'extenuating circumstances' would have rendered her 'confession' void according to Austin's criteria, since it is extorted under duress (see turn 24). In addition, a confession of guilt not only entails being guilty but suggests an attitude of the confessor – namely, that the person is sorry and repents. Does Tituba really believe that she is guilty, and, if not, how can she be sorry and repent?

In fact, Tituba neither explicitly denies the charge, nor confesses her guilt, yet her accusers interpret her utterances as a 'confession'. Austin's work so far has allowed us to consider the intentions of the speaker, and the securing of 'uptake' is seen to be the speaker's sole responsibility. In Hale's case, his threat is successful, since it results in (what he believes is) Tituba's confession. However, as we have seen, Tituba's continued attempts to deny her guilt appear to be irrelevant in the face of Hale's determination to interpret her utterances as a confession. In order to investigate fully the dynamics of conversational interaction, we must also consider the role of the hearer, thus moving to the opposite end of the communicative scale.

SEARLE AND SPEECH ACTS

Another language philosopher, J. R. Searle, developed speech act theory beyond Austin's original work. Although, like Austin, Searle is primarily interested in what the speaker does and not the hearer, his contribution (1975b) allows us to shift our focus from the intentions of the speaker to the way in which the hearer arrives at an *interpretation* of the speaker's intention. As we have seen with regard to Tituba, it is not always possible for the speaker to secure 'uptake'. Tituba and her co-conversationalists have different, and incompatible, conversational goals, since the accusers want Tituba to confess to an accusation which Tituba wants to deny. However, the more powerful status of her white male accusers renders Tituba's attempted denials futile. Evidently then, the hearer dimension of conversational interaction is crucial. Searle suggests a set of rules or conditions which might enable the hearer to arrive at a successful interpretation of what a speaker intends. For example, he considers the reasons why a question such as 'Can you reach the salt?' can be intended as a request, and interpreted as such. He argues that successful conversational interaction partly depends on shared linguistic and non-linguistic knowledge. Conventionally, we know that such utterances function as requests, and that questions concerning our *ability* to do something are preconditions to our being *asked* to do something. This kind of utterance is termed an 'indirect speech act', 'cases in which one illocutionary act is performed indirectly by way of performing another' (Searle 1975b: 60).

The ability of a speaker to perform an illocutionary act successfully is dependent on the presence of certain 'felicity conditions': 'Each type of illocutionary act has a set of conditions that are necessary for the successful and felicitous performance of the act' (Searle 1975b: 71).

A necessary precondition to *requesting* someone to perform an act is that they are *able* to perform that act. Similarly, a necessary precondition to making a promise is the ability of the speaker to perform the act anticipated by the promise (i.e. a future action of the speaker). Below are the felicity conditions for the successful execution of these two illocutionary acts (S = Speaker, H = Hearer, A = Act):

	Directive (Request)	Commissive (Promise)
Preparatory condition	H is able to perform A	S is able to perform A H wants S to perform A
Sincerity condition	S wants H to do A	S intends to do A
Propositional content condition	S predicates a future act A of H	S predicates a future act A of S
Essential condition	Counts as an attempt by S to get H to do A	Counts as the undertaking by S of an obligation to do A

(Searle 1975b: 71)

Asking someone about their *ability* to pass the salt is therefore a preparatory condition for (or preliminary to) *requesting* them to pass the salt. What is important for our analysis of the speech acts in *The Crucible* is that the preparatory condition for directives relates to the hearer's ability, whereas the remaining three conditions relate to the speaker.

We can use these felicity conditions to help us to explain how things have 'gone wrong' in *The Crucible*. Searle's felicity conditions for making a directive can apply to orders and threats, and the characters know that an accusation of witchcraft embodies the threat of being hanged for not confessing. The preparatory condition for threatening someone is that the hearer is able to perform the act (or is able to refrain from performing the act) that the speaker wants (or does not want) him or her to perform. An accusation is evidence that the accusers want the accused to confess, and counts as an attempt to make them confess, and so on. A confession entails less cost than a denial, and imprisonment, which is seen by some as preferable to losing their lives.

Tituba's case is different, however. It is not just that her utterances do not really constitute a confession. In addition, many of the felicity conditions for her performing the acts required of her are unfulfilled. For example, Hale says 'Tituba, I want you to wake this child' (turn 20), thereby presupposing Tituba's ability to wake Betty. The preparatory condition for Tituba performing the act of waking Betty (an act that no one else has been able to accomplish) is that Tituba is able to perform this act. However, it is not within Tituba's power to wake Betty because Betty is not really 'bewitched', she is only pretending to be asleep (Act I, p. 26). The sincerity, propositional content and essential condition, which relate to the wants of the speaker, are fulfilled, but the preparatory condition relating to the ability of the hearer, Tituba, to perform the required act is not. As Searle notes, 'it is a rule of the directive class of speech acts that the directive is defective if the hearer is unable to perform the act' (1975b: 72). Tituba's denial ('I have no power on this child', turn 21) is not accepted by Hale, but rather confirms her guilt in his eyes. Parris's subsequent directive 'You will confess yourself or I will take you out and whip you to your death, Tituba!' (turn 24) is a definite threat,[6] leading to a series of ambiguous utterances from Tituba which may *imply* her guilt but do not constitute a confession. Hale not only threatens Tituba, but promises her salvation and protection should she comply: 'open yourself and let God's holy light shine on you' (turn 42). 'We will protect you. The Devil can never overcome a minister' (turn 55). Promises are, of course, predicated on an action of the speaker, not the hearer, and Hale refers to the preparatory condition for his being able to fulfil his promise, i.e. 'The Devil can never overcome a minister', thereby intending to persuade Tituba to confess. The acts anticipated by Hale's promise (salvation and protection from evil) are assumed to be sufficiently desirable to persuade Tituba to confess, since the alternatives (damnation and abandonment to evil) are assumed to be more frightening than the imprisonment which results from confession.

We are now in a position to explain the reasons why Tituba's 'confession' is so 'unhappy'. Not only has she not confessed according to Austin's rules for 'happy' performatives, but the directives which are addressed to her are also defective, since they are based on invalid preparatory conditions relating to her ability to perform the act required of her. In fact, it is not within Tituba's power: Betty is the only person who is able to 'wake' Betty.

There is a difference therefore between what Hale believes, i.e. that Tituba is performing witchcraft on Betty and preventing her from waking, and what Tituba believes, i.e. that she has no power over Betty and cannot therefore wake her. This is a problem which is difficult to resolve since, as Danforth, one of the judges states:

> witchcraft is *ipso facto*, on its face and by its nature, an invisible crime, is it not? Therefore who may possibly be witness to it? The witch and the victim. None other. Now we cannot hope the witch will accuse herself: granted? Therefore we must rely upon her victims.
>
> (Miller 1986: 90)

The gap between what Tituba intends to achieve conversationally and her failure to do so results from this erroneous belief. The evidence against Tituba is based on something which cannot be proved or disproved, unless, of course, Betty herself reveals that she is only pretending. When Betty *does* eventually wake (Act I, p. 49), it appears to be a result of witnessing Hale's reaction to Tituba's 'confession'. Changing his conversational strategies from threatening and intimidating Tituba, Hale promises to save her. Abigail and Betty subsequently declare that they too want to be saved, thereby, ironically strengthening Hale's belief that it is Tituba's 'confession' that has broken the spell she has been exerting on the girls. This is why, subsequently, a denial can never prove that a character is innocent, and the only 'happy' outcome of an accusation, as far as the accuser is concerned, is a confession.

The 'unhappiness' of Tituba's 'confession' is a direct result of the Salem belief system and her lack of status in the community. The asymmetrical power relationships which exist in Salem are responsible for the (mis)interpretation of what she says by her accusers, and render Tituba unable to deny her guilt. The white characters who are accused can choose to deny the charge of witchcraft and at least keep their 'good names'. We can compare this exchange between Rebecca Nurse and Danforth, for example, with the earlier one between Tituba and Hale.

DANFORTH: I say, will you confess yourself, Goody Nurse?
REBECCA: Why, it is a lie, it is a lie; how may I damn myself? I cannot, I cannot.

(Miller 1986: 121)

Rebecca's refusal is not commented on by Danforth, who instead questions John Proctor, asking him to name Rebecca Nurse as part of *his* confession. Unlike Tituba, Rebecca is not threatened with a whipping for not confessing, and is instead hanged for denying the charge. Tituba's powerless position means that she is unable to deny her guilt, since she is treated as if she had indeed confessed. This impression is reinforced by Tituba's use of 'non-standard' English. Indeed, it is easy for Hale and Parris to apply their own interpretation to her utterances. For example, when Tituba says 'I tell him I don't desire to work for him, sir' (turn 26), Parris assumes that the pronoun (him) refers to the Devil (turn 27) and Hale comments, 'Then you saw him' (turn 28). This assumption is not confirmed by Tituba, whose next utterance is 'I do believe somebody else be witchin' these children' (turn 29), which is seen as confirming her guilt, rather than supporting her denial.

There is therefore differential treatment of denials according to social status. Those of the white characters are accepted, and taken as evidence of their involvement in witchcraft. They are able to realize their conversational intentions in a way which Tituba is unable to do. Because of her status of 'slave', whatever Tituba's *intentions* are, her words are interpreted by her accusers as a 'confession', and what she intends to 'do with words' is irrelevant, due to their ability to interpret her words in whatever way they choose.

CONCLUSION

Speech act theory provides a useful framework for an analysis of *The Crucible* due to the performative nature of the act of confession. It is possible to explain the feeling of dissatisfaction associated with Tituba's 'confession' due to the 'unhappiness' of the circumstances in which it occurs. The play exemplifies the potential gap between the effective realization of a speaker's intention and the actual consequences of her speech acts, and allows us to consider the reasons why some speakers are more successful than others. It also demonstrates the multiplicity and uncontrollability of perlocutionary effects associated with utterances, as illustrated by Abigail's accusation and Tituba's subsequent 'confession'. We are in the privileged position of being aware of the intentions (and 'unintentions') of the characters, something which is not always possible in everyday conversation. Some of the theoretical issues associated with speech act theory thus effectively form the plot of the play. Abigail's original intention may have been to rid herself of her rival by drinking a 'charm to kill Goody Proctor', but the consequence was to have devastating results for the population of Salem.

SUGGESTIONS FOR FURTHER WORK

1 I have argued that under Austin's rules for 'happy performatives', Tituba's 'confession' is void. If you examine the text immediately following the extract I have chosen, you may wish to argue that Tituba's words do suggest that she is guilty. To what extent do you agree with the suggestion that a confession must contain an explicit performative? Contrast Tituba's 'confession' with that of John Proctor (Miller 1986: 123). What processes must Proctor go through that are missing in Tituba's case? What do the differences tell us about the social status of the two individuals?

2 Look at the stage directions in the text of Tituba's 'confession' which Miller has supplied as an aid to interpretation. Austin argues that in order to show how speech acts can 'go wrong', 'We must consider the total situation in which the utterance is issued – the total speech act' (Austin 1962: 52). To what extent do the stage directions help us to assess the amount of duress to which Tituba is subjected? What do they tell us about the attitudes of the characters to one another? What difference would their absence make to your interpretation of Tituba's words?

3 In this chapter I have discussed the speech acts of 'confession' and 'denial', and suggested that the choice of each tells us something about the integrity of the characters. You may wish to look at the way in which the other speech acts (e.g. commands, questions) tell us about the relative power of the speakers. For example, in the extract examined in this chapter, Hale and Parris have power over Tituba, not only because they are white and male. Hale is a minister of the church and Parris is Tituba's employer. This power relationship may be compared to that between John Proctor and Mary Warren. Yet Mary feels able to defy John and Elizabeth Proctor. Look at the exchanges between Mary, John and Elizabeth (Act II, pp. 56–9) in terms of commands and refusals. What do they tell us about shifting power relationships in Salem?

NOTES

1 See Short (1996: Ch. 6), for a discussion of the similarities and differences between dramatic dialogue and 'normal' conversation, and analysis of sample texts.
2 All references are to the 1986 Penguin edition of *The Crucible*.
3 Thomas (1995: Ch. 3) deals specifically with speech acts, providing a useful summary of the work of Austin and Searle, and a discussion of the problems associated with their approaches.
4 From *The Crucible* by Arthur Miller. Copyright 1952, 1953, 1954 renewed © 1980 by Arthur Miller. Used by permission of Viking Penguin, a division of Penguin Books USA Inc.

5 At least in formal situations: arguably, a nod of the head may suffice in informal situations. We would expect for legal reasons, however, that this action would have to be translated into writing and a statement to that effect signed by the confessor.
6 The conditions for promising and threatening are similar, with the obvious exception that in the case of a threat, the hearer does not want the speaker to perform the future act. See Thomas (1995) for a full discussion.

11 The give and take of talk, and Caryl Churchill's *Cloud Nine*

Michael Toolan

EDITORS' PREFACE

In this chapter, Michael Toolan explores how people use linguistic acts of speech when they interact with one another, and how these acts indicate the interpersonal relations between speakers. In discussing the patterns and complexities in this area of the study of spoken discourse, Toolan bases his work on the contributions of Michael Halliday, John Searle and Malcolm Coulthard, all of whom have made distinctive contributions to the field, and also connects acts of speech to the Politeness Theory of Penelope Brown and Stephen Levinson. Toolan then goes on, through the detailed analysis of extracts from Act 2 Scene 1 of *Cloud Nine* by Caryl Churchill, to show how this style of analysis can be used in the study of dramatic texts. The analysis shows how we interpret the conversational exchanges in the particular dialogues, and also how the patterns of exchange help us to perceive the relations among the characters in the play.

TALK: THE BASICS

What are we actually *doing* when we talk to each other? And how many truly *different* things can we do in the course of talking to each other? In this chapter I would like to sketch a simple answer to these questions, and then use this answer in exploring some of the dynamics of passages of talk in plays. My sketched answer to the two questions heading this paragraph may well be flawed and inaccurate; it contains what amounts to a 'speech act' model of dialogue (I shall explain the term speech act more fully below), and such models have come in for plentiful criticism over the years. Nevertheless I think such speech act models continue to be one among an array of analytical tools useful to the study of dialogue – real or fictional – and it is in that guarded spirit that I present it here. But those first two questions are my underlying interest here: if we imagine a speaker saying each of the following remarks, in the typical kind of context in which that remark is usually heard, we know quite well that particular and different things are being done in each case:

Good morning, Mr Barnes.
I'm so sorry darling.
Love that coat on you.
Could you phone back before 5?
Does she have an email address?

These are, respectively and typically, a greeting, an apology, a compliment, a request, and a question. But just how long might be such a list of typical acts performed, each with its distinct label? And are there any overlaps once a longer list is devised? Could it be that, even if we accept that there are hundreds of distinguishable acts performable through speech, nevertheless that diversity emerges from a quite delimited core set of speech functions?

Many analysts, including Halliday (1994) have suggested that the language of dialogue involves, in essence, acts of *exchange*. I believe the term is not entirely satisfactory, largely because it suggests that there is normally a return, from interactant B to interactant A, in compensation for whatever A has supplied. But in practice talk is often far less reciprocal than this, so that it might be better to say that it involves *transfer* more consistently than *exchange* – although 'transfer' doesn't seem quite the right word either. With that caveat lodged, I shall continue to use the term 'exchange' below. The following paragraphs adopt and elaborate a number of ideas which have their source in Chapter 3 of Halliday (1994), to which the reader is referred for further discussion of the lexicogrammatical roots of the different kinds of act.

It should hardly need mentioning that this sketch of a simplest typology of speech act types, drawing on Halliday's work, is only one of a large number of possible ways of classifying discoursal moves. This chapter proceeds on the assumption that the reader has no background in the field. For those who wish to explore the area further, Coulthard's introductory survey remains invaluable (Coulthard 1985), as also is Burton (1980), perhaps the first book-length exploration of how a systematic or grammar-orientated discourse analysis might be applied to literary dialogue. Also to be recommended are Leech (1983), Thomas (1995), Tsui (1995), and the collection edited by Coulthard (1992). In recent years linguistic approaches to interaction have been deeply influenced by theories of face and politeness, and how face considerations shape our utterances, in predictable ways. The seminal text remains Brown and Levinson (1978); but, like Searle's foundational text in speech act theory (Searle 1969), this may be too technical to be a suitable introduction (for a very brief introduction to speech act theory, see Valerie Lowe in this volume).

When individuals talk to each other, they are enacting exchanges, and these exchange phenomena can be thought of as predominantly either mental or physical, and the grammar of English reflects this. If the enacted exchange is chiefly mental, the conversational contribution amounts to a giving of information or a seeking of information; if the exchange is chiefly physical, the contribution amounts to a giving or seeking of goods and services. So, four core conversational moves, or acts, thus amount to the giving, or seeking, of either information or goods and services. These can be represented as in the grid below, with example utterances likely to perform each of the acts:

	Goods and services	*Information*
Speaker is giving to addressee	Can I give you a hand with that?	I mustn't do any heavy lifting.
Speaker is seeking from addressee	Will you give me a hand with this?	Have you got a good hold at your end?

We can give familiar labels for the typical kind of conversational act performed in these four core categories:

	PROPOSALS	PROPOSITIONS
	Goods and services	*Information*
Giving	Offer	Inform
Seeking	Request	Question

We can also group Offers and Requests together, and Informs and Questions: since Offers and Requests both concern future proposed action by one interactant or the other, they are called Proposals; since Informs and Questions provide or seek information, they are called Propositions. The future action that a Proposal specifies is normally non-verbal (washing the dishes, closing the door, repaying a loan, etc.) although occasionally it can involve a verbal performance ('Billy, recite the present tense conjugation of *donner*, please'). The information sought or given in response to a Proposition is normally verbal, but replies to Propositions can be performed non-verbally (A: Where's the oil-can? B: [*points to far corner of garage*]).

Each of these labels (Offer, Request, etc.) covers a range of utterances. For example, under the Request category I include, as the figure above implies, any conversational act in which a speaker seeks goods or services from the addressee. Thus the Request category includes commands, demands, requests, begging, praying, etc.; for example:

Stand at ease!
Pull in to the side of the road, please.
Could you pass the salad?
Please don't tell Mummy.

At first glance one might be tempted to include threats within the Offer category, since these sometimes promise to give some service to the addressee, even if they are intended to be damaging to that addressee. But threats are always implicitly or explicitly subordinate to some superordinate Request which, in the threatener's view, is being unsatisfactorily addressed by the party being threatened: 'if you don't do/stop doing x, I will etc.' Furthermore, the speaker's preference is for the Request to be complied with and for the threatened consequence to be set aside, rather than for the Request to be dismissed so that the threatened negative consequence has to be performed. So threats are essentially Requests, not Offers. Much more can be said about threats and promises; here, only the broadest distinctions among discoursal acts can be sketched. Of the four primary classes, Offers seem to be the least extensively used. But they are a relatively well-defined group: they are proposed future actions or services on the part of the speaker, ostensibly to the benefit of the addressee, the undertaking of which is, significantly, made contingent upon the addressee's consent. This last point is arguably crucial, and distinguishes Offers from announcements ('I'm going to reorganize your bookshelves into some sort of order'), which are a kind of Inform. Grammatically, Offers are usually in the first person, often with one of the modal verbs *shall, can,* or *may,* where these can be interpreted as contributing to a proposal meaning 'Do you consent to me doing x for you?' A typical and expectable response to an Offer is a reply expressing consent – *OK; all right –* or a declination with a reason for so declining – *No thanks, I've just had one.*

Just as the Request category includes various subtypes, so too does that of Offers: these include promises, vows, some invitations, and offers of help. Informs include claims, warnings and compliments; they entail the imparting – at one level or another – of verbalizable information. Whether or not the addressee finds an Inform *informative* is a separate matter. Questions are acts designed to obtain the kind of information that Informs supply.

IDENTIFYING ACTS FUNCTIONALLY AND FORMALLY

So far I have been calling this utterance an Offer, and that utterance a Request, as if the labelling were simple and invariable. But the situation is a little more complex. With suitably different contexts, the same string of words can easily function as an Offer in one dialogue and as, say, a Question in another situation. Or, to give another example, consider the utterance you might hear when you phone the electricity company to complain about a bill: *Can you hold?* On functional grounds, since it is intended by the speaker to get the hearer to do something (and something more in the speaker's immediate interests than the hearer's), this is a Request. But now consider the following invented exchange:

A: Can you guess the only words from a real human being that I got out of the electricity company this morning when I 'phoned them to complain about the bill?
B: 'Can you hold?'
A: Exactly!

Here B's contribution serves as a Question (similar to 'Would it have been 'Can you hold?' by any chance?'). Now consider an exchange between a switchboard supervisor and a trainee receptionist:

SUPERVISOR: Now once you see that every adviser's line is busy, what is
the first thing you must say to new callers?
TRAINEE: 'Can you hold?'
SUPERVISOR: 'Can you hold, sir or madam.' Good.

Here the trainee's contribution is an elicited Inform – no less an Inform just
because, like many responses to teachers' questions, it informs the instructor
of something they know already.

I have supplied these examples to emphasize that the surface form of an
utterance taken separately cannot tell us which speech act is being performed;
we have to look at utterances in context to do this (and my earlier examples,
blithely labelled Offers, Informs, etc., have relied on your imagining the
utterances in a *stereotypical* context of use). The examples also serve to under-
line the fact that act-identification is guided by function, not form. This can
seem troublesome, since functions are sometimes less concrete and explicit
and more open to variant interpretation than forms. However, there are
ways, outlined below, in which functionalist interpretation can be usefully
underpinned, often with reference to formal and grammatical evidence.
These confirmatory criteria help ensure that disputes where analyst A says
'That's an Inform' and analyst B says 'No it's not, it's an Offer' are actually
quite rare. Similarly, in actual interaction, we are very infrequently forced
to pause and wonder 'Is he asking me or telling me?', 'Was that an offer or a
request?'; and the occasions when we *do* hesitate in this way are, clearly,
worthy of attention for that reason alone.

The four-way system of contrasts outlined above, then, arguably 'pins
down the four corners' of a schematic map charting the potential acts performed by interactants via language. And the four acts identified also seem
supported by various kinds of linguistic evidence. The first kind of evidence
to note is the established grammatical system of imperative, declarative and
interrogative:

Eat your spinach!
She ate her spinach.
Did she eat her spinach?

More often than not, grammatical imperatives express discoursal Requests,
declaratives express Informs, and interrogatives express Questions. But on
many occasions this simple matching is absent (to begin with, we have three
grammatical sentence types, but four act types). For example, despite being
in the declarative, the following utterance in a suitable context is more likely
to be a Request than an Inform:

I want you to eat your spinach this minute!

How do we know that the above is a Request, not an Inform? What kinds of
criteria might justify describing it as a Request? Two criteria which may be
particularly important here are:

1 '*please*-insertability', and
2 prospection.

With Requests, unlike Informs and Questions (the third and fourth examples below), you can usually insert the word *please* (or the slightly old-fashioned *kindly*) before the verb denoting the action to be performed, even if the Request is indirect, as in the second example:

> Please eat your spinach!
> I want you to kindly eat your spinach this minute!
> ?She please ate her spinach.
> ?Did she please eat her spinach?

The second criterion, prospection, refers to the kind of response – in terms of form and content – that we would expect to occur after the given act. For example, *Thank you* is often prospected by Offers, but not by Requests or Questions; instead Requests standardly prospect some compliant action on the part of the addressee, optionally preceded by a verbal acknowledgement of the request, such as *OK*, *Sure*, or a verbal declination, such as *No!* In the Conversational Analytic tradition (discussed in Coulthard 1985), this powerful tendency for certain kinds of first turns to be followed and 'completed' by certain second-turn partners is explained in terms of 'adjacency pairs'.

Act type	*Possible prospection*
Offer	'Thanks'/'No thanks'
Request	'OK' + action/'No!' + action
Inform	'Oh'
Question	'Yes'/'I don't know'

The items listed here as prospections are not cited as necessarily the normal or most usual response to the given act, but rather as entirely possible responses for that act which are in addition highly implausible as responses for any of the other acts. Consider *Oh*, a legitimate response to Informs. While this would be an awkward response to some kinds of Informs it remains a coherent one; but *Oh* as a complete and free-standing response to an Offer ('I'll put the garbage out') or a Request ('Put the garbage out, would you?') or a Question ('Did you put the garbage out?') would be decidedly odd.

At the same time, a more likely response to some kinds of Informs may well be *Thanks* and not *Oh*. Consider, for example, service-encounter enquiries in which you ask someone at an information-desk for a particular Inform (the desk may be 'virtual', as when we phone directory enquiries). Here, a Question (not a Request, since the act is intended to secure the supply of verbal information, rather than a particular – usually non-verbal – behaviour) is, as is to be expected, followed by an Inform and this Inform is in practice much more likely to be responded to by *Thanks* than by *Oh*. But then this is a particular kind of Inform, a contingent and non-Exchange-initial one. It is a solicited Inform. By contrast the specified prospections in the table above apply to Exchange-initial acts, ones which initiate a round of talk rather than respond to another party's already initiated exchange. And when someone 'spontaneously' or freely provides you with information, via an Inform, *Oh* amounts to a default acknowledgement that you have heard and understood; *Thanks*, in the acknowledgement of an Exchange-initial Inform, amounts to treatment of that Inform as relatively beneficial to the addressee, and a relatively 'unrecompensable' cost to speaker A:

A: Excuse me sir, but you've left your headlights on.
B: Oh yes, thanks very much.

The 'telephone enquiries' example, 'Can you hold?' above, highlights how carefully we must use genre labels like 'service-encounters', since the label may conceal differences and mislead us into thinking that these exchanges always involve a Request for a material service. For example, service-encounters may involve the seeking of either non-verbal goods and services (e.g. an airline ticket from a travel agency) or verbal information (e.g. a quoted price for a particular airline ticket, from the same agency); or, of course, a complex combination of both.

COMPLEX ACTS, MARGINAL CASES, AND PHATIC 'STROKING'

While Offers, Requests, Questions and Informs as defined above are the canonical discoursal acts, there are invariably occasions of speech which seem to be intermediate between these categories. Consider, for example, the following utterances, from someone wishing to go out on a date with the person addressed:

1 Would you be interested in going to a movie with me some time?
2 Can I buy you lunch?

These are interrogative in form, but surely convey a Proposal rather than a Proposition, hence either Requests or Offers. The first utterance, (1), is arguably a complex speech act, in which an underlying Request (because a non-verbal action beneficial to the speaker is sought, whether or not it is also beneficial to the addressee) is wrapped in a Question 'shell'. The Question is enough of a real one to prospect *Yes* as part of a possible compliant reply; by contrast a typical Request – such as *Please send me a brochure* – never prospects the response *Yes* as an adequate reply. Utterance (1) is a Request with Question-like trimmings, the kind of complexly designed utterance we can expect to find where a speaker wishes both to secure an addressee's co-operation and to minimize the sense of imposition or 'face-threat'. In other words, its complex exploitation of the basic system can be explained via recourse to politeness theory (see Brown and Levinson 1987). Utterance (2) is superficially a question checking the speaker's ability to do something – a question which the speaker is logically in a much better position to answer than the addressee; but the typical intent of this indirect formulation is to request that the addressee have lunch with the speaker. The act performed is therefore borderline between an Offer and a Request, but lying closer to the former prototypical category (unlike a Request, it seems to require some verbal response, of consent or declination). So (2) is an Offer with overtones of Requesting, and Question-like trimmings! I hope that such marginal cases show clearly enough how the specific dynamics of the situation of use, including the tenor of the relations between the parties involved, and the prosody (the stress and intonation) adopted, are all crucial to the classifying of utterances as particular acts.

While Offers, Requests, Informs and Questions are argued here to be central to discourse, they are not the only acts involved. But they are the central ones, I shall hypothesize, in that just one among these four can occur as the nucleus of a first move in an interaction. But interlocutors' responses also merit classification. And in fact each of the canonical initiating acts strongly specifies a particular kind of response:[1]

Offer – Acceptance
Request – (Acknowledgement +) Non-verbal Performance
Inform – Acknowledgement
Question – Inform

You will see that this elaboration introduces just two new kinds of act, Acceptances and Acknowledgements, of a quite secondary nature. Typical examples of Acceptances are: *thanks, OK*, and *very well*; typical examples of acknowledgements are *oh, thanks*, and *really?*; and non-verbal equivalents are often used instead. Acceptances and Acknowledgements are secondary in that they are semantically attenuated, as the above examples suggest, and in that they are contingent upon some prior, exchange-driving act from among the set of four described above. Relatedly, while we have characterized talk as kinds of give and take, very little is given (back) when an Acceptance or Acknowledgement alone is made; and a bare positive Acceptance is not very different from a bare negative one, i.e. a declination of an offer, even though the interactional implications and consequences may be great. Nor, taken as whole groups, are they profoundly different from each other in form or function. For these various reasons, I propose to treat all verbal Acceptances/ Acknowledgements as members of a single secondary class of act, abbreviated to A, alongside abbreviations for the four other primary acts: O, R, I, and Q.

The picture presented so far, of dialogue as a trading of Offers, Requests, Informs and Questions, seems to bias the picture towards a transactional view of talk, as if we were always intent on getting work done, of 'dealing', using our words and our physical capabilities. What about the interactional side to talk, where we give and take 'strokes' (or lashes)? Isn't verbal interaction peppered with greetings and partings, compliments, apologies, insults, and so on, many of them traditionally classified as phatic communication? Where do these fit into a picture of Offers, Requests, Informs and Questions? I suggest that all these interactional manoeuvres can fit within the system sketched so far, even if they are atypical cases. The following apology is two Informs – *I'm sorry; I shouldn't have done that* – even if the second of these is something the addressee knew already and the first is less than heartfelt. The compliments '*What a fabulous jacket!*' and '*Sharp haircut!*' are Informs with evaluation and other-attentiveness uppermost. Greetings and partings are often the most mechanical and routine parts of interaction, but they, too, can be characterized as in part Informs, disclosing the speaker's wishes or disposition towards the addressee (as indeed do insults, also). Very many of our more interactional speech acts (compliments, greetings, and so on) are Informs refracted by considerations of politeness: a compliment is an Inform that is noticeably and excessively attentive to the addressee's positive face (the wish to be approved of), while an insult is an Inform designed to be abnormally threatening to the addressee's positive face (cf. Brown and Levinson 1987 and Culpeper in this volume). Since an Inform is usually 'beneficial' to the addressee (see below), the insulting Inform is sharply at odds with normal patterns in this respect too.

We can use additional, clarifying descriptive terms about the four core speech acts: giving or seeking goods and services are Proposals, that something happen or be done; giving or seeking information are Propositions, that something be known. A proposal involves a speaker intent on some act of doing, a proposition involves a speaker intent on some act of knowing. Furthermore, as should be clear from the examples of an Offer, a Request, an Inform, and a Question, the relations of dependence or obligation between speaker and addressee are sharply different in the four basic cases. Let us think of speaker and addressee as Self and Other respectively. Then, clearly, a rather different dependence-relation is implied when a speaker Offers:

Can I give you a hand with that?

than when she Requests:

Will you give me a hand with this?

In an Offer, as the grammar reflects ('*I give you*'), the speech act is focused on the needs of the Other, the addressee – or at least on what the speaker *thinks* are the Other's needs. Other is cast as beneficiary, Self is presented as the giver who, as in any genuine act of giving, is likely to incur some costs. Indeed it is hard to think of a genuine Offer, a giving of goods or services, that doesn't involve one in some cost. Additionally, although less overtly, the speaker-Self who makes an Offer may be adopting a stance of deference or subordination to whoever the addressed Other is.

In a Request, on the other hand, the relations are broadly reversed: the utterance is Self-orientated, imposes some cost on the addressee, and may cast that Other in a subordinate stance. We can make similar characterizations of Propositions, whether Informs or Questions. On the assumption that knowledge is desirable, Informs involve a knowing Self going to the trouble or cost of informing an Other, primarily for the latter's benefit; and Questions typically involve a not-knowing Self imposing on an Other-addressee, to Self's benefit. So, unlike the cases in Proposals, in which the subordinate– superior roles match up with those of cost-incurrer and beneficiary, in Propositions the two pairs of roles diverge:

Offer – speaker cast as subordinate and incurs cost, addressee cast as superior and beneficiary;

Request – speaker cast as superior and beneficiary, addressee cast as subordinate and incurs cost;

Inform – speaker cast as superior (the Knower) but incurs cost, addressee cast as subordinate but beneficiary;

Question – speaker cast as subordinate but beneficiary, addressee cast as superior (Knower) but incurs cost.

Let me emphasize again that these characterizations are tendencies, fitting canonical instances fairly well and other instances more loosely or not at all. Thus in a canonical Inform, the speaker is a cost-incurring Knower, and the addressee is informationally subordinate and the beneficiary. But in an atypical Inform such as a compliment, these characterizations are obviously modulated or tweaked: the superior/subordinate contrast is minimized, speaker's cost is slight, and the extent to which the speaker is telling the addressee something they do not already know may range from great to small. Compliments are thus a kind of Inform with some characteristics approaching those of an Offer; nevertheless they are essentially Informs and not Offers. Propositions and Proposals contrast in other interesting ways. Offers and Requests specify actions scheduled to occur within a timespan that extends from the speaker's present into the future; their temporal reference is delimited to the non-past. Informs and Questions, by contrast, are quite unrestricted in their potential temporal reference: a Proposition can refer to a state of affairs sited in the distant past as easily as in the distant future.

ON *CLOUD NINE*

I am sharply aware that this outlining of the descriptive model may seem rather protracted, and that turning our attention to some actual dialogue is now overdue. By way of justification, I hope that you will find it useful to apply the model to other discourse texts in and beyond this volume, besides the one reproduced below. What follows is the opening of the second act of Caryl Churchill's farce-like overview of Anglo-Saxon attitudes 'then and now'. Her play ranges freely among themes familiar and highly controversial: colonialism, sexism, feminism, marriage, family, racism, classism, sexuality, sexual-orientation, gender-bending, paedophilia, and so on. Perhaps inevitably, many of the characters are as a result stereotypes, but they are interesting and funny rather than crude and boring. Their stereotypicality is shown rather than told. From Act 1 to Act 2 there is a chronological leap of about a hundred years, from Victorian colonial Africa to late 1970s London; so here at the Act's opening we effectively meet entirely new characters. My basic premise is that if we tag these characters' utterances in terms of the four speech act options Offer, Request, Inform, and Question, we can proceed fairly speedily to a more detailed understanding of their different temperaments, interests, and goals. But first the scene:

[*Winter afternoon. Inside the hut of a one o'clock club, a children's playcentre in a park,* VICTORIA *and* LIN, *mothers.* CATHY, LIN's *daughter, age 4, played by a man, clinging to* LIN. VICTORIA *reading a book.*]

(1) CATHY: Yum yum bubblegum.
     Stick it up your mother's bum.
     When it's brown
     Pull it down
     Yum yum bubblegum.

(2) LIN: Like your shoes, Victoria.

(3) CATHY: Jack be nimble, Jack be quick,
     Jack jump over the candlestick.
     Silly Jack, he should jump higher,
     Goodness gracious, great balls of fire.

(4) LIN: Cathy, do stop. Do a painting.

(5) CATHY: You do a painting.

(6) LIN: You do a painting.

(7) CATHY: What shall I paint?

(8) LIN: Paint a house.

(9) CATHY: No.

(10) LIN: Princess.

(11) CATHY: No.

(12) LIN: Pirates.

(13) CATHY: Already done that.

(14) LIN: Spacemen.

(15) CATHY: I never paint spacemen. You know I never.

(16) LIN: Paint a car crash and blood everywhere.

(17) CATHY: No, don't tell me. I know what to paint.

(18) LIN: Go on then. You need an apron, where's an apron. Here.

(19) CATHY: Don't want an apron.

(20) LIN: Lift up your arms. There's a good girl.

(21) CATHY: I don't want to paint.

(22) LIN: Don't paint. Don't paint.

(23) CATHY: What shall I do? You paint. What shall I do mum?

(24) VICTORIA: There's nobody on the big bike, Cathy, quick.
      [CATHY *goes out.*]

[. . .]

(32) LIN: I didn't get very far with that book you lent me.

(33) VICTORIA: That's all right.

(34) LIN: I was glad to have it, though. I sit with it on my lap while I'm watching telly. Well, Cathy's off. She's frightened I'm going to leave her. It's the babyminder didn't work out when she was two, she still remembers. You can't get them used to other people if you're by yourself. It's no good blaming me. She clings round my knees every morning up the nursery and they don't say anything but they make you feel you're making her do it. But I'm desperate for her to go to school. I did cry when I left her the first day. You wouldn't, you're too fucking sensible. You'll call the teacher by her first name. I really fancy you.

(35) VICTORIA: What?

(36) LIN: Put your book down will you for five minutes. You didn't hear a word I said.

(37) VICTORIA: I don't get much time to myself.

[. . .]

[CATHY *comes in with gun, shoots them saying Kiou kiou kiou, and runs off again.* LIN *watches the children playing outside.*]

(50) LIN: Don't hit him, Cathy, kill him. Point the gun, kiou, kiou, kiou. That's the way.

(51) VICTORIA: They've just banned war toys in Sweden.

(52) LIN: The kids'll just hit each other more.

(53) VICTORIA: Well, psychologists do differ in their opinions as to whether or not aggression is innate.

(54) LIN: Yeh?

(55) VICTORIA: I'm afraid I do let Tommy play with guns and just hope he'll get it out of his system and not end up in the army.

(56) LIN: I've got a brother in the army.

(57) VICTORIA: Oh I'm sorry. Whereabouts is he stationed?

(58) LIN: Belfast.

(59) VICTORIA: Oh dear.

(60) LIN: I've got a friend who's Irish and we went on a Troops Out march. Now my dad won't speak to me.

(61) VICTORIA: I don't get on too well with my father either.

(62) LIN: And your husband? How do you get on with him?

(63) VICTORIA: Oh, fine. Up and down. You know. Very well. He helps with the washing up and everything.

(64) LIN: I left mine two years ago. He let me keep Cathy and I'm grateful for that.

(65) VICTORIA: You shouldn't be grateful.

(66) LIN: I'm a lesbian.

(67) VICTORIA: You still shouldn't be grateful.

(68) LIN: I'm grateful he didn't hit me harder than he did.

(69) VICTORIA: I suppose I'm very lucky with Martin.

(70) LIN: Don't get at me about how I bring up Cathy, ok?

(71) VICTORIA: I didn't.

(72) LIN: Yes you did. War toys. I'll give her a rifle for Christmas and blast
Tommy's pretty head off for a start.
[VICTORIA *goes back to her book.*]
(73) LIN: I hate men.
(74) VICTORIA: You have to look at it in a historical perspective in terms of
learnt behaviour since the industrial revolution.
(75) LIN: I just hate the bastards.
(76) VICTORIA: Well it's a point of view.

(Churchill 1985: Act 2, scene 1)

The scene begins with Cathy's racy rhymes, a series of provocative and
unelicited – indeed, unwelcome – Informs (themselves containing embedded
fictional Requests, such as 'Jack jump over the candlestick'). Lin's inter-
jection, addressed to Victoria, is demonstrably not the kind of Acknowledge
that Informs prospect; as her next utterance, a Request, confirms – 'Cathy,
do stop' – she doesn't want to be in conversation with her daughter at all.
But Cathy is not easily 'managed': Lin's next Request to her is bounced
straight back, to be returned again – all routine parent–child friction. When
Cathy seeks guidance – via a Question – on just what to paint (even though
she has just implied she *won't* do a painting: such unannounced changes of
attitude and compliance are not rare in natural child–parent discourse),
Lin's suggestions (Requests) are unsurprisingly rejected. In terms of the 'preferred' prospections of the four canonical acts, we have yet to encounter a
single paired exchange in which a first act (of Requesting, Informing, etc.)
has been compliantly responded to. When Lin's exasperation point is
reached, she resorts to grim humour with the suggestion that Cathy paint a
car crash and blood everywhere. But more funny and ghoulish is Cathy's
Request reply, 'No, don't tell me', again refusing to be constrained as compliant addressee in 'request–comply' exchanges; her counter Request implies
that she wants to have come up with this 'excellent proposal' all by herself.

I shall shortly turn to later exchanges, but before leaving this opening it
may be worth noting that act-labelling is not always as unambiguous as it
has been so far here. Consider, for example, Lin's turn number 20, 'There's a
good girl.' It follows her Request that Cathy lift up her arms, evidently so
that the apron can be put on her. But does the apron actually get put on; and
relatedly, what act does 'There's a good girl' perform here? Does it approximate to 'please', and is thus a reiterated Request? Or does it approximate
'thank you', and is hence an Acknowledgement of performed requested behaviour? Both interpretations seem possible, and different productions of the
play may select either one. Ambiguous moves like this one are important to
reflect upon, since – in the cold print of literary dialogue, especially – they
highlight the genuine variability of uptake or interpretation that attends situated utterance; it is likely that where we can identify a series of such oblique
utterances, systematically interpretable in two contrasting but plausible

ways, we are looking at a key basis of alternative interpretations of the larger scene or story.

This first episode ends with Cathy's resumed Questions 'What shall I do?' . . . 'What shall I do mum?', and the tiresome prospect of another round of unproductive exchanges looms; but Victoria – nice, polite, middle-class, un-self-critiqued Victoria (as we shall soon learn) – diverts Cathy's attention by way of an Inform, in turn 24. There is no explicit Request in Victoria's words at all. Only the fact that the Inform is explicitly directed at Cathy (since Victoria names her), and the appended 'quick', overtly conveys that the Inform entails a suggestion. And clearly Victoria's instincts are right: any-thing more direct in the way of a Proposal to Cathy, we suspect, would be sure to receive nothing but some such reproof as 'No, don't tell me!' (of Requests) or 'I can do it myself!' (of Offers). Jumping ahead a little, notice how Victoria responds when Lin encourages Cathy to 'kill' Tommy with the toy gun. Lin (Requesting) says 'Point the gun, kiou, kiou, kiou. That's the way.' And Victoria, undoubtedly 'signifying' at her, Informs in turn 51: 'They've just banned war toys in Sweden.'

The first thing to notice about this putative Inform is that it is not *directly* relevant to the ongoing interaction between the two children and the two mothers. That is, neither *Sweden* nor *war toys* nor banning things nor *They* has been the explicit or implied topic of the foregoing interaction. So the listener, like Lin, has to assess in what way, if at all, Victoria's contribution here is indirectly relevant to the situation. In the established context, it is clear that Victoria doesn't wish to turn the conversation to Sweden, as such; the link, rather, is with the *war toy* that Cathy is playing with, and the focus of Victoria's remark is on the *banning* of such toys in another country. So we can begin an appropriate interpretation of what Victoria's remark conveys by recognizing that it must be delivered with the dominant intonational empha-sis on *banned* – perhaps a pronounced falling tone on *banned* and a low rising tone on *in Sweden*.

A significant interpretative step clearly remains to be taken: why does Victoria here invite mutual attention to the banning of war toys in Sweden? She might wish to suggest that she finds this deplorable, or ridiculous, or problematic, or admirable: it is difficult to decide which attitude is intended, if the utterance is viewed removed from its context. Perhaps the strongest clue within the utterance is the description *war toy* which, for detailed lexico-grammatical reasons I lack room to explore here, arguably treats the item referred to as more to do with real war, and less to do with toys and play, than do the descriptions like 'toy gun' or 'toy weapon' (compare *war toy* with 'car toy', used to describe a mobile phone: the mobile phone is actually real rather than a toy, and the car in which it sits is also real rather than pretend). But more important than any utterance-internal clues are the indications we gather from the surrounding co-text and context, which cumulatively suggest not merely that Victoria approves of Sweden's banning of war toys but also that, in approving that ban, she herself disapproves of such toys. Hence

Victoria's remark is a good example of what in politeness theory is called an 'off-record' strategy, an indirect hint (Brown and Levinson 1987). There is no overt Request here, and any implicit Request we might postulate ('You shouldn't encourage children to play with toy weapons') is so 'off-record' that we cannot be sure it is intended: what Victoria actually intended might have been a much stronger or much weaker imposition – that is the beauty of indirect hinting speech acts. None of this complexity is lost on Lin, whose immediate Inform rejoinder is certainly worth considering. That is to say, well beyond the confines of this scene, it leads to such questions as the following: 'Is it better for children to really hit each other than to play at killing, if this leads them to grow up still hitting but not killing?' At the same time, Lin does not ignore the unspoken Request we have suspected in Victoria's Inform: much later in the scene she breaks away from the current topic (men) to make the blunt Request: 'Don't get at me about how I bring up Cathy, ok?', and is undeflected by Victoria's denial. Thus the specificities of how characters interact – how Lin Requests and Cathy Requests or Questions back, and of how Victoria implies Proposals by actually uttering mere Informs – provide a rapid and revealing illumination of their contrasting natures. Even this early, a broad pattern is beginning to emerge: working-class and less-educated Lin tends to interact via Proposals (Offers and Requests), which also means doing things and (trying to) get things done; middle-class and educated Victoria tends to interact via Propositions (Informs and Questions), even when particular Proposals are her goal; so on the latter occasions, there is inevitably an indirectness, subtlety, or 'non-face-threatening' politeness to her discourse. These systematic contrasts, which are part of what characterize Lin and Victoria, persist and are exploited in later scenes.

   Limitations of space prevent me from going through the entire dialogue at a similar level of detail. But in the exchanges between Lin and Victoria which lead up to turn 34 it becomes clear, from her minimal Informs and Acknowledgements, that Victoria is a reluctant conversationalist here: while Lin wants to be talking with Victoria, Victoria would evidently rather be reading. This is not lost on Lin; at the end of a lengthy rehearsal of her anxieties about Cathy, evidently wasted on Victoria since she neither expresses sympathy nor even pays attention, Lin daringly and amusingly breaks out of the conventionalities and resets the interactional footing with an entirely *un*prospected Inform: 'I really fancy you.' The fact that in response to Victoria's checking Question 'What?' Lin does not repeat or reformulate this Inform (as usually happens following checking Questions) leaves us uncertain as to whether 'I really fancy you' was said only as a joke, as an attention-getter; and uncertain whether, if sincere, the declaration is un-repeated due to some lapse in Lin's confidence. But like any *powerful* speech act (by which I mean, broadly, any act with the potential to trigger multiple significant interactional consequences) that 'I really fancy you' resonates long after in this scene and beyond it, long after its lack of local uptake has been forgotten. This is partly so since the entire play thematizes elected and spontaneous shifts in sexual and emotional affiliation, but also because in later scenes we find that Lin and Victoria have become lovers.

There is not space here to look at length and in appropriate analytical detail at how humour is created in the passage. Some comments on just one instance will have to suffice – namely, the humour generated in the course of Lin's and Victoria's final turns in the reproduced passage, turns 73–6. Again, speech act analysis seems relevant. Turns 73, 75 and 76 are Informs, while in turn 74 Victoria produces a modalized Request concerning how we *have to* understand the historical basis of men's behaviour. But Lin will have nothing to do with this suggestion, as her use of 'just' makes clear. But before commenting further, we can sensitize ourselves to the importance of the specific way in which turn 75 is phrased by comparing it with other possible responses which Lin could have used but did not:

LIN: I hate men.
VICTORIA: You have to look at it in a historical perspective in terms of learnt behaviour since the industrial revolution.
LIN: I hate men.
  or I just hate men.
  or I just hate them.
  or I loathe the bastards.
  or I just loathe the bastards.
  or I hate the way that they blame you for everything wrong with their lives and claim all the credit for everything that's right with their lives.
  or No I don't.
  or Why should I?
  or What's that got to do with my ex-?

And so on. None of these, I would suggest, is as funny or works quite the same effect as Lin's actual reply. And those alternatives which are closest to the actual reply, such as 'I just loathe the bastards', may be the most illuminating of what sets the actual reply apart.

The first thing to note about turn 75 is that, in the context of turn 74, it is thoroughly unprospected. But it would not be both unprospected and funny if it did not exploit (a) speech act logic and (b) cohesion logic in quite the way it does. In terms of speech act logic, turn 75 is unexpectedly redundant, and therefore significant in its redundancy: it is an Inform which is virtually a copy of Lin's prior Inform, turn 73. In terms of cohesion logic, where it does not link to turn 73 by means of simple repetition it links by means of substituting a general term for an evaluative epithet, introduced by the definite article. The effect of this is that speaker (and attending listener) skip over an intermediate proposition, that 'men are bastards', which is then 'taken as read'. Lin's 'point of view', as Victoria gamely calls it, is thus all the more succinctly encapsulated (Victoria here does more of that middle-class relexicalizing of abuse as 'opinion' to which she is prone). And Lin's succinctness in comparison with Victoria's lengthy and wordy abstraction is already a source of humorous contrast.

Here I must end, with an invitation to the reader to analyse further *Cloud Nine* and its ingenious exploitations of speech-act sequences and pre-suppositions, and to apply the model sketched here to a range of fictional and actual dialogues. Some readers may still be asking: Why should we bother with all this laborious and fallible classification? And why, in particular, should it be thought that this has any relevance to the reading and appreciation of literature? A decent reply to these doubts should begin by considering how one might proceed to study drama dialogue *without* recourse to systems, methods, and inventories. What is likely to happen is that, on a step-by-conversational-step basis, you notice how Lin 'shares' while Victoria is more reserved; how Lin tells her child to do things while Victoria barely does at all, and quickly gives up the effort; how Lin pesters and prods Victoria. But what you would be unable to do would be to locate these tendencies – however acutely recognized and described in their particularity – within a *general* scheme of interactional possibilities. It is one thing to note that one character makes a series of impositive requests of another character; but we cannot grasp the full significance of this unless we have a clearer understanding of the complete range of possible discourse acts that an interactant could perform; this is what any general description of discourse acts attempts to articulate. By analogy, to describe a shirt as cyan is only fully understood if speaker and addressee have a shared grasp of the full set of colour terms, and in particular the set of terms for shades of blue, that is being assumed. Our general description of discourse acts attempts to map, in themselves and relative to each other, the foundational colours to be found on the spectrum of interactional possibilities.

SUGGESTIONS FOR FURTHER WORK

1 By way of getting practice at teasing out the range of acts performable with a single, variously inflected and variously contextualized utterance, consider the following turn:

> Can I help you?

Sketch at least three different scenarios in which this utterance might be used, perhaps delivered with a different prosody in each case, so as to perform a distinct kind of act (now a Question, now an Offer, and so on).

2 What follows is an extract from Kazuo Ishiguro's novel, *The Remains of the Day* (1990), a novel which in part charts the undeveloped and unexplored human relationship of two people in service in England between the world wars (Mr Stevens, the butler, and Miss Kenton, the housekeeper). There are many indications in the novel that Miss Kenton would have welcomed a personal relationship with Mr Stevens – namely, marriage – which, it transpires, Mr Stevens is incapable of proposing. Stevens is dehumanized

by his mindset of deference. But these are rude summaries, while the text itself is subtle and suggestive. Work through the dialogue provided below, taken from fairly late in the book, commenting on the kinds of speech acts which predominate, noting to what extent these seem to be oblique or indirectly expressed and why. To what extent is the dialogue shaped by Informs *about* prior Informs, and similar reflexive or backward-looking commentary? If at the back of this conversation is Miss Kenton's tacit wish that Stevens come out with a very particular kind of Proposal, what are the discoursal means by which – seemingly unconsciously, on Stevens's part – this proposal remains irretrievably buried?

'We did agree to my taking this evening off a fortnight ago, Mr Stevens.'

'Of course, Miss Kenton. I do beg your pardon.'

I turned to leave, but then I was halted at the door by Miss Kenton saying:

'Mr Stevens, I have something to tell you.'

'Yes, Miss Kenton?'

'It concerns my acquaintance. Who I am going to meet tonight.'

'Yes, Miss Kenton.'

'He has asked me to marry him. I thought you had a right to know that.'

'Indeed, Miss Kenton. That is very interesting.'

'I am still giving the matter thought.'

'Indeed.'

She glanced down a second at her hands, but then almost immediately her gaze returned to me. 'My acquaintance is to start a job in the West Country as of next month.'

'Indeed.'

'As I say, Mr Stevens, I am still giving the matter some thought. However, I thought you should be informed of the situation.'

'I'm very grateful, Miss Kenton. I do hope you have a pleasant evening. Now if you will excuse me.'

[. . .]

'Mr Stevens, do I understand that you are wishing me to remain on duty this evening?'

'Not at all, Miss Kenton. As you pointed out, you did notify me some time ago.'

'But I can see you are very unhappy about my going out tonight.'

'On the contrary, Miss Kenton.'

'Do you imagine that by creating so much commotion in the kitchen and by stamping back and forth like this outside my parlour you will get me to change my mind?'

'Miss Kenton, the slight excitement in the kitchen is solely on account of Mr Cardinal coming to dinner at the last moment. There is absolutely no reason why you should not go out this evening.'

'I intend to go with or without your blessing, Mr Stevens, I wish to make this clear. I made arrangements weeks ago.'

'Indeed, Miss Kenton. And once again, I would wish you a very pleasant evening.'

(Ishiguro 1990: 215–16)

NOTES

1 The organization of speech acts into connected sequences, where certain sequences are particularly common, is usually called 'preference organization'. See Levinson (1983: 332).

12 Advice on doing your stylistics essay on a dramatic text

An example from Alan Ayckbourn's
The Revengers' Comedies

Peter K. W. Tan

EDITORS' PREFACE

For the final chapter of this book, Peter Tan discusses how to go about writing a stylistics essay on an extract from a dramatic text. First of all, he discusses factors to consider when choosing a text to analyse and the most appropriate methods of analysis to apply to that text. He then exemplifies how to do the analytical research for the essay by examining the beginning of Alan Ayckbourn's *The Revengers' Comedies* from the perspective of a series of different discoursal and pragmatic approaches to textual analysis. During the course of his discussion, he relates his various analytical findings together in order to show in detail the basis for the pre-analytical views about the play, and its characters, which he had formed on first seeing the play. Tan's description itself provides an exemplification of how to write up a stylistics essay after having carried out the analytical research.

INTRODUCTION: CHOOSING A TEXT TO ANALYSE

In this chapter, I want to explore how best to write a stylistics essay on a dramatic text. I will go through the steps from choosing an extract to writing up the final analysis. I am not suggesting, of course, that the process I describe is the only way of doing the job; though I would argue that a systematic approach generally yields the best results.

It may be that a particular excerpt has been assigned for analysis, or you might be required to choose your own passage. You may have been asked to perform an analysis using a particular framework, e.g. politeness theory; or you may have been left to choose whatever frameworks are appropriate.

Let's assume that the choice of passage and framework has been left to you. (If it hasn't, then the task will be more straightforward.) Should you choose an 'established' and familiar play, perhaps a text that you studied at school, or a text which has already attracted a large amount of critical attention? Some students are understandably modest about their own reactions and intuitions, preferring to rely on established texts, and corroborating their interpretations by what eminent critics have said. The problem with this strategy is that it is potentially stultifying. It is usually more helpful to think of your stylistics essay not as an exercise in exemplifying established opinion but as an attempt to interpret or re-interpret a text systematically. It is only in that way that you can develop your own critical skills. If you do feel the need to look at an extract which others have already commented on, it is often a good idea to choose one which has a critical commentary with which you disagree, at least to some extent. This will help you to sharpen up your own critical and analytical ideas, and to demonstrate your independent thoughts, supporting them by analysis.

I generally find it helpful to let my reactions guide me in the choice of text. What is interesting, amusing, significant, problematic or enigmatic often makes for a very good text to analyse. Significant moments in plays usually have lots of things going on textually, and your 'game plan' is to try to show how important meanings and effects are created through your interaction with the words on the page. But note that not all texts allow you easily to display your analytical wares. Our intuitive understanding runs far in advance of our ability to demonstrate that understanding through analysis. So it is important to choose an extract which you find attractive both for itself and which you can also cope with in analytical terms. This is particularly the case if you are being asked to analyse a text using a restricted set of analytical approaches: the text needs to be interesting to analyse in terms of those particular approaches, as well as for its own sake.

Another significant factor in text selection is the length and 'shape' of the extract. You want something which forms a coherent whole, but which at the same time is no longer than one to two pages. If it forms a coherent dramatic 'unit', you will be able to describe how its parts 'add up' to produce its overall meaning and effect. But it is just as important not to choose too long an extract. If you do, you will find that, because stylistic analysis takes up a lot of words, either you will have an unacceptably long essay, or you will not be able to go into enough analytical detail, thereby running the risk of being accused of being vague and imprecise. I have chosen to deal with a very short opening scene from Alan Ayckbourn's *The Revengers' Comedies*. I have chosen it partly because I enjoyed watching it on stage in London in 1991, and then listening to it when it was broadcast on the BBC World Service in 1995.[1] It is a relatively successful play in box-office terms, with plenty of humour and action. So, one of our main objectives will be to explain this humour and dynamism.

I have chosen the *beginning* of the play for analysis for two reasons. The first is an eminently practical one: there will be no need for me to provide background information as to what has happened before the extract analysed. The second reason is to do with dramatic impact: opening scenes are usually crucial for playwrights because it is here that they can manipulate the audience's or readers' initial reactions to the characters, and first impressions are always important dramatically. Characterization, and how it is achieved, will therefore be central in the analysis.

Below, I present the text to be analysed, and follow it, first by a statement of some general interpretative impressions, and then by a more detailed analysis, concentrating on analytical aspects which are relevant to that initial statement (i.e. those aspects which support, and 'flesh out' that general statement). This ordering will help you to be able to follow my argument better. It is usually best for you to go from the general to the particular, and I would recommend this overall structure for when you write up your essay.

Note, however, that the 'structure' of your research leading to the writing of your essay will be a bit different. After reading the text a few times, and jotting down your first impressions, you will need to analyse the text carefully and systematically in terms of all the linguistic aspects that would appear to be interpretatively relevant. You should be on the look-out for linguistic evidence which (a) supports your initial interpretative hypotheses, (b) helps you to 'flesh out' your interpretation in more detail, and with more analytical sophistication, or (c) goes against your initial hypotheses in either a minor or a major way. You shouldn't assume that all you will find will be proof for your views. The evidence of careful stylistic analysis, if used well, can often lead you to modify your initial views, and so improve your overall interpretation. Interpretation is generally not static, and there have been many occasions when I have revised my first impression of a text after analysis; on other occasions, the analysis has been useful in explaining why I reacted to the text the way I did.

Finally, once you have arrived at a fully formed interpretation, you will need to *select*, from the mass of data you have collected, those aspects which are most crucial interpretatively. If there are important linguistic aspects which you have uncovered, and which you still can't properly account for, my advice would be to state them in your essay rather than disguise them. Most tutors prefer students who can be rationally critical of their own work, as well as that of others!

THE EXCERPT

[*Midnight.*]

[*Albert Bridge, SW3. Perhaps a little river mist. Distant traffic, a ship's siren. Henry, a man in his early forties, appears in a pool of street light on the bridge. He is wrapped in an overcoat and scarf. He is hunched and miserable. He stares over the edge, deciding whether to jump. From his expression, it's evidently a long way down. He says a little silent prayer, as though asking forgiveness, and makes to climb over the railing. He is uncomfortably straddled across the railing and in some discomfort when he hears a woman's voice from the darkness.*]

(1) KAREN: [*Calling*] Help ... Help ... Please help me ...
           [HENRY *stops and listens, rather startled.*]
(2) HENRY: [*Calling, tentatively*] Hallo?
(3) KAREN: [*Calling back*] Hallo ...

(4) HENRY: [*Calling again*] Hallo?
(5) KAREN: Would you stop saying hallo and come and help me, please? I've got myself caught up here . . .
(6) HENRY: Oh, right. Hang on, there . . . Just hang on . . .
[*He starts to clamber back on to the bridge.*]
(7) KAREN: I don't have any option. I've been hanging here for hours.
(8) HENRY: Just one very small second . . .
[HENRY *moves to the source of her voice. As he does so, we make out* KAREN *for the first time. She is in her mid-twenties. She wears a woolly hat and a lightweight coat over an evening dress. She is hanging outside the bridge railing. All that seems to be keeping her from falling is the belt of her coat, which has become entangled with the ironwork.* HENRY *reaches her.*]
Oh, Lord. How can I . . .?
(9) KAREN: [*Trying to indicate*] Do you see? Something's caught – I think it's the belt of my coat . . .
(10) HENRY: Oh, yes, yes. Look, I think I'd better . . . [*Flustered*] Look – er . . . Yes, yes. I think I'd better try and – er . . . Would you mind if I – tried to lift you . . .?
(11) KAREN: You can do what you like – just get me off this bloody bridge . . .
(12) HENRY: Yes, yes, right . . . [*He studies the problem.*]
(13) KAREN: Can you see? I think it's my belt . . .
(14) HENRY: Yes, yes, so it is. I think I'd better get that free before I . . .
[*He starts to untangle the belt.*]
(15) KAREN: Careful –
(16) HENRY: Yes. Only I don't want to tear your coat, you see. If I tried to lift you over as you are, I might damage it . . . It's a very nice coat . . .
(17) KAREN: [*Sarcastically*] Well, that's very considerate of you . . . Thank you.
(18) HENRY: [*Finally freeing the belt*] Right. There you go, all free.

(Ayckbourn 1991: 1–2)

GENERAL IMPRESSIONS

One important concern, particularly if you have watched a performance of the play in question, is being able distinguish between the text and the stage version of the text. I follow Short (1989: 139–43) and Elam (1980: 2–3) in using the term 'drama' to refer to the text or the 'fiction', and 'theatre' to refer to the performance. The term 'dramatize' itself is interesting in that it suggests a change of state, a transformation of the original genre. There is also a sense in which a dramatic text is 'incomplete' without a performance because the stage directions frequently make overt references to the props or the movement of characters on the stage. Interestingly, although most of the Ayckbourn excerpt's stage directions are explicit, some of them appear only to be tentative suggestions (e.g. *Perhaps a little river mist*), allowing the director some leeway in the creation of appropriate stage effects (for a consideration of the relation between text and performance, see Short, this volume).

If you have already watched the play, it might be useful to try to separate what is in the text and what is not – i.e. which of your impressions result from the particular performance you saw. If you haven't, it might be useful to try to 'see' and 'hear' the scene mentally, letting the stage directions evoke mental pictures for you. Let me try to put down my own general impressions:

1 the opening seems rather melodramatic, even a little clichéd (midnight, mist, person praying for forgiveness);
2 the melodrama seems to disintegrate into buffoonery (cf. the awful 'hang on' pun);
3 Henry seems to be a bumbling idiot;
4 although her situation appears to be desperate, Karen seems rather acerbic.

WHICH APPROACH?

We are now ready to move on to the analysis itself. I said earlier that I shall assume that the approach has not been prescribed. We now need to decide what sort of linguistic framework should be used in our analysis. One of this book's earlier companion volumes, *Twentieth-Century Poetry: From Text to Context* (Verdonk 1993), for example, deals with the analysis of phonological, grammatical, lexical and pragmatic elements in poetry, together with other discussions of interpersonal relationships and of the cultural context. Poetry and prose have been thought of as being amenable to approaches that emphasize the ideational function of language: language used to convey experience and information about the context. Analyses based on the structuring of sound, sentence and semantic patterns have been used to discuss the meanings and themes of poems and prose passages. All of these are potentially useful frameworks for analysing dramatic texts too, but clearly the pragmatic and discoursal frameworks explored in the other chapters in this volume are likely to have most relevance. The choice of which approach or approaches to use depends on which will bear the most fruit, as it were. And this, in turn, depends on the nature of the text chosen for analysis.

Although we should not forget that there is dialogue in the novel, or that many poems have 'conversations' within them, it is dramatic texts that are usually thought of as giving more emphasis to the interpersonal function of language (cf. Halliday 1994) because drama is prototypically the literary genre which is composed almost entirely of face-to-face interaction between characters. The interpersonal function relates to how language is used as a resource for developing relations, or for hindering relations from developing. Approaches based on pragmatics, discourse analysis or conversation analysis are frequently used to throw light on interpersonal relations, and could therefore help us analyse the dialogue in plays, as the earlier chapters in this volume have shown.

Many of Shakespeare's plays and some of T. S. Eliot's (e.g. *Murder in the Cathedral*) are composed in verse, and even some of Stoppard's plays (e.g. *Rosencrantz and Guildenstern are Dead*) rely on word play and patterning for their effect. So, extracts chosen from plays like these would need 'poetic' analysis as part of an overall account. But, by and large, *The Revengers' Comedies* does not exploit the poetic function of language. I will therefore make use of a number of frameworks that focus on the interpersonal function of language, making tentative 'local' interpretations based on the analyses of the excerpt, in turn linking the analyses to the general impressions noted above.

THE ANALYSIS

The situation portrayed is a very dramatic one – two characters, both apparently contemplating suicide, happen to meet on the same bridge in London. Karen has presumably tried to throw herself off the bridge but has got her belt caught in the ironwork. Henry is shaken out of his own thoughts of suicide by the need to rescue Karen. Given these dramatic circumstances, it is highly likely that these two are central characters in the play, and therefore we should be watching them closely. We need to know what they are like, by observing the way they interact with each other.

There is nothing 'poetic' or 'lyrical' about the excerpt. Instead, we have two characters who are keen on interacting and doing things to and for each other. There is also plenty of action, and we shall need to take this into account whilst trying to work out what the characters are like.

TURN-TAKING

We know that whenever there is dialogue, turn-taking mechanisms must be in operation. If the mechanisms operate well, there should be minimal overlaps or instances of pauses or interruptions (see Herman and Simpson, this volume).

One turn that might possibly be less well-constructed is turn 10, where Henry appears to have problems completing his turn. Three of the sentences are incomplete:

* Look, I think I'd better . . .
* Look – er . . .
* I think I'd better try and – er . . .

We need to interpret how the punctuation is used here, as Ayckbourn is distinguishing systematically between '–' and '. . .'. Among other things, the dash can be used to indicate a break in the sentence, or a pause; it could indicate both here. Similarly, the trailing dots could just indicate an incomplete sentence, or a trailing off of the voice at the end of a grammatically complete structure, suggesting a lack of discourse cohesion at the turn-boundary. In both cases, in performance these graphological markers will probably be realized as pauses – what Stenström (1994: 1) calls 'silent pauses'. But it looks as if Ayckbourn is distinguishing brief pauses ('–') from longer ones ('. . .') in order to help the reader and actor establish the rhythm of hesitant incoherence which he wants Henry to have. Henry also uses 'er' – what Stenström (1994: 1) calls a filled pause. Henry's contribution in turn 14, with its incomplete sentence and trailing dots is similar in effect to 10, but less extensive in its use of the pause. The stage directions tell us that Henry is 'flustered', and his problem in completing his turn is apparently complicated by the fact that he is so embarrassed by working out how to free Karen without 'interfering' with her that he is not able to concentrate enough on what he is saying. Karen's utterances also often end with '. . .', but her contributions are direct and grammatically complete, suggesting that the silent pause indicated is because Henry does not respond as quickly as we would normally expect, again indicating his undue hesitancy. However, there are no complete breakdowns in the turn-taking mechanism.

SPEECH AND DISCOURSE ACTS

I mentioned earlier that there seems to be a lot happening in the excerpt, and that Karen and Henry are doing things to, or for, each other. A useful starting point in stylistic analysis is to consider the speech acts being performed (see Lowe and Toolan, this volume), not only at a local level but also more globally. Henry is performing the overall *physical* act of rescuing Karen from her predicament, specifically pulling her up from the bridge, which in turn comes about as a response to the overall *speech* act performed by Karen – that of requesting help, a request to which he must have effectively acceded. These speech acts can therefore be seen as necessary preliminaries to the physical act of the rescue.

Under normal circumstances, we would have expected that, as the need for the physical action to be completed is fairly urgent, the preliminary local speech acts would be kept to the minimum, and that more expansive speech acts would be left for after the physical action has been completed. Talk should be kept to the minimum under such circumstances, and where there is talk the speech acts should normally serve to facilitate physical actions. As such, directives[2] and commissives would not be surprising, as these speech acts serve to effect physical change. Representatives, on the other hand, would not be expected; Henry's explanation in turn 16 seems redundant (and this is confirmed by Karen's reprimand in turn 17). Even more surprising is that some of the earlier turns constitute *metalinguistic* speech acts (see Chapter 4 in this volume), i.e. speech acts that comment on other speech acts (cf. Henry's requests for repetition in turns 2 and 4, and Karen's sarcastic response, in turn 17, to Henry's inappropriate concern for her coat). It is not surprising in these circumstances that the characters talk to one another, but it is surprising that so much of it is talk about talk. These instances when, somehow, our expectations as readers are not met[3] generally call for some interpretation on our part. The author appears to be trying to convey something about the relationship between the situation and the characters, for example that one or both of them do not appreciate the seriousness of the circumstances, something which leads to near absurdity.

CO-OPERATION

A lot of the work done in pragmatics discusses the way in which participants exchange information (see Cooper, this volume). This is an obvious starting point for our estimation of how Karen and Henry relate to the situation and to each other. To the extent that Karen and Henry are talking relevantly to each other, we can say that they are engaged in a co-operative exchange. In other words, each turn does relate to the previous turn.

But there does seem to be too much talk, and therefore this excerpt fails to observe Grice's (1975) quantity maxim. Although Henry talks too much, he does not appear to intend Karen to notice this. However, because we know that the dramatic text has been written, and, indeed, has probably gone through several stages of revision, we can assume that, from the point of view of the author, the breach of the quantity maxim is deliberate and open. In other words, the author has flouted the maxim of quantity in order to help us to infer something about Henry. We could thus conclude that Henry's over-wordiness and inappropriate remarks are part of Ayckbourn's characterization of him as a somewhat ineffectual person – a rather timorous character who tries to cover up his fear and social inadequacy with unnecessary and inappropriate words. Henry's non-fluency, which I discussed in the turn-taking section, can also be seen as a flout by the author of Grice's maxim of manner, leading to an interpretation in line with what we have already noticed.

Given the emergency situation, we might also expect Karen not to talk as much as she does. Her ironic and sarcastic remarks (turns 7 and 17) do not seem likely to ameliorate her situation. From her flouting of the quantity maxim (and the quality maxim as well in turn 17), it would appear that Karen cannot stop herself from making caustic remarks, no matter how dire the circumstances – perhaps because this is part of her character, or because of some bitterness as a result of how life has treated her.

POLITENESS

Most requests (for attention, for action, for permission, etc.) are accompanied by politeness strategies because they are inherently face-threatening: they seek the hearer to do something for the benefit of the speaker (see Bennison and Culpeper, this volume).

Karen's initial request, as we would expect, given the situation, is uttered directly ('Help . . . Help'), without any politeness strategies. The pay-off of direct requests is their efficiency, and in emergency situations there are more important things than face to worry about (Brown and Levinson 1987: 72). The *urgent* need for action to be taken – i.e. help to be given to Karen – and the relatively small cost to Henry both make it unsurprising that the direct strategy is used. However, when Henry and Karen get stuck in the groove and keep repeating 'Hallo', Karen makes another request – but this time for Henry to stop talking. She uses the conventionally indirect way of phrasing her request ('Would you . . . ?'), because of the threat (a) to Henry's negative face in requiring him to do something and (b) his positive face in her criticism that his echo-speech is inappropriate in the circumstances.

Henry also begins by using direct requests ('Hang on, there . . . Just hang on . . .'), as is appropriate given the context. Even here, though 'just' is a hedge (normally used to mitigate in negative politeness), and in any case what he is commanding Karen to do is clearly in her interest and so is negatively polite. Given the context, the appropriate response would be to accept the request, but instead Karen criticizes it ('I don't have any option . . .'). The criticism seems gratuitous because it doesn't help to expedite the task to hand. Henry's next request, 'Would you mind if I . . . tried to lift you . . . ?' is conventionally indirect and therefore polite; and again the action he proposes to carry out is beneficial rather than 'costly' to Karen. This, and the fact that this is an emergency situation, makes Henry's politeness unnecessary, and therefore comic. Karen's response is again critical, this time emphasized by the expletive 'bloody'.

This pattern repeats itself. In turn 16, Henry explains his tardiness as being due to his not wanting to damage Karen's 'nice coat' – a positive evaluation, and therefore polite, but clearly inappropriate, given the need to get on and save Karen. Her response, as stated in the stage direction, is sarcastic.

We therefore have one character, Henry, who is overly and unnecessarily polite, and another, Karen, who is unnecessarily impolite, even though she is in dire need of help. I have already suggested that Henry seems to be portrayed as being ineffectual, and his being overly polite underlines this. Karen's bitterness could well be related to her earlier, unsuccessful, attempt to throw herself off the bridge (we learn subsequently that she conceives this act as her 'revenge' on Anthony Staxton-Billings, who apparently 'betrayed' her). We have clearly been introduced to two dramatically contrasting characters; and it is this oppositional mismatch which will generate much of the impetus for the development of the play.

COMPARING THE ANALYSIS WITH THE GENERAL IMPRESSION

It will now be helpful if I compare my analysis with what I said in the 'General Impressions' section of this chapter. I made two related points about the nature of the play and two points about the characters. The first point about the melodramatic nature of the excerpt is perhaps difficult to give concrete linguistic evidence for; it may be that I should give examples of other plays (or films and television dramas) that make use of this formula. My second point related to how I thought we weren't supposed to take the play too seriously. I think the analysis of the characters' exchanges can be used to support this point – the fact that they talk so much in an emergency situation and that Henry is so polite and Karen so sarcastic. The analysis has also shown how Henry's and Karen's conversational behaviour contrasts with one another, and this clearly provides support for my initial impressions of the two characters.

When analysing dramatic texts, it is also important to remember that inter-action seems to happen at two levels at least. There is, on the one hand, character-to-character interaction; and, on the other hand, author-to-reader/audience interaction (see Short 1989, and 1996: 168–72) As we ana-lyse dramatic texts we need to come to terms with these two levels and how they interact. Earlier, I mentioned (a) the rather excessive talk between the characters; (b) Henry's tendency towards over-politeness and (c) Karen's tendency towards rudeness. We find out later in the play that it is Henry's ineffectualness that caused him to lose his job. It is this aspect of his character that he has to overcome by the end of the play. Karen's sharpness helps pre-pare us for her rather warped view of life, and her inability to come to terms with her family and other relationships (the play suggests that she had a hand in the death of her parents). The way the play has been set up to portray a potential clash of characters might also lead us to expect some sort of treat-ment about how to deal with this; and this is, in fact, what happens.

CONCLUSION

Once you have completed your research and analysis stage, you can plan the structure of your essay and write it up. There are several ways of organizing an essay. You can summarize your interpretation first, and the rest of the essay will mainly provide proof or evidence for your interpretation (this will be a deductive essay; see Colomb and Williams 1985: 122.) Or you can analyse the excerpt first, pointing out its main features. Then, based on this, you can interpret the passage in its own terms, and in relation to the rest of the play. (This will be an inductive essay.) The former structure is often easiest for a reader to follow, and it is probably a good idea to marshal your evidence so that the most salient points come first, as this will help to strengthen the argument-flow of your writing. Whichever kind of essay you write, it is essential that throughout you relate your interpretation to your analysis in a clear and concrete manner. You can do this by quoting relevant parts of the text, or by giving appropriate line or turn numbers, and then pro-viding the detailed linguistic analysis to support your interpretative points. It is important, however, that you do not just quote, or refer to, the relevant part of the text and stop there. It is the detailed analysis of the text in relation to meaning and effect that is the *modus vivendi* of stylistic analysis.

Sometimes it might be appropriate to provide statistical accounts of the text (e.g. number of words spoken by each character; number of different kinds of speech acts), particularly if you are wanting to contrast different parts of a play or different character-behaviours over stretches of text large enough to make statistical work appropriate. Sometimes it is helpful to provide this sort of evidence in the form of a table, as it provides summary information in a clear form which can be referred to in different parts of the essay. I haven't provided statistical information in this chapter as the extract is too short to yield reliable statistical data.

Finally, when you have completed the writing up, don't forget to check that your essay holds together well, is free of mechanical errors and has the relevant bibliographical information and an attached copy of the text analysed. After having put in all that thought and complex analytical work, you don't want to irritate your tutor by forgetting to do the simple and obvious things!

NOTES

1 *The Revengers' Comedies* was first staged in Scarborough (in the North of England) in 1989. One reviewer described it as a 'ripping yarn' that would keep the audience 'on [their] seat[s] waiting to find out what happens next' (Edwardes 1991, cited in Kalson 1993: 165).
2 I use Searle's (1969) five categories of speech acts here: representatives (e.g. stating); directives (e.g. ordering, requesting, questioning); commissives (e.g. undertaking, promising); expressives (expressing emotional state); and declarations (effecting a change in status).
3 The mismatch between the reader's expectations and what is there in the text is generally discussed under the term 'foregrounding': see, for instance, the relevant entry in Wales (1989: 181–2). The related term 'deautomatization' emphasizes the fact that readers are to some extent estranged from the text, and therefore that the element of surprise or counter-expectation is crucial.

Bibliography

Apte, M. L. (1985) *Humor and Laughter*, London and Ithaca: Cornell University Press.

Aston, E. and Savona, G. (1991) *Theatre as Sign-System: A Semiotics of Text and Performance*, London: Routledge.

Austin, J. L. (1962) *How to do Things with Words*, London: Oxford University Press.

Ayckbourn, A. (1977) *Between Mouthfuls*. In *Confusions: Five Inter-Linked One Act Plays*, London: Samuel French.

Ayckbourn, A. (1991) *The Revengers' Comedies*, London: Faber and Faber.

Bach, K. and Harnish, R. M. (1979) *Linguistic Communication and Speech Acts*, Cambridge, Mass.: MIT Press.

Bartlett, F. C. (1932) *Remembering: A Study in Experimental and Social Psychology*, Cambridge: Cambridge University Press.

Berkoff, S. (1983) 'Greek', in *Decadence and Greek*, London: Calder.

Bernstein, B. (1971) *Class, Codes and Control 1*, London: Routledge and Kegan Paul.

Birch, D. (1991) *The Language of Drama*, London: Macmillan.

Bradley, A. C. (1904) *Shakespearean Tragedy*, London: Macmillan.

Brecht, B. (1964) *Brecht on Theatre* (translated by J. Willett), London: Methuen.

Bremond, C. (1966) 'La Logique des Possibles Narratifs', *Communications* 4: 4–32.

Bremond, C. (1973) *Logique du récit*, Paris: Seuil.

Brooke, N. (ed.) (1990) *The Tragedy of Macbeth*, Oxford: Clarendon Press.

Brown, G. and Yule, G. (1983) *Discourse Analysis*, Cambridge: Cambridge University Press.

Brown, P. and Levinson, S. (1978) 'Universals in Language Usage: Politeness Phenomena', in E. Goody (ed.) *Questions and Politeness Strategies in Social Interaction*, Cambridge: Cambridge University Press, 56–289.

Brown, P. and Levinson, S. C. (1987) *Politeness: Some Universals in Language Usage* Cambridge: Cambridge University Press.

Bruce, B. (1981) 'A Social Interaction Model of Reading', *Discourse Processes* 4: 273–311.

Buck, R. A. and Austin, T. R. (1995) 'Dialogue and Power in E.M. Forster's *Howards End*', in P. Verdonk and J. J. Weber (eds) *Twentieth-Century Fiction: From Text to Context*, London: Routledge, 63–77.

Burton, D. (1980) *Dialogue and Discourse*, London: Routledge and Kegan Paul.

Calvo, C. (1997) *The Year's Work in English Studies 76 (1995)*, Oxford: Blackwell, Chapter 2, Section 9.

Camus, A. (1984 [1955]) *The Myth of Sisyphus*, Harmondsworth: Penguin.

Chafe, W. (1985). 'Some Reasons for Hesitating', in D. Tannen and M. Saville-Troike (eds) *Perspectives on Silence*, Norwood, N.J.: Ablex, 77–93.

Churchill, C. (1991 [1984]) *Top Girls*, London: Methuen.

Churchill, C. (1985) *Plays-one*, London: Methuen.

Colomb, G. G. and Williams J. M. (1985) 'Perceiving Structure in Professional Prose: A Multiply Determined Experience', in L. Odell and D. Goswami (eds) *Writing in Nonacademic Settings*, New York: Guilford, 87–128.

Cook, G. (1990) 'Goals and Plans in Advertising and Literary Discourse', *Parlance* 2: 48–71.

Cook, G. (1994) *Discourse and Literature: The Interplay of Form and Mind*, Oxford: Oxford University Press.

Coulthard, M. (1985) *An Introduction to Discourse Analysis*, London: Longman.

Coulthard, M. (ed.) (1992) *Advances in Spoken Discourse Analysis*, London: Routledge.

Coupland, N., Wiemann, J. and Giles, H. (1991) 'Talk as "Problem" and Communication as "Miscommunication": An Integrative Analysis', in N. Coupland, H. Giles and J. Wiemann (eds) *'Miscommunication' and Problematic Talk*, London: Sage, 1–17.

Csicsila, J. (1995) 'Review of Oleanna', *The David Mamet Review* 2: 5–6.

Culpeper, J. (1996) 'Towards an Anatomy of Impoliteness', *Journal of Pragmatics* 25: 349–67.

Daniels, S. (1984) *Masterpieces*, London: Methuen.

De Quincey, T. (1897 [1823]) 'On the Knocking at the Gate in Macbeth', in D. Masson (ed.) *The Collected Writings of Thomas De Quincey*, 10, London: A. & C. Black, 389–94.

Downes, W. (1988) 'Discourse and Drama: King Lear's "Question" to his Daughters', in W. van Peer (ed.) *The Taming of The Text: Explorations in Language Literature and Culture*, London: Routledge, 225–57.

Drew, P. and Wootton, A. (eds) (1988) *Erving Goffman: Exploring the Interaction Order*, Cambridge: Polity Press.

Durant, A. and Fabb, N. (1990) *Literary Studies in Action*, London: Routledge.

Eagleton, T. (1967) *Shakespeare and Society*, London: Chatto and Windus.

Edelsky, C. (1993) 'Who's Got the Floor?', in D. Tannen (ed.) *Gender and Conversational Interaction*, New York and Oxford: Oxford University Press, 189–227.

Edwardes, J. (1991) 'Time Out', *Theatre Record* XI, 21: 1293–4.

Elam, K. (1980) *The Semiotics of Theatre and Drama*, London: Methuen.

Erickson, B., Lind, A. E., Johnson, B. C. and O'Barr, W. M. (1978) 'Speech Style and Impression Formation in a Court Setting: The Effects of "Powerful" and "Powerless" Speech', *Journal of Experimental Social Psychology* 14: 266–79.

Esslin, M. (1965) 'Introduction', in M. Esslin (ed.) *Absurd Drama*, Harmondsworth: Penguin, 7–23.

Esslin, M. (1980) *The Theatre of the Absurd*, Harmondsworth: Penguin.

Everett, B. (1989) 'Macbeth: succeeding', in B. Everett, *Young Hamlet: Essays on Shakespeare's Tragedies*, Oxford: Clarendon Press, 95–105.

Fairclough, N. (1989) *Language and Power*, London: Longman.

Fairclough, N. (1995) *Critical Discourse Analysis*, London: Longman.

Findlater, R. (1967) *Banned! A Review of Theatrical Censorship in Britain*, London: MacGibbon and Kee.

Forster, E. (1987 [1927]) *Aspects of the Novel*, Harmondsworth: Penguin.

Fowler, R. (1977) *Linguistics and the Novel*, London: Methuen.

Fowler, R. (1985) 'Power', in T. A. van Dijk (ed.) *Handbook of Discourse Analysis* 1, London: Academic Press, 61–82.

Fowler, R. (1986) *Linguistic Criticism*, Oxford: Oxford University Press.

Franklin, R. W. (ed.) (1981) *The Manuscript Books of Emily Dickinson*, Cambridge, Mass.: The Belknap Press of Harvard University Press.

Freeman, D. C. (1993) ' "According to my Bond": King Lear and Re-cognition', *Language and Literature* 2(1): 1–18.

Freeman, D. C. (1995) ' "Catch[ing] the Nearest Way": Macbeth and Cognitive Metaphor', *Journal of Pragmatics* 24: 689–708.

Gass, S. and Varonis, E. (1991) 'Miscommunication in Nonnative Speaker Discourse', in N. Coupland, H. Giles and J. Wiemann (eds) *'Miscommunication' and Problematic Talk*, London: Sage, 121–45.

Gilmore, P. and Glatthorn, A. (eds) *Children in and out of School: Ethnography and Education*, Washington, DC: Center for Applied Linguistics.

Goffman, E. (1969) *The Presentation of Self in Everyday Life*, Harmondsworth: Penguin.

Goffman, E. (1974) *Frame Analysis*, New York: Harper and Row.

Goffman, E. (1979) 'Footing', *Semiotica* 25: 1–29.

Grice, H. P. (1975) 'Logic and Conversation', in P. Cole and J. L. Morgan (eds) *Syntax and Semantics* 3, New York: Academic Press, 41–58.

Grice, H. P. (1981) 'Presupposition and Conversational Implicature', in P. Cole (ed.) *Radical Pragmatics*, New York: Academic Press, 183–98.

Gumperz, J. J. (1982) *Discourse Strategies*, Cambridge: Cambridge University Press.

Gumperz, J. J. (1992) 'Interviewing in Intercultural Situations', in P. Drew and J. Heritage (eds) *Talk at Work: Interaction in Institutional Settings*, Cambridge: Cambridge University Press, 302–27.

Halliday, M. A. K. (1971) 'Linguistic Function and Literary Style: An Enquiry into William Golding's *The Inheritors*', in S. Chatman (ed.) *Literary Style: A Symposium*, Oxford: Oxford University Press, 330–65.

Halliday, M. A. K. (1994) *An Introduction to Functional Grammar*, London: Edward Arnold.

Hare, D. (1988) *The Secret Rapture*, London: Faber and Faber.

Harris, S. (1984) 'Questions as a Mode of Control in Magistrates' Courts', *International Journal of the Sociology of Language* 49: 5–27.

Hayman, R. (1977) *How to Read a Play*, London: Methuen.

Hazlitt, W. (1939 [1817]) *Characters of Shakespeare's Plays* (A. Quiller-Couch, ed.) Oxford: Oxford University Press.

Heilman, R. B. (1972) 'Introduction to *The Taming of the Shrew*,' in S. Barnet (ed.) *The Complete Signet Classic Shakespeare*, New York: Harcourt Brace Jovanovich.

Herman, V. (1991) 'Dramatic Dialogue and the Systematics of Turn-taking', *Semiotica* 83: 97–121

Herman, V. (1995) *Dramatic Discourse: Dialogue as Interaction in Plays*, London: Routledge.

Hinchliffe, A. (1969) *The Absurd*, London: Methuen.

Hubert-Leibler, P. (1992) 'Dominance and Anguish: The Teacher–Student Relationship in the Plays of David Mamet', in L. Kane (ed.) *David Mamet: A Casebook*, New York: Garland, 69–85.

Hymes, D. (1972) 'On Communicative Competence', in J. B. Pride, and J. Holmes (eds) *Sociolinguistics*, Harmondsworth: Penguin, 269–93.

Ionesco, E. (1958) 'Victims of Duty' in *Plays: Volume 2* (translated by Donald Watson), London: Calder.

Ishiguro, K. (1990) *The Remains of the Day*, London: Faber and Faber.

Jakobson, R. (1960) 'Closing Statement: Linguistics and Poetics', in T. A. Sebeok (ed.) *Style in Language*, Cambridge, Mass.: MIT Press.

Jakobson, R. and Jones, L. G. (1970) *Shakespeare's Verbal Art in 'Th' Expence of Spirit'*, The Hague: Mouton.

Johnson, M. (1987) *The Body in the Mind*, Chicago: University of Chicago Press.

Kahn, C. (1977) 'The Taming of the Shrew: Shakespeare's Mirror of Marriage', in A. Diamond and L. R. Edwards (eds) *The Authority of Experience: Essays in Feminist Criticism*, Amherst: University of Massachusetts Press.

Kalson, A. E. (1993) *Laughter in the Dark: The Plays of Alan Ayckbourn*, Rutherford, N.J.: Fairleigh Dickinson University Press; London: Associated University Press.

Kureishi, H. (1995) 'My Son the Fanatic', in A. S. Byatt and A. Hollinghurst (eds) *New Writing* 4, London: Vintage, in association with the British Council, 100–11.

La Belle, J. (1980) 'A Strange Infirmity', *Shakespeare Quarterly* 31: 381–6.

Lakoff, G. (1987) *Women, Fire, and Dangerous Things*, Chicago: University of Chicago Press.

Lakoff, G. and Johnson, M. (1980) *Metaphors We Live By*, Chicago: University of Chicago Press.

Leech, G. N. (1969) *A Linguistic Guide to English Poetry*, London: Longman.

Leech, G. N. (1983) *Principles of Pragmatics*, London: Longman.

Leech, G. N. (1985) 'Stylistics', in T. A. van Dijk (ed.) *Discourse and Literature*, Amsterdam: John Benjamins, 39–57.

Leech, G. N. (1992) 'Pragmatic Principles in Shaw's *You Never Can Tell*', in M. Toolan (ed.) *Language, Text and Context: Essays in Stylistics*, London: Routledge, 259–80.

Leech, G. N. and Short, M. H. (1981) *Style in Fiction*, London: Longman.

Levinson, S. (1983) *Pragmatics*, Cambridge: Cambridge University Press.

Levinson, S. C. (1988) 'Putting Linguistics on a Proper Footing: Explorations on Goffman's Concepts of Participation', in P. Drew and A. Wootton (eds) *Erving Goffman: Exploring the Interaction Order*, Cambridge: Polity Press, 161–227.

Low, L. (1983) 'Ridding Ourselves of Macbeth', *The Massachusetts Review* 24: 826–37.

Lucretius, T. (1982 [1st century BC]) *De Rerum Natura* (M. Smith, ed.), Loeb Classical Library, No. 181, Cambridge, Mass. and London: Harvard University Press and Heinemann.

Mamet, D. (1993 [1992]) *Oleanna*, London: Methuen.

Miller, A. (1986) *The Crucible*, Harmondsworth: Penguin.

Milroy, L. (1984) 'Comprehension and Context: Successful Communication and Communicative Breakdown', in P. Trudgill (ed.) *Applied Sociolinguistics*, London: Academic Press, 7–31.

Monty Python's Flying Circus (1971) BBC Television/Kettledrum Lownes Productions Ltd.

Muir, K. (ed.) (1984) *Macbeth*, The Arden Shakespeare, London and New York: Routledge.

Ng, S. H. and Bradac, J. J. (1993) *Power in Language*, London: Sage.

Osborne, J. (1965 [1957]) *Look Back in Anger*, London: Faber and Faber.

Paton, G. (1988) 'The Comedian as Portrayer of Social Morality', in C. Powell and G. Paton (eds) *Humour in Society*, London: Macmillan, 206–33.

Piette, A. (1995) 'The Devil's Advocate: David Mamet's *Oleanna* and Political Correctness', in M. Maufort (ed.) *Staging Difference: Cultural Pluralism in American Theatre and Drama*, New York: Peter Lang, 173–87.

Pinter, H. (1981 [1959]) *The Birthday Party*, London: Eyre Methuen.

Raskin, V. (1987) 'Linguistic Heuristics of Humor: A Script-based Semantic Approach', *International Journal of the Sociology of Language* 65: 11–25.

Rochester, S. and Martin, J. R. (1979) *Crazy Talk: A Study of the Discourse of Schizophrenic Speakers*, London: Plenum Press.

Rumelhart, D. E. (1975) 'Notes on a Schema for Stories', in D. G. Bobrow and A. M. Collins (eds) *Representation and Understanding*, New York: Academic Press, 211–36.

Rumelhart, D. E. (1980) 'Schemata: The Building Blocks of Cognition', in R. J. Spiro, B. C. Bruce and W. F. Brewer (eds) *Theoretical Issues in Reading Comprehension*, Hillsdale, N.J.: Lawrence Erlbaum, 33–58.

Sacks, H., Schegloff, E. A. and Jefferson, G. (1978). 'A Simplest Systematics for the Organization of Turn Taking in Conversation', in J. Schenkein (ed.) *Studies in the Organization of Conversational Interaction*, New York: Academic Press, 7–55.

Schegloff, E. and Sacks, H. (1973) 'Opening up Closings', *Semiotica* 8: 289–327.

Schenkein, J. (ed.) *Studies in the Organization of Conversational Interaction*, New York: Academic Press.

Schiffrin, D. (1987) *Discourse Markers*, Cambridge: Cambridge University Press.

Searle, J. R. (1969) *Speech Acts: An Essay in the Philosophy of Language*, Cambridge: Cambridge University Press.

Searle, J. R. (1975a) 'The Logical Status of Fictional Discourse', *New Literary History* 6(2): 319–32.

Searle, J. R. (1975b) 'Indirect Speech Acts', in P. Cole and J. L. Morgan (eds) *Syntax and Semantics* 3, New York: Academic Press, 59–82.

Semino, E. (1977) *Language and World Creation in Poems and Other Texts*, London: Longman.

Semino, E. (1995) 'Schema Theory and the Analysis of Text Worlds in Poetry', *Language and Literature* 4: 79–108.

Shaw, G. B. (1984 [1898]) *Plays Pleasant*, Harmondsworth: Penguin, 214–17.

Sherzer, D. (1978) 'Dialogic Incongruities in the Theater of the Absurd', *Semiotica* 22: 3–4, 269–85.

Short, M. (1989) 'Discourse Analysis and the Analysis of Drama', in R. Carter and P. Simpson (eds) *Language Discourse and Literature*, London: Unwin Hyman, 139–68.

Short, M. (1996) *Exploring the Language of Poems, Plays and Prose*, Harlow: Longman.

Showalter, E. (1992) 'Acts of Violence: David Mamet and the Language of Men', *Times Literary Supplement* 4675: 16–17.

Shultz, J., Florio, S. and Erickson, F. (1982). 'Where's the Floor?: Aspects of the Cultural Organization of Social Relationships in Communication at Home and at School', in P. Gilmore and A. Glatthorn (eds) *Children in and out of School: Ethnography and Education*, Washington, DC: Center for Applied Linguistics, 88–123.

Simpson, N. F. (1960) *One Way Pendulum*, London: Faber and Faber.

Simpson, P. (1989) 'Politeness Phenomena in Ionesco's The Lesson', in R. Carter and P. Simpson (eds) *Language, Discourse and Literature*, London: Routledge, 170–93.

Simpson, P. (1993) *Language, Ideology and Point of View*, London: Routledge.

Simpson, P. (1997) *Language through Literature*, London: Routledge.

Stanislavski, C. (1968) *Building a Character* (translated by E. R. Hapgood), London: Methuen.

Stenström, A-B. (1994) *An Introduction to Spoken Interaction*, London: Longman.

Stoppard, T. (1978 [1977]) *Professional Foul*, London: Faber and Faber.

Styan, J. L. (1971 [1965]) *The Dramatic Experience*, Cambridge: Cambridge University Press.

Talmy, L. (1988) 'The Relation of Grammar to Cognition', in B. Rudzka-Ostyn (ed.) *Topics in Cognitive Linguistics*, Philadelphia and Amsterdam: John Benjamins, 165–205.

Tannen, D. (1979) 'What's in a Frame? Surface Evidence for Underlying Expectations', in R. O. Freedle (ed.) *New Directions in Discourse Processing*, Norwood, N.J.: Ablex, 137–82.

Tannen, D. (1993a) *Framing in Discourse*, New York: Oxford University Press.

Tannen, D. (ed.) (1993b) *Gender and Conversational Interaction*, New York and Oxford: Oxford University Press.

Tannen, D. and Saville-Troike, M. (eds) (1985) *Perspectives on Silence*, Norwood, N.J.: Ablex.

Thomas, J. (1995) *Meaning in Interaction: An Introduction to Pragmatics*, London: Longman.

Tillyard, E. M. W. (1963 [1943]) *The Elizabethan World Picture*, Harmondsworth: Penguin.

Tsui, A. (1995) *English Conversation*, Oxford: Oxford University Press.

Turner, M. (1987) *Death is the Mother of Beauty*, Chicago: University of Chicago Press.

Turner, M. (1991) *Reading Minds: The Study of English in the Age of Cognitive Science*, Princeton: Princeton University Press.

Turner, M. (1996) *The Literary Mind*, New York and Oxford: Oxford University Press.

Verdonk, P. (ed.) (1993) *Twentieth-Century Poetry: From Text to Context*, London: Routledge.

Wales, K. (1989) *A Dictionary of Stylistics*, London: Longman.

Wandor, M. (1987) *Look Back in Gender: Sexuality and the Family in Post-War British Drama*, London: Methuen.

Watanabe, S. (1993). 'Cultural Differences in Framing: American and Japanese Group Discussions', in D. Tannen (ed.) *Framing in Discourse*, New York: Oxford University Press, 176–209.

Watson, R. (1984) *Shakespeare and the Hazards of Ambition*, Cambridge, Mass.: Harvard University Press.

Weber, J. J. (1992) *Critical Analysis of Fiction*, Amsterdam: Rodopi.

Weber, J. J. (ed.) (1996) *The Stylistics Reader*, London: Arnold.

Weber, J. J. and Verdonk, P. (eds) (1995) *Twentieth-Century Fiction: From Text to Context*, London: Routledge.

Wells, S. (1970) *Literature and Drama*, London: Routledge and Kegan Paul.

West, C. and Zimmerman, D. H. (1985) 'Gender, Language and Discourse', in T. A. van Dijk (ed.) *Handbook of Discourse Analysis* 4, London: Academic Press, 103–24.

Young, D. (1990) *The Action to the Word: Structure and Style in Shakespearean Tragedy*, New Haven: Yale University Press.

Index